АMERICAN BUSINESS CYCLES, 1865-1897

AMERICAN BUSINESS CYCLES

1865-1897

/\/\/\/\/\

BY RENDIGS FELS

GREENWOOD PRESS, PUBLISHERS
WESTPORT, CONNECTICUT

The Library of Congress has catalogued this publication as follows:

Library of Congress Cataloging in Publication Data

Fels, Rendigs, 1917-
    American business cycles, 1865-1897.

    Reprint of the ed. published by the University of North Carolina Press, Chapel Hill.
        Bibliography: p.
        1. Business cycles. 2. United States—Economic conditions—1865-1918. I. Title.
[HB3743.F4 1973]   338.5'4'0973   73-3924
ISBN 0-8371-6863-5

Copyright 1959 by The University of North Carolina Press

Originally published in 1959
by The University of North Carolina Press, Chapel Hill

Reprinted with the permission
of The University of North Carolina Press

First Greenwood Reprinting 1973

Library of Congress Catalogue Card Number 73-3924

ISBN 0-8371-6863-5

Printed in the United States of America

TO MOTHER

WHO HAS WAITED A LONG TIME

(The next one will be dedicated to Bee,
who has waited a long time too.)

PREFACE

NOT ALL OF THOSE to whom I am indebted in connection with this study will be named here. Even so, I hesitate to acknowledge obligations that are heavy compared to achievement, lest failure to take full advantage of help reflect on those who were so generous. But with the hope that the shortcomings of the study will be blamed solely on me, I wish to express gratitude to Seymour E. Harris, my principal teacher during the years I was at Harvard, and George W. Stocking, who as Department Chairman at Vanderbilt gave me friendship, encouragement, and support not only in connection with this study but in a thousand other ways as well. I regret that I cannot here name all the others who helped me nor describe the nature of the help given by the following individuals: Moses Abramovitz, Robert A. Gordon, Gottfried Haberler, Earl Hamilton, and Geoffrey Moore. I am indebted to the Social Science Research Council and to the Institute of Research and Training in the Social Sciences of Vanderbilt University for financial assistance; to the National Bureau of Economic Research for generously making available their unparalleled collection of business cycle statistics; to the following for permission to use copyrighted material: American Economic Association, Macmillan & Co., Inc., McGraw-Hill Book Company, Inc., National Bureau of Economic Research, Inc., Oxford University Press, the President and Fellows of Harvard College, *Review of Economic Studies,* the Southern Economic Association, the University of Chicago Press, and W. W. Norton & Company, Inc.; and to the Ford Foundation for a grant under its program for assisting American university presses in the publication of works in the humanities and the social sciences.

CONTENTS

	PAGE
Preface	vii
1. Methodology	3
2. Theoretical Framework	22
3. Price and Wage Flexibility during Cyclical Contraction	44
4. External Events	55
5. Long-Wave Depression	62
6. The Cycles of 1865-79	83
7. The Cycle of 1879-85	113
8. The Cycle of 1885-88	137
9. The Cycle of 1888-91	159
10. The Cycle of 1891-94	179
11. The Cycle of 1894-97	193
12. The Depression of the Nineties	209
13. Conclusions	220

Appendices

    1. Twenty-Year Cycles   229
    2. The Month of the 1887 Peak   233

Index   239

LIST OF CHARTS

	PAGE
Chart 1. Four-Cycle Schema	28
Chart 2. Prices and Wages	63
Chart 3. Interest Rates, 1865-97	64-65
Chart 4. Construction and Immigration, 1865-97	86
Chart 5. Gold Premium and Exchange Rate, 1865-78	88
Chart 6. Agriculture, 1869-97	91
Chart 7. Output, 1865-97	93
Chart 8. Bond Issues and Railroad Bond Yields, 1865-97	116-17
Chart 9. Merchandise Exports and Imports, 1865-97	119
Chart 10. Federal Receipts and Expenditures, 1865-97	121
Chart 11. Freight Ton-Miles, Outside Clearings, and Pig-Iron Output, 1875-97	160
Chart 12. Iron and Steel and Railroad Gross Capital Expenditures, 1884-1900	216

LIST OF TABLES

Table 1. Rate of Change of Output, Prices, and Interest Rates, 1869-1913	66
Table 2. Miles of Railroad Track Laid on Main Lines, 1886 and 1887	145

AMERICAN BUSINESS CYCLES, 1865-1897

1

METHODOLOGY

AN ANALYTIC HISTORY of business cycles in the United States of America between the years 1865 and 1897 constitutes the core of this study. I hope that this in itself, together with the paucity of work on the subject, justifies the undertaking. But I have felt bound to try to do something more. I am not an economic historian working on the cyclical aspect of his field; I am a specialist in business cycles working on a historical topic. I am interested not only in the light that present understanding of business cycles can throw on a historical period but also in the light that period can throw on the nature of business cycles. This interest makes it advisable to start with an extended discussion of methodology.

The methodology of business cycle research has been a battleground for contending partisans. There are several competing methods, each of which offers a guarantee of slow progress, a hope of great achievement, and reason for fearing the hope will never be fulfilled. Each research worker selects a method according to his training, temperament, and abilities; but once he has made his choice he is apt to crusade for his own method and try to discredit the others.

The controversies that ensue have positive rather than negative value: they do not succeed in shelving the method under attack but do help to clarify the value of the methods under discussion. But the controversial approach to the subject is apt to lead to confusion. A balanced appraisal is in order, partly for its own sake, mainly to clarify what is being attempted in the present study.

Before the issues are discussed, some terms need to be explained. Certain economists say there are no such things as business cycles, arguing that the term should be abandoned in favor of something like "economic fluctuations." Now, since the purpose of words is to convey meaning, I persist in talking about "business cycles" because there is no doubt in any economist's mind as to the class of phenomena I am referring to. No other excuse for using the term is needed, any more than there is need to apologize for calling a man "Knight" who does not wear a suit of armor.

The terminological dispute is, however, based on real differences of opinion. Those who use the term "business cycles" usually believe that there is a generating mechanism that can be called cyclical without much deviation from the meaning of the word as used outside economics. Those who object to the term deny that a cyclical mechanism exists. The issue of substance is important and will have to be faced later in this study. But arguing over terms is not fruitful, since it drags in lexicographical disputes which cloud the issue. I need now say only that the term "business cycles" is used here solely as a label and does not imply any opinion on issues of substance.

The word "theory" in this chapter will mean a general explanation that combines or accounts for what in physical science are called "laws," just as Newton's theory explained Kepler's laws. In this sense the acceleration principle model, although an analytical tool, is not a theory, but Hicks's explanation of the trade cycle, which includes the acceleration principle as one of its elements, is a theory. All approaches to the study of business cycles aim at achieving a satisfactory theory in this sense.

There are four principal approaches: the inductive, the deductive, the econometric, and the historical. The inductive approach of the National Bureau of Economic Research (N.B.E.R.) is that described by Burns and Mitchell in *Measuring Business Cycles*.[1] By "deductive approach" I mean the building of models, whether literary or mathematical, by making simplifying assumptions and deducing their logical conclusions. By "econometric," I mean the statistical estimation of parameters for a dynamic model.[2] By "historical approach," I mean the attempt to explain business cycles of the past as individuals.[3]

1. Arthur F. Burns and Wesley C. Mitchell, *Measuring Business Cycles* (New York, 1946).
2. This is a narrow definition of the term "econometric," but for my purposes it is the most convenient. What makes the approach distinctive is the joining of economic theory, mathematics, and statistics.
3. There are two minor approaches that deserve mention. I call the survey method "minor" (despite its recent rise to importance) because it aims only at discovering laws or regularities important for business cycles, not at a general theory. I call the regional approach "minor" because one who studies business cycles of particular regions must choose one or more of the four major approaches.

METHODOLOGY

The Statistical Approaches

Let us begin with the Koopmans-Vining controversy over the relative merits of the two statistical approaches—that of the N.B.E.R. and the econometric.[4] In his review of *Measuring Business Cycles,* Koopmans described the N.B.E.R. methods[5] as analogous to the Kepler stage of research in celestial mechanics, in which observation proceeded almost independently of theory and discovered empirical laws that in turn ultimately led to Newton's theory of gravitation. Although conceding that Mitchell had made "an important contribution to the 'Kepler stage,' "[6] Koopmans claimed that faster progress in business cycle research could be made by combining the Kepler stage with the Newton stage, i.e., by combining observation with theory. He had three arguments: first, that theory is needed to decide which variables are relevant for study; second, that prediction without theory is not possible because "economic variables are determined by the simultaneous validity of an equal number of 'structural' equations" so that "the mere observation of regularities in the interrelations of variables . . . does not permit us to recognize or to identify behavior equations among such regularities";[7] and third, that greater wealth, definiteness, rigor, and relevance to specific questions of information can be obtained by specifying the form of the joint probability distribution of the variables and testing hypotheses according to modern methods of statistical inference.

Koopmans' review apparently casts doubt on any method other than econometrics.[8] Viewed from this angle, Koopmans' criticisms can be considered as arguments for econometrics. And cogent arguments they are, too; for if variables are determined by many simultaneous relationships, it may be possible to identify significant regularities only with a set of structural equations representing the entire cyclical movement.

---

4. Tjalling C. Koopmans, "Measurement Without Theory," *Review of Economic Statistics,* XXIX (Aug. 1947), 161-72; Rutledge Vining, "Koopmans on the Choice of Variables to Be Studied and of Methods of Measurement," *Review of Economics and Statistics,* XXXI (May 1949), 77-86; Koopmans, "A Reply," *ibid.,* pp. 86-91; and Vining, "A Rejoinder," *ibid.,* pp. 91-94.

5. Of course, only a part of the Bureau's work is under discussion here. The Bureau's statistical work has made large contributions to economics in general and would have made large indirect contributions to business cycle research even if it had never taken up the subject directly at all.

6. "Measurement Without Theory," p. 162.

7. *Ibid.,* pp. 166 and 167.

8. Vining, "Koopmans," p. 77.

There are many other arguments in favor of econometrics. Cyclical turns may result not from specific factors like a shortage of capital, which literary theorists can put their fingers on, but simply from the particular values of the parameters of a set of equations;[9] and if so, the problem of the business cycle can scarcely be solved by any other method than econometrics. If economists ever arrive at a theory capable of predicting business cycles quantitatively, they will want to express it in econometric form; and the more practice the econometricians get in solving their technical problems, the better prepared they will be for that happy day. Econometric models have already thrown light on the cyclical mechanism (even though there is room for disagreement as to how bright the light has been).

Unquestionably econometrics will continue to make progress which will be steady even if it is slow. Moreover, econometrics is like a football play that will go for a touchdown if every player does his part perfectly: each new set of structural equations carries the hope that it will successfully predict not only what would happen in the absence of policy changes but also the consequences of any contemplated change of policy.[10]

Unfortunately, the hope is probably illusory. Econometric equations have repeatedly failed to provide good predictions. It is questionable whether the underlying statistics are sufficiently accurate to bear the burden econometrics throws on them. The observations available usually constitute a very small sample for determining the parameters. The methods now in use usually involve linear equations; if curvilinear relationships are introduced, the problem of the number

---

9. Jan Tinbergen, "Econometric Business Cycle Research," reprinted in American Economic Association, *Readings in Business Cycle Theory* (Philadelphia, 1944), pp. 77-78, from *The Review of Economic Studies*, VII (1940), 87-88.

10. Scientific predictions in economics at best can only be conditional—some assumptions must be made about external events, and failure of the prediction on account of an unexpected change in external events does not decrease our confidence in the method used. No scientific predictor of business cycles as of June 1, 1950, could have been expected to predict the Korean War, although he might answer the question as to what would happen if war leads the government to adopt certain specific policies. On account of external events alone, prediction of business cycles cannot be as spectacularly successful as predictions of eclipses of the moon.

"Scientific" is used here in the sense of a positive science, where accurate predictions can be made by deductions from a limited number of fundamental propositions or theories. The word "science" is sometimes used in the broader sense of any organized body of knowledge. In the broad sense, history is a science; and a prediction that is nothing more than an informed guess could be called "scientific." It seems better to regard such prediction as art rather than science.

METHODOLOGY

of observations may be intensified.[11] Econometric methods are open to question because the parameters do not remain sufficiently steady.[12] In order for a model to be workable, the number of equations and variables must be small; but in a matter as complex as the business cycle, a small number of equations is inadequate.[13] "Models such as those of Tinbergen and Klein produce cycles only with the aid of frequent outside shocks. That may well be the explanation of the cycle, but if one is impressed with its regularity, then something more basic is required."[14] Econometrics must use relationships given by economic theory. If these relationships are not correct, the models will not be correct either; and econometrics has no certain superiority over other methods for discovering correct relationships. Although a set of structural equations might be ideal for predicting the effects of certain consequences of government policy like the mechanical effects of government spending, they would be of little value for others, such as the effect of guaranteeing bank deposits on the incidence of runs on banks. It may be an advantage to explain all phases of the cycle by a single argument, thus dispensing with separate theories for individual phases, but this also "may result in misconstructing the whole phe-

---

11. The use of linear relationships can be justified on grounds that for short distances a curvilinear relationship can be approximated by a straight line. Moreover, there are techniques available for dealing with situations where the assumption of linearity does too much violence to the facts. See Tinbergen, "Research," pp. 69-71.

12. John R. Hicks, *A Contribution to the Theory of the Trade Cycle* (Oxford, 1950), p. 6, n. 2 (hereafter cited as *Contribution*); Robert A. Gordon, "Business Cycles in the Interwar Period: The 'Quantitative-Historical' Approach," *American Economic Review*, XXXIX (May 1949), 52. There are ways of dealing with parameters that change over time, provided that we know the rules governing their changes, but we have reason to fear that in practice econometricians have a bias in favor of avoiding the discovery of changes in the values of parameters and in any event could handle such changes only if they were not very numerous. To borrow a figure from Nicholas Georgescu-Roegen, an econometrician could very easily operate in the same fashion as a man who says, "There is a madonna in that log," and proceeds to prove his point by carving the log until a madonna does indeed appear.

13. Tinbergen, "Research," p. 68; Gordon, "Approach," p. 52. Cf. Milton Friedman in N.B.E.R., *Conference on Business Cycles* (New York, 1951), pp. 112-13 (hereafter cited as *Conference*): "Limitations of resources—mental, computational, and statistical—enforce a model that, although complicated enough for our capacities, is yet enormously simple relative to the present state of understanding of the world we seek to explain. Until we can develop a simpler picture of the world, by an understanding of interrelations within sections of the economy, the construction of a model for the economy as a whole is bound to be almost a complete groping in the dark. The probability that such a process will yield a meaningful result seems to me almost negligible."

14. James J. Duesenberry, "Hicks on the Trade Cycle," *Quarterly Journal of Economics*, LXIV (Aug. 1950), 476.

nomenon."[15] It would not be advisable for the N.B.E.R. to abandon its own methods in favor of econometrics.[16]

For the N.B.E.R.'s method produces steady accretions to knowledge. Unlike econometrics, the Bureau does not hope to make a touchdown in one play; it is content to gain a few yards at a time in the hope that eventually it will score. That is to say, after observing many regularities, it hopes to produce the theory everybody is looking for. Unfortunately, this happy result is not likely to occur at any time soon. It took the Bureau a quarter of a century to mature its technical methods. It promises a long series of monographs to lay the groundwork for the theory. Just as it took much longer to produce *Measuring Business Cycles* than Wesley Mitchell anticipated,[17] so the series of monographs may stretch out further than anyone now expects.

Methodological criticism is more likely to be helpful if it is constructive rather than destructive. Impatience for quicker results ought not to lead to condemnation of the Bureau's method but rather to the suggestion that it and the econometricians should concentrate on the middle ground between them.[18]

Econometrics has tried to do too much, the Bureau too little. More testing of limited hypotheses is needed so that a set of propositions (analogous to the "laws" of the physical sciences) can be built up that are proved as certainly as anything can be proved in the difficult field of business cycle research.

As illustration, take the last four chapters of *Measuring Business Cycles*. They are not tests of a group of hypotheses revolving around the general question of whether there have been changes in cyclical behavior over a span of time.[19] Burns and Mitchell did not test such hypotheses as the existence of a Kondratieff cycle or of Schumpeter's combination of Kitchin, Juglar and Kondratieff. They tested the more limited question of whether such longer cycles are so clearly evident as to impair the usefulness of the Bureau's technique for analyzing statistical time series. Inevitably their tests have provided interesting evidence on the more fundamental hypotheses, but this was incidental. Hence, the results—mostly adverse to the hypotheses—are

15. Joseph A. Schumpeter, "Historical Approach to the Analysis of Business Cycles," in *Conference*, p. 153n.
16. I do not mean to imply that Koopmans favors such as drastic course.
17. Arthur F. Burns, "Wesley Mitchell and the National Bureau," *29th Annual Report of the National Bureau of Economic Research* (New York, 1949), p. 36.
18. Friedman, *Conference*, p. 114.
19. Koopmans, "Measurement Without Theory," p. 167, was incautious in this respect.

inconclusive except for the specific purposes of the N.B.E.R. In the case of Schumpeter's three-cycle schema, the tests are virtually worthless except for the specific purpose Burns and Mitchell had in mind. In other cases, the tests merely throw doubt on the hypotheses.

Some research of recent years gives encouraging evidence that both the econometricians and the Bureau are moving into the middle ground. On the econometric side, a number of studies have appeared that, rather than try to explain the whole cycle, explore limited relationships such as investment in particular industries or the acceleration principle.[20] On the Bureau side, the study of inventory cycles by Abramovitz (one of the series using the method described by Burns and Mitchell) contains an illuminating discussion of theoretical issues.[21] Whatever the prospects that either of the approaches will achieve a satisfactory theory, both can make valuable contributions to understanding business cycles.

The Deductive Approach

Let us now turn from the two statistical approaches to the purely theoretical approach. It will be convenient to use Hicks's theory[22] as an illustration, since it has been highly praised by commentators with a theoretical bent and roundly condemned by those skeptical of the value of simplified models. Moreover, it will be used in the rest of this volume, so that discussion of it here will serve other purposes besides illustration.

In his theory, Hicks assumes a value of the accelerator so high that its interaction with the multiplier produces explosive upward movements and would produce explosive downward movements if disinvestment could exceed the rate of depreciation. He introduces the concept of a ceiling beyond which output cannot be raised in order to explain why the upswing does not continue forever. Once the ceiling is reached, the decline in the rate of increase of output causes the downturn via the acceleration principle.

Duesenberry in his review raises considerations leading to the con-

---

20. See the contribution by Lawrence R. Klein to *Conference*, pp. 233-303; and John Meyer and Edwin Kuh, "Acceleration and Related Theories of Investment, An Empirical Inquiry," *Review of Economics and Statistics*, XXXVII (Aug. 1955), 217-30.
21. Moses Abramovitz, *Inventories and Business Cycles, with Special Reference to Manufacturers' Inventories* (New York, 1950).
22. *Contribution*.

clusion that the existence of the ceiling "is extremely doubtful."[23] Duesenberry's evidence is direct and indirect. In the indirect argument, he first shows that a shortage of equipment amounts to a shortage of labor, so that the latter can be taken as the main if not the only ingredient in the ceiling. He then shows that in the United States there has been a reserve army of low-paid labor in agriculture which has been willing to move into industry as jobs became available there. In the nineteenth century the reserve army was even larger than now, on account of immigration. Hence, "in the United States at least, there is never an effective ceiling on the *level* of output. The ceiling, if any, is on the rate of increase of output."[24]

Now, Duesenberry's reserve army is entirely relevant to the discussion, but is less important than appears at first sight. Although in Hicks's theory there is an effective ceiling at any instant of time, the ceiling rises over time. For all practical purposes the ceiling for Hicks, as for Duesenberry, is on the rate of increase of output.[25] The reserve army makes a quantitative but not a qualitative difference. The line FF in Hicks's chart[26] representing the ceiling on income as it rises over time will be drawn more steeply if account is taken of the reserve army; i.e., the possible rate of increase of output will be greater. And the steeper the FF line, the less plausible does Hicks's theory appear; for if the ceiling is to be effective, the rate of increase of income possible at the ceiling must be less than that actually achieved during the upswing. But Hicks's theory, in principle at least, can withstand Duesenberry's criticism.

Duesenberry's direct test of whether the ceiling exists (or rather, whether it is likely to be reached) proceeds by inquiring "how many booms have ended because of shortages in investment goods? There do not seem to be many cases of that sort. In particular it seems very

23. "Hicks," p. 472. Duesenberry also argued that the ceiling concept was unnecessary for Hicks's theory, apparently unaware that Hicks on p. 106 had made the very same point.
24. *Ibid.* (Duesenberry's italics).
25. There is a difference between the two. For Hicks, barring cases where the upswing dies out before it reaches the ceiling, a point is actually reached at which output is at the maximum possible at that point of time, and output can expand thereafter only as the maximum rises over time. For Duesenberry, while there presumably would be a theoretical maximum which would be reached when the reserve army was entirely absorbed in industry, in history this maximum is never reached and the ceiling is set only by the rate at which the reserve army can in fact move.
This conceptual difference between Hicks and Duesenberry is without significance for the problem in hand. For both, the ceiling is on the rate of increase of output.
26. *Contribution*, p. 121.

hard to argue that the boom of the 1920's ended in the way Hicks suggests."[27]

Duesenberry is to be commended for doing what Hicks himself should have done—namely, to devise factual tests of the theory.[28] At the Universities–National Bureau Conference on Business Cycle Research, someone stated that every theorist should devote a few pages to describing factual tests that could conceivably prove the theory wrong. This is a sound methodological principle, and one could wish that it had been universally followed during the past thirty years. The next best procedure is for someone else to devise tests, but Duesenberry's tests of Hicks's theory show that this is not entirely satisfactory.

Duesenberry's direct test no more "disproves" Hicks's ceiling than the indirect test. True, few cases, if any, can be found of upper turning points that seem to have been caused in Hicks's fashion. In the cases I have examined in detail, I have often found good evidence for other explanations, never for this one.[29] That does not dispose of the matter. The evidence is rarely sufficient to establish one explanation beyond a reasonable doubt. What is more important, the ceiling could cause a downturn without ever making itself obvious. Although bottlenecks and shortages can be spectacular and provide concrete evidence of a Hicksian mechanism, the ceiling may quietly lead to rising prices, unfilled orders, and a decline in the rate of increase of output that brings about the downturn via the accelerator—all without anyone's being aware of what is going on. In such cases, other explanations will seem more plausible.

This discussion can lead to any of three conclusions. Perhaps economics is not very far advanced in the technique of testing business cycle theories; and until more is learned about how to proceed, only the author of a theory can be depended on to devise tests that could definitely disprove his theory.

But another, less hopeful conclusion suggests itself. Do the difficulties in testing theory stem from the nature of the field of investigation? Isn't there danger that all possible tests are either trivial or impossible to apply? (By "trivial" I mean that confidence in the theory is not much advanced by its passing the test; by "impossible to apply,"

---

27. "Hicks," p. 468.
28. Actually the tests are applicable only to a part of Hicks's theory. One could hardly expect more of Duesenberry in a review.
29. In the case of 1882, however, I have found evidence supporting another variant of Hicks's theory. See below.

that the information needed to apply the test is not available.) If such is the case, business cycle theory is more like philosophy than science. In philosophy, hypotheses are not infrequently put forward which cannot possibly be tested factually.[30] Cycle theory would not on this conclusion be wholly worthless. Aside from the pleasure some economists get from pure theory for its own sake, it could still be justified on the same grounds that will be used below for the historical approach, namely, that the practical decisions which governments must make on business cycle problems demand that economists do the best they can to provide some basis for informed judgments. But economists clearly cannot base their methodology on the defeatist assumption that they will never be able to test business cycle theories adequately.

Rejecting such a counsel of despair, one could still say that Hicks has indulged in a speculative flight of fancy having little or no roots in factual studies—a kind of worthless speculation that has characterized too much of business cycle literature in the past and that could well be omitted in the future. Now, no one is likely to say this in such bold and unqualified form, but it probably typifies the unexpressed reaction a good many economists have to Hicks's *Contribution*.

Moreover, it is in line with the much more politely phrased verdict of Arthur F. Burns:

> The sophistication of Hicks's work derives from the pressures of a subtle and inquiring mind, not from a large knowledge of practical affairs or the teachings of history and statistics. The result is a closely reasoned and attractively written essay about a possible cycle, but—as far as I can see—a dubious aid to students seriously concerned with the actual alternations of good and bad trade to which the Western world has been subject in modern times.[31]

This represents an application of the general attitude to a specific case Burns had expressed earlier:

> Whereas the theorists have ordinarily speculated on the basis of only vague knowledge about economic qualities and relations, the National Bureau has sought to determine the magnitude of the leading economic variables, their characteristic movements over time, and their actual relations to one another. The ground covered has been smaller, but the findings have been better supported by evidence.[32] . . . the habit of insisting upon evidence is spreading, and today evidence less often means deduction from

---

30. A. Wolf, *Essentials of Scientific Method* (London, 1925), p. 14.
31. "Hicks and the Real Cycle," *Journal of Political Economy*, XL (Feb. 1952), 24.
32. "The Cumulation of Economic Knowledge," *28th Annual Report of the National Bureau of Economic Research* (New York, 1948), p. 6.

untested premises. Economic models continue to receive hopeful attention; but mere logical consistency or aesthetic appeal now counts for less, and performance under tests for more, than a generation ago.[33]

Is Hicks's book a throwback to an earlier, unfortunate day? Before passing judgment, it is necessary to state what the model-builders are trying to do.

To imagine any connection between such a [simplified] model and economic history seems grotesque. . . . The fact that this tendency to alternation in levels of economic activity has appeared more or less uniformly in all advanced capitalist countries argues that there is some typical set of relations which would tend, in the absence of disturbance, to produce a regular cycle. . . . There must be basic features of capitalism which will explain why these fluctuations have appeared in so many different countries over such long periods. It is these features which we must seek to isolate by ingenuity and perspicacity, even though they are hidden by the stormy history of capitalism. These elements must be capable by themselves of producing a cycle, and they will explain what uniformity there is in cycle after cycle. But any such theory must have many "open ends" through which we may insert the impact of historically given events, which will explain the enormous variability and irregularity of the cycle. Thus it is not that we can expect any simple, mathematical model to explain the wave-like character of economic history, but rather merely to explain the remarkable fact that there is some degree of uniformity in the otherwise unique course of development.[34]

The difference between the inductive and deductive methods is more than a dispute over two alternative routes to the same goal. For the goals are not precisely the same. The N.B.E.R. seeks a theory that will explain the full complexity of cyclical experience in all its details. The theorist seeks those few fundamental characteristics that explain why there are cycles at all. The N.B.E.R. might contend that its route is the best one toward the model-builders' goal; but it is nevertheless true that should the N.B.E.R. produce the theory it seeks, the pure theorists would want to simplify that theory, throw away regu-

---

33. *Ibid.*, p. 17. Burns's statement that "today evidence less often means deduction from untested premises" must be interpreted carefully. Burns should not be understood as holding the fallacious view that the assumptions of a model should be tested directly. As Friedman has pointed out, the appropriate test is indirect and involves testing the predictions that can be deduced from the model, i.e., from the premises. Burns is quite properly objecting to regarding the deductions themselves as evidence. See Milton Friedman, *Essays in Positive Economics* (Chicago, 1953), chap. 1.

34. Richard M. Goodwin, "A Model of Cyclical Growth," in Erik Lundberg, ed., *The Business Cycle in the Post-War World* (London, 1955), pp. 207-8.

larities that are not essential, and reduce it to a compact model. By the same token, should someone succeed in capturing the essence of the cycle in a model, the N.B.E.R would want to elaborate it until it embraced all the complex cyclical phenomena. Success in one task would immeasurably speed success in the other but would not render it superfluous.

The model-builder has a task of his own. The question remains: should he pursue it now? Or should he wait until the N.B.E.R finishes its task? The deductive approach probably cannot be as successful in the field of business cycles as in some other branches of economics. The fact that there is no orthodox theory of the business cycle, whereas there has been a reasonably satisfactory theory of the international gold standard since the days of Hume, may be a symptom of this. Economic theory usually makes progress by using the concept of stable equilibrium together with some drastically simplifying assumptions such as economic rationality. Anything that happens is treated as a displacement from equilibrium or a change of the equilibrium position itself. If the theory can foretell roughly the goal of the ensuing movement, it can ignore the complications determining the exact path of the movement. This is why highly simplified models work. But the essence of the business cycle is a dynamic process that is just as apt to move away from equilibrium as toward it. Where it goes depends on the full characteristics of the system, including leads and lags, so that it is extraordinarily difficult to find simplifications that perform the classic function of stripping the problem of complications and exposing the fundamental process.

Under the circumstances it might seem advisable to fall back on the Kepler-Newton method of accumulating dependable regularities. If the regularities in this field were really dependable, such a conclusion might be justified. They are not. A symptom of their undependability is the scanty use made, not only in cycle literature but in other branches of economics as well, of the word "law." There are very few economic laws, and those few are not formulated in precise quantitative terms.

Three reasons can be given for the irregularity of our regularities. The first is external events. Because all cycles are disturbed, the N.B.E.R. may never answer what for the theorist is the fundamental question—what would happen in the absence of disturbances? Second, there is the point stressed by Schumpeter—the invention of products, processes, and institutions that in a fundamental sense are new. Third, people learn from their unique historical experiences; but how their behavior will change as they learn is also fundamentally new. Regularities of the past cannot be counted on in the future and were not even entirely regular in the past.

In a sense, the justification of every approach to the study of cycles consists of the doubts about the others. But more positive reasons have to be adduced. Like the other approaches, the theoretical guarantees a certain amount of progress when employed by a first-rate theorist and holds out some small hope of spectacular achievement. The clarification of logical relations contributes to immediate understanding, assists in framing limited hypotheses for testing, provides stepping-stones for building better theories, and (what is very much to the point for present purposes) gives historians hints as to what to look for. A model must be the starting point for econometric structures; if there is justification for proceeding with econometric work, there is *ipso facto* justification for model-building. And we must do our best to construct theories now because it cannot be taken for granted that anticyclical policy can proceed with no better understanding of the causes of cycles than is now available.

Moreover, at this stage there is no way of telling whether a theory is a flight of fancy or a miraculous flash of insight. When, as, and if perfect understanding of the cycle is achieved, it may turn out that one of the model-builders was right—and that happy day would be hastened if we could have the correct explanation before us now, even though untested and unproved. A theory closely related to historical fact like Schumpeter's has a better chance of being right than one that, like Hicks's, gives only occasional hints of historical origins; but this is by no means certain. A long line of pure theorists have preceded Hicks. No doubt, others will follow him. It is not for the rest of us to discourage them. We profit even from their failures; and though only one of them could be wholly successful, we must keep on the lookout for that one.

The Historical Approach

This study follows the historical approach. The case for pursuing other methods is good but not so strong as to establish a *prima facie* case against any alternative. The historical method has two essential characteristics: systematic use of nonstatistical as well as quantitative information, and tailor-made explanations of individual cycles.

What does this alternative have to offer? Some sort of historical reseach is inevitable. Much cyclical knowledge cannot be adequately understood in purely statistical terms. For instance, the bank crisis of 1933 affects the time series of the N.B.E.R and the equations of the econometricians, but who would expect to understand that event through statistics and equations alone? The same can be said for the stock market boom and crash of 1929, the inventory boom of 1919-20, and all phenomena where psychology plays a large role.

One can see in the work of the N.B.E.R., of the econometricians, and of the theorists historical labor behind the scenes. Although Wesley Mitchell's first great study of business cycles was a monument to the importance of collecting statistics, the book dealt with a great many matters of a nonstatistical variety;[35] one of the early works of the Bureau on cycles was Thorp's study of annals;[36] and the discussions in the Bureau's monographs make use of general historical knowledge. Similarly, the elements that go into the work of theorists contain much that is nonstatistical history.[37] This element also forces itself on the econometricians.[38]

But something more systematic is needed. A systematizing principle for conducting historical research is provided by the attempt to frame a tailor-made explanation for each cycle.[39] Tailor-made explanation inevitably uses as much statistical information as is available—so much that it has been quite appropriately called the "quantitative-historical approach,"[40] inasmuch as the statistical material should predominate. It is nevertheless the systematic search for nonstatistical information, together with an effort to understand cycles individually, that distinguishes this from other avenues of study.

Historical research would be sufficiently justified as a supplement to other kinds. It is also a possible avenue to a general theory. If enough explanations for individual cycles are accumulated, they may give the basis for formulating a general explanation. This route com-

35. *Business Cycles* (Berkeley, Calif., 1913).
36. Willard L. Thorp, *Business Annals* (New York, 1926).
37. This is particularly obvious in Joseph A. Schumpeter, *Business Cycles: A Theoretical, Historical, and Statistical Analysis of the Capitalist Process* (2 vols.; New York and London, 1939), hereafter cited as *Business Cycles*.
38. Jan Tinbergen, "On a Method of Statistical Business Cycle Research," in Alvin H. Hansen and Richard V. Clemence, eds., *Readings in Business Cycles and National Income* (New York, 1953), pp. 343-44 (hereafter cited as *Readings*).
39. Sumner H. Slichter, "The Period 1919-1936 in the United States: Its Significance for Business Cycle Theory," *Review of Economic Statistics*, XIX (Feb. 1937), 1-19.
40. Gordon, "Approach."

METHODOLOGY 17

mends itself to those who are impressed with the differences among cycles. Any single one of the existing theories may be applicable only to one or a limited number of cycles, so that the general explanation toward which everyone is working may be a compound of the alternative explanations now called "theories."

The hope for success is no better than in the case of the other approaches. The historical method has been criticized as ineffective for explaining cyclical movements except

> ... where in the series to be explained a sudden rather marked change occurs at the same time, or shortly after, some sudden change in another series, or some new event happens. Just because the changes are rather sudden ones, we have approximately the situation that all other factors remain almost constant. Hence, in that short interval there is a simple correlation between the variable to be explained and the one explanatory variable that suddenly changes. It is evident that this method can be successful especially for the analysing of the influence of new events. ... It is far more difficult, if not impossible, to apply it to the ever-present factors that do not change suddenly.[41]

The criticism, which has considerable force, can be made even more pointed.[42] Examining one cycle at a time means always dealing with a sample of one. For this reason, the ideal historical study would take one or more good econometric structures as its starting point. The catch is in the word "good." Historians have in the past done no more than make occasional references to the conclusions drawn by econometricians, because they had little confidence in such studies; and no econometric structure is used in this book because none is available for the period here studied.

For the same reason, the historian does well to study the results of the N.B.E.R. to determine to what extent the individual cycle is typical. This study has perhaps not gone as far in this direction as it should. But I have made some attempt and in addition I am greatly indebted to the N.B.E.R. for making available to me its collection of statistics.

The dependence of historical work on deductive theory is more obvious and insistent than its dependence on the two statistical approaches. Although each theorist hopes he has found a general explanation, the historian can regard the aggregate of business cycle

---

41. Tinbergen, *Readings,* p. 82.
42. The criticism should not, however, be overdone. Historians can deal with the ever present factors that do not change suddenly, even though the historical approach without the aid of theory and/or econometrics is not likely to discover how they operate.

theories as a toolbox from which he can select whatever tool is appropriate for each occasion.[43] The tools serve the double purpose of showing the historian what to look for and helping him understand what went on. And the historian ought to serve the theorist by showing to what extent his model is useful—in other words, by providing a kind of test of the model's validity.

Experience has taught me that the proper relationship between the deductive and the historical approaches is even more intimate. In trying to apply the extensive literature on price and wage flexibility to the cyclical contraction of the 1870's, I found to my surprise that previous research, voluminous though it was, had not provided tools in usable form. I therefore was obliged to rework the theory for my own purposes; the results appear in a subsequent chapter.

I also found it advisable to do some work on cycle theory. In keeping with the standard research procedure of building on the work of predecessors, it is necessary in this study to pay close and continuing attention to Schumpeter's work. True, the historical sections of his work have a different purpose from mine. Whereas my purpose is a history of what actually happened with the help of all theories that seem relevant, his intent was to test a particular theory. Nevertheless, his work is not only illuminating but also constitutes the only important attempt to deal with my subject. His theory has been subjected to some searching criticism, so that I felt pushed, if not driven, into trying in the next chapter to rework the theory as a prelude to the historical studies. It was also necessary to incorporate into his framework some of the more recent theoretical work on cycles. All this adds up to a conviction that historical and theoretical research should go hand in hand.

The particular period I have chosen for study—from 1865 to 1897 in the United States—itself requires justification. Quite aside from the difficulties inherent in the historical approach, the amount of data is limited. Although the N.B.E.R. has collected a large amount of statistics, and research keeps adding to the stock, there are still very

43. The text uses the word "tool" in a broader sense than is sometimes the case in economics. The kind of tool discussed is also an explanatory hypothesis. But tools need not be hypotheses: the most obvious case of theoretical tools which are not is the field of statistical theory; the theory of the stationary state is another case. Nobody imagines that such a state ever existed, but its theory can nevertheless be used, for example as Schumpeter used it in constructing his explanatory hypothesis (or theory) of the business cycle. Similarly, the Keynesian system can be stated in such a way as to involve no hypotheses about the real world, in which case it is a tool pure and simple—neither right nor wrong but only more or less useful.

large gaps; for instance, there are not even annual estimates of national income in print, let alone quarterly estimates. For the nineteenth century one cannot talk in the same terms or employ the same kind of analysis as for the twentieth, leaving serious doubts whether the present study can have any validity at all. The comments available in nineteenth-century sources are similarly inadequate compared to what is available for recent periods. Understanding of the cyclical mechanism then was comparatively meager and often naïve. Conclusions expressed here will be based not on conclusive proof but on a preponderance of evidence, and often flimsy evidence at that.

The problem is not peculiar to the subject but is common to history of many kinds. Historians, including economic historians, have usually been granted a great deal of freedom to reach conclusions on the basis of meager evidence. This can be justified on grounds that it is better to do the best one can than not try at all. In the course of doing so, some significant conclusions are reached that appear to be well established.

Moreover, much of our useful knowledge is not strictly scientific. Practical men are used to making decisions on the basis of inadequate information. They find it helpful to accumulate as much information as possible, however inadequate it may be. Many practical decisions in the field of business cycles have to be made by the President and Congress with the help of economic advisers. At present, these decisions can be nothing better than informed judgments. The more literature turned out by economists who have done their best to solve the cycle problem, the better the hope for wise decisions.[44] Similarly, historical studies contribute to the art as distinguished from the science of prediction. Historical studies have undoubtedly contributed to the skill of some individuals in the art of forecasting. If scientific prediction ever becomes possible, this justification for historical research will be greatly weakened, but at present it is sufficient for continuing the historical approach.

The size of the sample of business cycles available for investigation is necessarily small in any case. Counting from the first trough in the N.B.E.R. list of cyclical turns, there are only twenty-five Ameri-

---

44. We should not push this line of reasoning too far. The principle that a little knowledge is a dangerous thing can readily be illustrated in economics, e.g., the way that economists formerly advocated strict adherence to the rules of the gold standard game regardless of the cost. Nevertheless, it is clear that we must work on the methodological principle of assuming that more knowledge will lead to wiser policy decisions, even though we know that the assumption is not always correct.

can cycles open to study. If economists were to limit themselves to those for which there is a good deal of information, i.e., those since the end of World War I, the sample would be reduced to nine. Where the field is so limited, one cannot afford to discard any of it. Besides, one of the important questions for investigation is how far modern cycles resemble those of the nineteenth century and how far the large changes in economic structure have affected the nature of the cycle.

Granted that the case for studying American cycles from 1865 to 1897 is sound, there are two ways to deal with the problem of inadequate information. One is to confine oneself to those questions that can be answered with a high degree of confidence. The other is to ask the significant questions and try to answer them as best one can. There is merit in both. It would be unfortunate if all economists made the same choice. My choice has been to try to answer the significant question of what caused the cycles between 1865 and 1897. In so far as the justification for this has not already been given, it lies in the hope that this procedure will facilitate the efforts of future research workers. One may not have great confidence in the answers that can now be given, but if they lead somebody else to better answers, they are worth while.

In carrying out the policy of using whatever evidence is available, I have avoided elaborate manipulations of statistical data, since they are apt to lead to conclusions not implied by the evidence. For example, I see no merit in deflating outside clearings by an index of wholesale prices, preferring to consider the two series separately. The chief exception to this policy is a general, although not universal, preference for data adjusted seasonally.

The particular span chosen for study coincides with a period of falling prices. This makes the period a natural unit. It also embraces a period in which severe depressions were unusually frequent.[45] The years from 1865 to 1897 taken as a whole constitute a problem for explanation in addition to the problem of explaining the individual cycles.

45. At first sight, one might think that the period of severe depressions which ended in 1897 should be taken as beginning with 1873 rather than 1865. But it would be distortion to define such a period as beginning with the first year of a depression and ending with the last year of a depression. Moreover, one cannot deal with the depression of the seventies without dealing with the events leading up to it; this means starting with the end of the Civil War.

METHODOLOGY

Conclusion

Business cycles are so complex and disorderly—i.e., the regularities are so undependable—that it is an exceedingly difficult field in which to make progress. The doubts that can be raised about all approaches reflect this. These doubts should not lead to abandoning any of them, for they are complementary. Each has something to contribute. The greatest hope for a satisfactory theory lies in pursuing all approaches at once.

The real issue in the methodological disputes is not whether one method should be pursued to the exclusion of others, but how much research should be devoted to each. It is the eternal economic problem of the allocation of scarce resources. In these terms, the statistical approaches are rather expensive, since they require a great deal of computation, all of which must be carefully checked. To concoct a new model may be less expensive in terms of money, but the opportunity cost is apt to be large. It requires a high order of abilities which might better be devoted to branches of economics where deductive methods are apt to make more progress. In spite of the increasing amount of historical work that has been done in recent years, this approach is the one that has been most neglected. Nor is it particularly expensive. With this modest justification, I shall proceed with my subject.

2

THEORETICAL FRAMEWORK

THIS CHAPTER WILL develop a theoretical framework useful in the historical part of the study. The historian looks on deductive models as tools. He must rework the tools for his own purposes. In particular, it is helpful to synthesize the theories he will use most in order to clarify their interrelationships. They thus can be adapted for analyzing history at the same time that the task of assessing their relative usefulness is facilitated.

There are so many existing theories that it will be necessary to be highly selective. Those theories omitted from the present chapter will not necessarily be omitted from the historical discussion. Only three theories will be taken up here. The choice of Schumpeter was inevitable, since Schumpeter did the only previous important work on the period 1865-97 and found that it confirmed his theory to his own satisfaction.[1] Hicks's theory has been chosen as an elegant species of a genus that has loomed too large in recent discussions to be left out —the multiplier-accelerator models.[2] Gordon's work on major and minor cycles was selected to represent the most advanced species of another important genus—the investment opportunities theories.[3]

1. *Business Cycles*. See also Schumpeter, *The Theory of Economic Development*, trans. Redvers Opie (Cambridge, Mass., 1934), chap. 6; Schumpeter, "The Analysis of Economic Change," *Review of Economic Statistics*, XVII (May 1935), 2-10, reprinted in American Economic Association, *Readings in Business Cycle Theory* (Philadelphia, 1944), pp. 1-19; and Schumpeter, *Capitalism, Socialism and Democracy* (rev. ed.; New York, 1947), *passim*.

2. *Contribution*.

3. Robert A. Gordon, "Investment Behavior and Business Cycles," *Review of Economics and Statistics*, XXXVII (Feb. 1955), 23-34. An earlier version of his ideas appeared in his *Business Fluctuations* (New York, 1952), pp. 266-69.

THEORETICAL FRAMEWORK

These three theories embrace such a large amount of previous work that together they leave very little out of account.

Schumpeter

I am omitting from this volume the extended summary of Schumpeter's theory that I prepared for my own use.[4] The professional literature includes many discussions of Schumpeterian theory by excellent economists whose knowledge of the subject is lamentably superficial.[5] This makes me fear that clarity requires a lengthy restatement of it. Unfortunately, an adequate summary would be unjustifiably long. I can only warn the reader that the theory is unusually involved and peculiarly liable to misinterpretation.[6]

---

4. An excellent summary is available in Richard V. Clemence and Francis S. Doody, *The Schumpeterian System* (Cambridge, Mass., 1950), Part II.

5. The difficulties in the way of mastering Schumpeter are so formidable that I would be rash indeed to claim that I had done so, and in offering examples to back up the statement in the text, I am not trying to be critical, righteous, or vindictive but am merely illustrating the point.

Those who are interested in economic development generally cite *Theory of Economic Development* and *Capitalism, Socialism and Democracy* but ignore Schumpeter's most important work on the subject, presumably because it was entitled *Business Cycles*. See, for example, W. Arthur Lewis, *The Theory of Economic Growth* (London, 1955), p. 21.

Arthur R. Upgren in a paper apparently written in the spring or early summer of 1957 used Schumpeter's *Theory of Economic Development* to predict correctly that some time during autumn inflation would cease to be a problem. But he made the mistake of predicting that the outcome would be equilibrium, whereas anyone basing his forecast on Schumpeter ought to have predicted what actually came about—cyclical contraction. "The Forthcoming Economic Equilibrium," *The Journal of the American Society of Chartered Life Underwriters*, XI (Fall 1957), 294-302.

The discussions of Schumpeter by Thomas and Rostow are comparatively sophisticated, yet each of them makes a criticism in seeming ignorance that Schumpeter had dealt with the point raised. Brinley Thomas, *Migration and Economic Growth* (Cambridge, Eng., 1954), p. 28: "If Schumpeter had brought in fluctuations in the level of employment he would have had to recognize that consumption in real terms increases during prosperity and declines during recession." Schumpeter did bring in fluctuations in employment but not with the consequence anticipated by Thomas. W. W. Rostow, *British Economy of the Nineteenth Century* (Oxford, 1948), p. 29 (hereafter cited as *British Economy*): "there are grave ambiguities [in Schumpeter's system] as to just what fluctuates in the course of the long cycle: employment, real wages, interest rates, the rate of increase in production, prices?" Schumpeter in fact formulated the expectations implied by his model for the behavior of those variables. But perhaps Rostow was merely careless—he would have been on defensible ground had he said there were ambiguities in how those variables were expected to fluctuate.

6. A very brief reminder of the theory's main features is the most that can be offered here. Schumpeter's model starts from a position of general (Walrasian) equilibrium, which gets upset by innovation. Entrepreneurs are assumed to be new men in new firms who obtain money for innovation directly or indirectly through credit creation. Innovation comes in bursts because it is easier to imitate another

Not all commentators on Schumpeter have been superficial.[7] Kuznets criticized Schumpeter's theory for "the failure to forge the necessary links between the primary factors and concepts (entrepreneur, innovation, equilibrium line) and the observable cyclical fluctuations in economic activity."[8] This means several things. First, Schumpeter did not explicitly tie up his theory to a theory of income, output and employment. This was remedied by Bennion, who grafted it upon a Keynesian type of apparatus.[9] Second, there is no obvious relationship between the peaks and troughs marked off by the N.B.E.R. and the cyclical phases of Schumpeter's theory. Schumpeter himself dated a depression trough in the summer of 1932, by which he presumably meant about the same thing the Bureau means by a trough;[10] yet his dating of cyclical phases shows a transition from depression to revival at that time for neither Kondratieff, Juglar nor Kitchin.[11] Aside from differences in interpreting the facts, there are at least three reasons for expecting his dating of transitions from prosperity to

---

entrepreneur than to pioneer. During the prosperity phase of the cycle, investment associated with innovation adds to the spending stream without as yet increasing output. Prices rise. Noninnovating firms make windfall profits and speculate on the basis of expectations of continued inflation.

Prosperity gives way to recession and inflation to deflation when the innovating firms start to pour their output onto the market. The innovating firms make profits, whereas noninnovators in the aggregate suffer losses. The excesses associated with the boom require so much liquidation that the economy may (but in principle need not) overshoot equilibrium and enter into a depression phase. Once the vicious spiral ends, revival to a new equilibrium follows as a matter of course. Now the stage is set for another cycle.

In principle, Schumpeter would expect an indefinitely large number of cycles, inasmuch as different innovations have different gestation periods. For historical purposes, he found it convenient to work with a three-cycle schema, consisting of Kitchins (forty-month cycles), Juglars (ten-year cycles) and Kondratieffs (sixty-year cycles).

7. For some useful discussions, see the reviews of *Business Cycles* by Simon S. Kuznets (*American Economic Review*, XXX [June 1940], 257-71), Oscar Lange (*Review of Economic Statistics*, XXIII [Nov. 1941], 193), Jacob Marshak (*Journal of Political Economy*, XXVIII [Dec. 1940], 889-94), and E. Rothbarth (*Economic Journal*, LII [1942], 223-29); and the discussion by William Fellner, *Trends and Cycles in Economic Activity* (New York, 1956), pp. 43-54 (hereafter cited as *Trends*).

8. *American Economic Review*, XXX (June 1940), 270.

9. E. G. Bennion, "Unemployment in the Theories of Schumpeter and Keynes," *American Economic Review*, XXXIII (June 1943), 336-47.

10. *Business Cycles*, II, 926 and 995. To be sure, the Bureau dates the trough as March 1933, but it had a close decision to make between that date and the summer of 1932 (Arthur F. Burns and Wesley C. Mitchell, *Measuring Business Cycles* [New York, 1946], p. 82). Schumpeter chose the other alternative because he believed that the banking troubles of early 1933 were an avoidable accident. (*Business Cycles*, II, 926-27 and 943-44).

11. *Business Cycles*, II, 983, n. 2.

recession and from depression to revival to deviate from the Bureau's dates for peaks and troughs. (1) There are interferences among his three types of cycles, the phases of which rarely coincide. (2) One can expect some time to elapse before the recession phase breaks the secondary wave and produces a downturn in income and employment. (3) Schumpeter believed that "incipient recovery is . . . compatible with some further shrinkage of total dollar volume of business operations."[12]

There can be no question about the usefulness of the peaks, troughs, and cyclical phases marked off by the N.B.E.R. The only issue is whether it is fruitful to use in addition the phases of Schumpeter's model. I believe the answer to be yes, provided that we modify his three-cycle schema in ways to be described. But it is necessary to distinguish clearly between the two kinds of turning points and to put the Bureau's kind into the forefront.

Third, Schumpeter did not have a serviceable statistical technique to use in conjunction with his model. This is a real difficulty but one with which I shall not try to cope.

Probably the most serious weakness of Schumpeter's theory is the three-cycle schema.[13] Strictly speaking, the schema is not an integral part of the theory. The model implies multiplicity of cycles without specifying any definite number. But Schumpeter said that it is most convenient to proceed as if there were three kinds of cycles—Kitchin or forty-month cycles, Juglar or ten-year cycles, and Kondratieff or sixty-year cycles. His theory is plausible for the Juglar cycles of the period 1865-97. But is the same true for Kondratieffs and Kitchins?

To examine the Kondratieffs first, there are three reasons given by Schumpeter for expecting multiplicity of cycles. First, the gestation period is longer for some innovations than for others. This does not apply to Kondratieffs in any significant degree; e.g., it would be difficult to find innovations the gestation period of which extended from 1898 to 1914, which was the prosperity phase, according to Schumpeter's reckoning, of the third Kondratieff. Second, sequences of cycles bearing family resemblances occur because major innovations like railroads hardly ever "cover in one throw the whole field that will ultimately be their own."[14] This does apply to sixty-year cycles, particularly the Kondratieff of 1842-97. But this does not justify applying Schumpeter's four cyclical phases to the Kondratieff. It means

12. *Ibid.*, II, 945.
13. *Ibid.*, I, 161-74.
14. *Ibid.*, I, 167.

only that it is convenient to think of Juglars as coming in related groups.

The third reason for multiplicity of cycles is the long time it takes for the ultimate effects of, say, the railroads to work themselves out—new production opportunities must be developed and others annihilated; new cities must arise and old ones decay; and population must shift. This applies to Kondratieffs. It implies prosperity and recession phases—prosperity when the major innovation and the opportunities it opens up are going through gestation periods, recession as the ultimate effects annihilate old production and cause cities to decay. Does it also imply a secondary wave during prosperity and abnormal liquidation subsequently? Not necessarily.

Let us review what is meant by the various phases of the Kondratieff. A Kondratieff is like any other cycle in the Schumpeterian theory. Starting from equilibrium, prosperity is a period of innovating activity, with innovators borrowing money from banks and bidding factors away from other industries. This holds down the rise in output of finished goods, generates rising prices, and stimulates speculation based on the assumption that prices will go on rising indefinitely. Recession is the period when, innovation having stopped, the fruits of the innovation of prosperity are reaped. Output of finished goods rises rapidly, prices fall (the more so because innovators repay bank debt), and obsolete firms get competed out of existence. Depression (if there is any) means abnormal liquidation—liquidation of firms that could survive in equilibrium. It results from the speculation of the prosperity phases (without which recession would end in equilibrium, setting the stage for another period of prosperity). It carries the economy below equilibrium. It means falling prices. Although in the case of Juglars it means vicious spirals, panics and falling output, output does not fall in Kondratieffs.[15] Revival is a return to equilibrium, with rising prices and output.

In the historical sections of his treatise Schumpeter always worked with four-phase cycles, but in his theoretical discussion he made it

15. Schumpeter's theory includes the paradoxical concept of a depression with rising output: "total output will increase through all phases of the cycle, 'deep' depression alone excepted. . . , the exception hardly ever extending over the whole of the depressive phase, since it is due to panics and vicious spirals, which as a rule do not last more than one year" (*ibid.*, II, 500-1). The paradox is not troublesome for Juglars, for which the theory normally expects lower output at the end of depression than at the beginning. For the Kondratieff, the theory predicts rising output during depression as a whole. I prefer the two-phase Kondratieff in part because it avoids the paradox.

THEORETICAL FRAMEWORK

clear that depression and revival are not necessary parts of the model. Whether these phases appear at all he considered to be a question of fact.[16] Chapter 5 will take up the question of whether a two-phase or a four-phase Kondratieff fits the facts better. To anticipate, it will conclude that a two-phase cycle works better, with prosperity dated from 1843 to 1869 and recession from 1870 to 1897.[17]

Now for the Kitchins. Of the three reasons for expecting multiplicity of cycles, only the first applies to the forty-month cycle—namely, that the gestation period is different for different innovations. Kitchins will have prosperity and recession phases. But will they also have a secondary wave and abnormal liquidation, i.e., depression and revival? It is possible. But a Kitchin that occurs during revival or prosperity phases of a Juglar is not likely to experience a significant amount of abnormal liquidation, for the Juglar will swamp any tendency in that direction; and in the downward phases of the Juglar, there would be no opportunity for a secondary wave and therefore no abnormal liquidation. Expectation is generally in favor of Kitchins with two rather than four phases.

Schumpeter found in most Juglars exactly three Kitchins, although the latter often appear only in rates of change, not in absolute movements. But the theory can accommodate as many Kitchins in a Juglar as the facts warrant: there need not be any Kitchins at all; and the schema is flexible enough to fit a wide variety of cases.

But were the minor cycles of history really caused by innovations? Schumpeter himself had doubts on this point, mentioning that they may be "adaptive" fluctuations. One need not choose. Short cycles of

---

16. *Ibid.*, I, 150.

17. Fellner, *Trends,* paid almost no attention to the possibility of a two-phase Kondratieff, but I regard his discussion of the first two Kondratieffs as confirming my view. He had less objection to Schumpeter's four-phase Kondratieff for 1898-1953; here I disagree. If one makes due allowances for external events (the two world wars and their aftermaths), a two-phase Kondratieff fits quite well.

Although the two-phase Kondratieff generally works better, the idea of a secondary wave (or boom) is worth retaining even though it cannot be fitted neatly into a schema in a manner that also fits the facts. The basic idea of the secondary wave is speculation on the expectation that prosperity will last forever. If this concept is coupled with the well-known hypothesis that the longer good times last, the more reckless business behavior becomes, the unusually violent boom of 1928-29 (cf. also the boom of the early 1870's) falls nicely into place in a two-phase Kondratieff but not into the four-phase Kondratieff, the prosperity phase of which Schumpeter dated as ending in 1914. Unfortunately, a secondary wave implies depression and revival phases, contradicting the two-phase model. However awkward the idea is for the model, it seems worth retaining.

either type may occur. Factual investigations must determine which is right in any particular case.[18]

Statistical investigations of the past thirty years have turned up evidence of twenty-year cycles, or swings, in a number of different spheres, of which building is the best known. Schumpeter never dealt with them satisfactorily. His comments on the building cycle imply that it can be traced to innovation in other fields. This scarcely meets the problem, since it does not account for a cycle twice the length of the Juglar. Elsewhere, in discussing his choice of three classes of cycles, he wrote, "Five would perhaps be better, although, after some experimenting, the writer came to the conclusion that the improvement in the picture would not warrant the increase in cumbersomeness."[19] The better fit referred to may have been with reference to the twenty-year cycle, but evidently Schumpeter gives little help on this point. The problems are primarily empirical, making it inappropriate to try to deal with them fully now. Twenty-year cycles can be incorporated into the schema, if necessary, by adding a fourth kind of cycle, having two phases (prosperity and recession). There would be three such cycles to a Kondratieff, the greater part of two of them falling in our period—1861-79 and 1879-97. With due allowance for the Civil War and the effects of the Juglar cycles, this does not give too bad a fit to the building cycle. The meaning of the two phases is strictly Schumpeterian—recession was the period when the housing services

CHART 1. Four-Cycle Schema (Kitchin cycles are omitted).

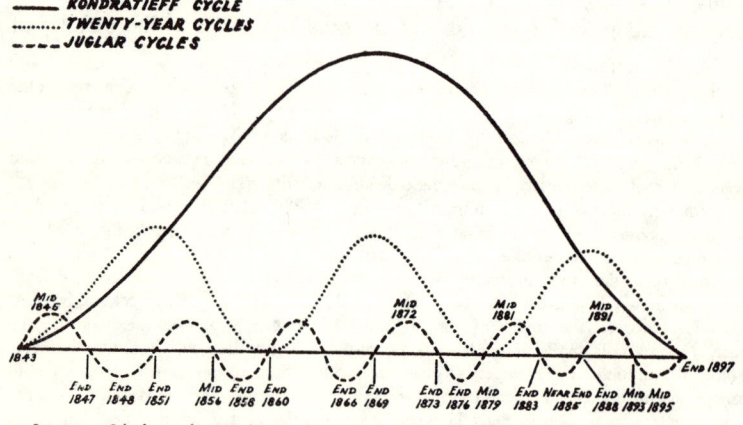

SOURCE: Of dates for Juglar cycles, Schumpeter, *Business Cycles*, I, 396-97.

18. Cf. *Conference*, p. 154.   19. *Business Cycles*, I, 169.

from the investment of prosperity were reaped. Chart 1 illustrates the revised schema.

The major weaknesses of Schumpeter's theory have now been dealt with. Kuznets criticized the theory on grounds that clustering of innovations does not follow from scarcity of entrepreneurial ability; but as Lange pointed out, clustering occurs because the risks of innovating are at a minimum in the neighborhood of the equilibrium that terminates the revival phase. Nevertheless, it should be noted that multiplicity of cycles implies that innovations may come at almost any time.

At first glance, Schumpeter's use of Walrasian equilibrium appears to be poles apart from anything that appears in most modern theories. Such, however, is not the case. To demonstrate this, let us use as an example the simplest type of multiplier-accelerator theory, that of Samuelson, and unlike him take it as a theory of the business cycle instead of a theory of the effects of marginal increments of public expenditure.[20] Samuelson's model yields cycles that may be anti-damped, damped, or undamped except for values of the multiplier and the accelerator that he considered most improbable. These cycles fluctuate about a line of equilibrium. The revival phase (in Schumpeter's sense) is a return to equilibrium in both the Samuelsonian and the Schumpeterian models. Samuelson's model, however, overshoots equilibrium because of the values of the multiplier and the accelerator (together with certain assumptions about lags), whereas Schumpeter called on innovation to explain the prosperity phase. Why doesn't Schumpeter's model overshoot equilibrium in the absence of innovation?

He had two answers. First, he thought there was nothing comparable to the breakdown of the secondary wave during recession to cause the economy to overshoot equilibrium. This can be interpreted in terms of Samuelson's model as meaning the accelerator will not in fact have a stable value but will become progressively lower as equilibrium is approached. Second, he said that if the economy does overshoot equilibrium, in the absence of innovation and external factors fluctuations about equilibrium will eventually die down, i.e., they will be damped. This can be interpreted as meaning either that the values of the multiplier and accelerator will be such as to produce

---

20. Paul A. Samuelson, "Interactions between the Multiplier Analysis and the Principle of Acceleration," *Review of Economic Statistics*, XXI (May 1939), 75-78, reprinted in *Readings in Business Cycle Theory*, pp. 261-69.

damped cycles or that buffers that Samuelson has not included in his simplified model will have the same effect.

Schumpeter's first reason is less convincing than the second. There is a mechanism that makes the economy overshoot equilibrium, namely, the reciprocal stimulation of investment and consumption, but in the absence of innovation the cycles might eventually die down.

The subject of equilibrium involves another problem. Unemployment is compatible with Schumpeter's (Walrasian) equilibrium, but it is different in kind from Keynesian equilibrium unemployment. Schumpeter's unemployment resulted largely from imperfections of competition; Keynes's came from oversaving. Schumpeter appeared to feel that equilibrium with no more than "normal" unemployment would have been reached in 1897 even without innovation; the Keynesian system opens the possibility that the equilibrium reached might have involved "abnormal" unemployment in Schumpeter's terminology (although in such a year as 1897 growth and the deepening of capital might have provided sufficient investment to generate full employment). This involves no difficulty, for Keynesian oversaving can be introduced into Schumpeter's model as a special case.[21]

Hicks

The purpose of the discussion above has been to rework Schumpeter's theory to make it a better hypothesis for historical work. What follows is on a different plane. In view of the chronically unsettled state of business cycle theory, historical research ought not be conducted in terms of a single analytic framework, unless it be highly eclectic. Now, there are advantages in synthesizing different approaches prior to coming to grips with history. The chief advantage concerns the ultimate aim of cycle research—namely, to arrive at a theory that is more than a mere hypothesis, that satisfactorily explains the business cycles of the capitalist world. Although this study cannot be expected to come remotely close to the ultimate aim, it is desirable to indicate as clearly as possible what kind of theory it points to. Since *a priori* there is no reason for excluding the possibility that it will point to some combination of existing theories, it will be useful to know at the outset how they fit together—to what extent they are complementary and can be combined, to what extent they offer alter-

---

21. Cf. Arthur Smithies, "Schumpeter and Keynes," *Review of Economics and Statistics*, XXXIII (May 1951), 164.

natives among which a choice must be made. The synthesis that will be offered is not a hypothesis but a tool, not a theory but a step toward a theory. It becomes a theory in the full sense only when either a choice has been made among the alternatives or the conditions are specified under which each alternative comes into play.

Cyclical theories that combine the multiplier and the accelerator are highly controversial. Some distinguished economists have developed and refined them; other distinguished economists have disparaged them. Why consider Hicks's theory at all in connection with historical work is the question adherents of the latter group will ask, whereas if I omitted them altogether adherents of the former group would be just as wondering. The reason for considering a multiplier-accelerator model is the fact that such theories are controversial. Whatever one's preconceptions, it is desirable to consider seriously whether such a theory is helpful in historical work. Even if the results turn out largely negative, the question needs to be taken up. Science progresses by discrediting theories.

Hicks's theory has a strongly eclectic element. It offers no less than five separate explanations of the downturn. But often the basic issue in cycle analysis is emphasis; and the distinctive element of Hicks's theory is its emphasis on real factors, particularly a high accelerator leading to collision with a full employment ceiling.

The first question to ask about Hicks's theory is whether the accelerator is relevant for business cycle analysis. No one questions the basic proposition underlying it, namely, that increased demand calls forth increased output, which necessitates greater capacity, and vice versa. In the long run, investment and capacity get geared to output. But in the short time periods relevant for business cycles, a host of other considerations bear on decisions to invest—expectations as to how long the increased demand will endure, amount of excess capacity, possibility of output's temporarily exceeding capacity, cost and availability of investment funds, cost and availability of capital goods, size of stocks, reaction of customers to higher prices, etc. Empirical studies of the relation between demand and investment in particular industries have generally been unfavorable to the acceleration principle. Many students of the business cycle have felt that the accelerator was worthless.

As a description of what goes on in the real world, the acceleration principle is far too simple. But the test of a theory is never whether it is descriptively accurate. Simplification is essential to theorizing. Uneasiness about simplification in the acceleration principle means no more than a guess about whether it might lead to a good theory and it does not mean that anybody who formulates a theory on the basis of it has been proved wrong. The test of a theory is in its implications.

In the context of Hicks's theory the usual objections to the accelerator do not hold. Take, for example, the situation at the end of the downswing. The problem of excess capacity is taken account of: income remains at the lower limit until excess capacity gets worked off. Thereafter, when Hicks calls on the accelerator to drive income up, all the complications that might interfere are, or shortly become, favorable to investment. Interest rates are low, capital goods are obtainable on favorable terms, confidence is increasing, stocks are low, labor is available, and by hypothesis excess capacity no longer prevails. It is true that each firm and industry will react differently, some faster than others; and the acceleration principle might provide a poor prediction of individual behavior. But in such circumstances the economy as a whole reacts by increasing capacity in response to increased demand. However drastically the acceleration principle simplifies the case, the considerations adduced against it do not destroy Hicks's theory.

One might believe that Hicks has not made adequate allowance for changes in the value of the accelerator. In one sense, changes in the accelerator's value are basic to the theory, inasmuch as induced investment (or disinvestment) is limited at the upper turning point, during the downswing, and in the period (called "depression" by Hicks[22]) during which output creeps along the lower limit. But all such changes may be looked on as deviations from the accelerator's "true" value; and the "true" value must be in a constant state of flux, of which it can be argued that Hicks has not taken adequate account.[23] It seems to me that this need not disturb us. In only one phase, upswing, does the true value of the accelerator fully assert itself. In this phase, an increase in the value of the accelerator would be of no

---

22. *Contribution*, p. 111.

23. The methodological basis of this discussion needs to be stated. Ideally, Hicks's theory would be tested by its predictions, not its assumptions, so that the discussion in the text above would be irrelevant. But on account of, e.g., external events, testing is so difficult that empirical workers are confronted with an unmanageably large legacy of cycle theories that have not been disproved. As a practical matter one must select a limited number for intensive consideration; and for each theory selected one must satisfy oneself on the basis of such points as are discussed here that it is a reasonably promising hypothesis. Or, to put the matter another way, I am at the moment developing tools of analysis and must inquire whether this particular tool is likely to be useful.

THEORETICAL FRAMEWORK

consequence, since it would reinforce the explosive behavior that is the essence of the theory. A decrease might bring about a downturn, but this would be only a variant of one of Hicks's own variants, the weak (anti-damped) cycle.

The next question to ask about Hicks's theory is whether the assumption of an explosive value of the accelerator is a useful tool. As Hicks himself said, "one's first reaction is to reject it out of hand."[24] But this reaction probably stems from the failure of pump-priming in the nineteen thirties, and such failure is precisely what Hicks's model would predict at that time of widespread excess capacity.[25] Moreover, Hicks's assumption corresponds very well with the traditional view of the business cycle mechanism. If there is any received doctrine in this field at all, surely it is the proposition that expansions and contractions cumulate like a snowball rolling downhill. The history of business cycles affords enough evidence for the hypothesis to warrant taking it seriously.

In the downswing especially there is little reason for skepticism. Any businessman who replaces equipment that there is no current use for does not remain a businessman long. The difficulty is to understand not why the decelerator should be explosive but why the downswing comes to an end short of zero employment. Hicks shows that because disinvestment cannot exceed depreciation, the downswing converges on a lower limit.

For the expansion phase one has difficulty resolving one's doubts about the explosive accelerator. It just does not seem likely that businessmen react as strongly to a rise in demand as the theory requires. On the other hand, the cumulative mechanism is at least plausible. Moreover, Hicks made a test based on statistics for the United States between 1869 and 1914 that, although admittedly crude, makes the explosive hypothesis appear reasonable.[26] The test indicates that the accelerator would have been high enough to induce antidamped cycles, provided that induced net investment exceeded one sixth of total net investment; and I infer that if it amounted to as much as one third, the accelerator would have been explosive. Such a proportion of induced investment to the total is well within possibility.

The one clearly unsatisfactory feature of Hicks's theory is the variant in which autonomous investment undergoes independent cycles of its own. Hicks has made no attempt to explain what causes cycles of autonomous investment. He has only shown how they

24. *Ibid.*, p. 91.   25. *Ibid.*, p. 52.
26. *Ibid.*, pp. 92-94. See also pp. 71 and 87.

can be inserted into his analysis if they occur. A satisfactory hypothesis must do more than this. But the weakness will be no great problem for this study. The variant in question is a subordinate one, not the essential part of Hicks's thought. What is more, there are ready to hand two possible explanations, Schumpeter's and Gordon's, for variations in what to Hicks is autonomous investment.

Now let us compare and reconcile, where possible, the theories of Schumpeter and Hicks. Hicks deals with only one kind of cycle, which lasts for seven to ten years and may therefore be regarded as comparable to Schumpeter's Juglar.[27] Since Schumpeter's could be put in terms of a Keynesian framework (however inadequate that framework would be for the purpose) and Hicks's could be put into a Walrasian framework (however unnecessarily complex that framework would be for the purpose), there is no problem of combining features of both theories if one wishes and no need to work out rigorously and completely how it would be done. Both theories start from an equilibrium line about which the business cycle fluctuates. The two equilibria are quite different. Schumpeter's is Walrasian, meaning that every single firm and individual is in equilibrium. With due qualification for imperfections, multiplicity of cycles, etc., the economy actually reaches a neighborhood of equilibrium at certain times. Hicks's equilibrium is merely aggregative; and although a turning point is the start of a movement toward equilibrium, the explosive accelerator dominates what happens from there on. Hicks explicitly states that the economy is never in equilibrium.

What is for Schumpeter the prosperity phase, for Hicks the latter part of the upswing, and for both the rise above equilibrium is motivated differently in the two theories. In Schumpeter it comes about because equilibrium creates conditions favorable to innovation, which induces credit creation and the secondary wave. In Hicks it comes about because the interaction of multiplier and accelerator in the first part of the upswing carries the economy beyond equilibrium. The two kinds of motivation are not mutually exclusive. In fact, *a priori* one might expect both to come into play. Moreover, there is not a great deal of difference between Schumpeter's secondary wave and Hicks's induced investment. In fact, Hicks's accelerator can be regarded as a simplification, helpful for mathematical manipulation, of the diverse factors that go into the secondary wave.

To Hicks's five explanations for the downturn (most of them not

27. *Ibid.*, p. 2.

mutually exclusive[28]) must be added that of Schumpeter, which involves increasing risks for innovators, exhaustion of innovating opportunities, autodeflation, and the competing-down process. This requires a further word on equilibrium. Disequilibrium enters into Hicks's model only as purely aggregative, whereas Schumpeter went behind the aggregates to discover disequilibria of particular firms and industries, disequilibria that grew out of the innovating process but eventually affected the aggregates. This idea should be incorporated in a synthetic theory, because it utilizes and explains Mitchell's discovery that costs overtake prices in the upswing and bring about a decline in profits. The competing-down process creates untenable situations that sooner or later must be liquidated. Their liquidation may be an element in the downturn. Consequently, equilibrium should be thought of in the Walrasian and not just in the aggregative sense.

Oddly enough, what in Hicks's principal variant is called the "full boom"—the period when output is creeping along the ceiling but has not yet turned down—comes in what for Schumpeter is the beginning of recession. The two names and analyses point to two different characteristics commonly found just before what the N.B.E.R. regards as a peak: full employment in the one case, increasing competition and failures in the other. The two explanations for the downturn are not mutually exclusive; both could be at work.

All analyses of what happens after the downturn (in the N.B.E.R. sense) are pretty much alike qualitatively. The distinctive feature of Schumpeter's is scrapping and rearranging—correction of partial disequilibria—during the remainder of recession and their contribution to monetary breakdowns. Another feature is autodeflation, the automatic repayment of bank loans by successful innovators out of their profits.

Schumpeter's analysis of why the downswing comes to an end is vague. He could see no reason in principle why the downswing should not go on indefinitely, but said that in practice buffers tend to limit it. Hicks is more precise in the way he analyzes the buffers, which are the Keynesian law that consumption falls less than income, autonomous investment (which may be depressed by the processes of the downswing but does not go to zero), and the limit imposed on induced disinvestment by its inability to fall below zero. The Key-

---

28. The exception is that the weak-cycle variant, which brings about a downturn without output's colliding with a ceiling, is inconsistent with the two variants in which there is a collision and with the monetary variant.

nesian law is one of Schumpeter's buffers (although not called by that name), and Hicks's autonomous investment is like the investment opportunities opened up by Schumpeterian innovation in the preceding prosperity. The limit on disinvestment did not explicitly enter into Schumpeterian analysis. The analysis of Hicks seems to offer a better hypothesis because it includes this factor and has greater rigor.

There is no counterpart in Schumpeter for what Hicks calls "depression," the period when output is creeping along the lower limit before it starts to rise toward equilibrium. Hicksian upswing must wait till excess capacity gets worked off through failure to replace capital and through the upward trend of autonomous investment.[29] For Schumpeter, no phase of this sort was necessary. A good deal of the excess capacity at the end of the downswing would be obsolete either technologically or in terms of the structure of demand, so that in effect it was already eliminated. Also, Schumpeterian revival is not powered by the accelerator. For present purposes, Hicksian depression can be retained in the synthesis, leaving it to empirical investigation to discover (if possible) whether it occurred.

For both authors, the first part of the upswing represents a return toward equilibrium; and in a broad sense, this is the undoubted explanation of why output, if ever it stops falling in the downswing, revives: the cumulative mechanism of the downswing has driven output below equilibrium. Nevertheless, Schumpeter and Hicks offer two quite different explanations, based on two quite different concepts of equilibrium—the one stable, the other unstable; the one depending on equilibrating adjustments of wages, interest rates, prices, investment, and saving, the other denying that such equilibrators are effective.

Post-Keynesian economists have a hard time accepting Schumpeter's account of revival. They no longer believe in the power of equilibrators, particularly in the short run, and are bound to inquire where the investment will come from that is needed to generate higher output. Yet there is more merit in the Schumpeterian view than they are apt to accord it. First, disequilibria of wages, prices, interest rates, etc., can depress output, and their correction is a necessary element of revival. Secondly, the answer to where the investment comes from has been provided. It comes from the new economic space opened up by the innovation of the preceding prosperity.[30] Thirdly, the

---

29. In the short time that Hicksian depression could be presumed to last, it is doubtful if either of these factors would be quantitatively significant.

30. Schumpeter, *Business Cycles*, II, 501.

THEORETICAL FRAMEWORK

equilibrators may have been more adequate in the nineteenth century than now.

Despite Schumpeter, there is no reason to doubt that rising demand and output induce increased investment, which in turn generates still more demand. To all intents and purposes, Schumpeter put this mechanism into the secondary wave of his prosperity phase, although he would have repudiated Hicks's method of dealing with it. That he did not allow for it also in revival appears to be a shortcoming.

To conclude, the analyses of Schumpeter and Hicks supplement each other. Investment that Hicks might regard as induced by a preceding rise of output might be interpreted by Schumpeter as moving into economic space opened up by previous innovation—and both could be right.

Gordon

Interaction of multiplier and accelerator represents one line of development from the work of Keynes. Another is analysis in terms of investment opportunities. The latest and most useful work along this line has been done by R. A. Gordon.[31]

Gordon defines the stock of underlying investment opportunities as the difference between the existing capital stock and that which businessmen would find it most profitable to have if they were well informed regarding all current cost and demand relationships and also the forces making for long-run growth in the economy. . . . The appropriate capital stock is to be considered with respect not to the present level of income but to that level which would result from attempts to achieve the appropriate capital stock. . . . What capital stock is appropriate also depends on what capital stock now exists, as well as on relative factor prices (including interest rates), the nature of consumers' preference maps, existing and foreseeable technological possibilities, and the nature of competitive relationships.[32]

The stock of investment opportunities must be distinguished from the inducement to exploit them. To the extent that a decline in actual investment has been caused by a cyclical decline in output, the stock of investment opportunities cannot be said to have declined. Rather, the inducement to take advantage of them has been impaired.[33]

Both exogenous and endogenous factors bring about changes in the stock. Among the forces giving rise to investment opportunities are technological change (foremost as a source of investment that "does

31. "Investment." 32. *Ibid.*, p. 25. 33. *Ibid.*, p. 26.

not depend on the behavior of aggregate output in the economy as a whole"[34]); population growth relative to the stock of housing; wear, tear and obsolescence,[35] giving rise to replacement needs; growth in output (the acceleration principle).[36]

Investment opportunities need not be used up at the same rate that they are created. The more the opportunities, the greater the inducement to invest *ceteris paribus,* but there are necessarily lags between creation of opportunities and their exploitation—the time it takes to perceive them, to make financial arrangements, to place orders, to produce the investment goods. The amount of investment that can be carried out at any time is limited by inelasticity in the supply of loanable funds and of capital goods. Further, investment is influenced by the cyclical situation.[37] Gordon assumes that an industrialized economy can finance and produce or import enough capital goods in the boom to use up investment opportunities more rapidly than they are being created.[38]

Gordon develops a threefold classification of cycles. In the pure minor cycle, neither the stock nor the inducement to exploit long-term investment opportunities becomes impaired. "The downturn comes because of a downward revision in short-period production plans. . . ."[39] This is the so-called inventory recession.[40] It is short and mild.

There are two types of hybrid cycles. In one, the stock of investment opportunities remains adequate but the inducement to exploit them becomes impaired. A downward revision of short-period production plans may initiate a decline in output that damages business confidence so that investment opportunities are not correctly evaluated.[41] In the other type of hybrid, the downturn results from shortage of capital—either loanable funds or investment goods—which temporarily reduces investment opportunities.[42] Hybrid contractions may be sharp but are not likely to last long.

In major cycles, investment goes on long enough so that the stock of opportunities becomes seriously impaired. Such a situation leads to depressions that are long and severe, even though secular stagnation is not envisaged.[43] The deficiency of investment opportunities is temporary. "During the depression we can assume that the stock of investment opportunities will begin to accumulate until it is again

---

34. *Ibid.*
35. This appears to overlap with technological change.
36. *Ibid.*, pp. 26-28.   37. *Ibid.*, p. 28.   38. *Ibid.*, p. 29.
39. *Ibid.*   40. *Ibid.*, pp. 23-24.   41. *Ibid.*, p. 29.
42. *Ibid.*, p. 30.   43. *Ibid.*, pp. 30-31.

THEORETICAL FRAMEWORK

able to support a high level of employment...."[44] One set of investment stimuli sometimes follows so closely on another that the intervening downswing, if any, is short. In such cases Gordon speaks of incomplete or overlapping major cycles.[45]

Some comments are in order. Even short-run changes in interest rates and other cost relationships are interpreted as changing the stock of investment opportunities rather than the inducement to exploit them. For my purposes, I prefer to define the stock in terms of long-run or equilibrium cost relationships so that short-run changes affect the inducement to exploit it.[46] This means that in both types of hybrid cycles, not just one, the stock remains unimpaired. This makes it easier to show how Gordon's ideas fit into Hicks's analysis.

Although Gordon makes some allowance for irrational investment[47] (as well as irrational failure to invest), his concept of opportunities embraces only rational investment, i.e., investment that would be profitable under correct appraisal. For the American economy of today this is appropriate. By and large, investment decisions are made on the basis of staff work and careful investigation. For the nineteenth century, a strictly rational concept of opportunities is awkward. It is hard to tell even in retrospect how much of the investment in railroads was rational in any long-run sense; I suspect that a substantial part was not. In such a situation, major cycles in a sense close to but not identical with Gordon's may result from long-continued investment seriously impairing a stock in which genuine investment opportunities are mingled with spurious ones; and the exhaustion of spurious opportunities could be a significant element. Fortunately, I have not in practice been able to tell spurious from genuine, and can pretend that they are all the latter.

In Gordon's major depressions, the stock is temporarily too low to support a high level of employment. It is very difficult to know in any historical case how large the stock is or whether it is deficient. One must guard against the error of inferring inadequate opportunities from inadequate realized investment. Particularly for the last third of the nineteenth century, it will be difficult to refute those who argue that investment opportunities are never deficient. But Gordon's statement that the greater the stock of opportunities, the greater is the inducement to invest, points the way to a useful and less

---

44. *Ibid.*, p. 31.   45. *Ibid.*, p. 32.
46. More precisely, fluctuations of interest rates within major cycles affect the inducement; fluctuations between major cycles, the stock.
47. *Ibid.*, p. 30.

controversial generalization. Although one cannot tell whether the total stock is deficient relative to the propensity to save, one can often form some notion as to the stock's fluctuations; and a decline in the stock can always be interpreted as an unfavorable force even though one may not be able to tell if it is a sufficient cause of depression.

Whereas the theories of Schumpeter and Hicks are strictly endogenous,[48] Gordon's analysis includes a large measure of external events. Quite aside from technological change, the factors creating investment opportunities are often exogenous—wars, for instance. Beyond the difference this implies between Gordon's major cycles and Schumpeter's Juglars, Gordon's concepts look more like a set of tools and less like a cyclical theory. He does, to be sure, sketch a complete theory of the major cycle: investment opportunities get used up in the boom and accumulate during depression. But the accumulation need not come about for internal reasons; and depression may not be longlived—in fact, it may not occur at all.

The relation between Gordon and Hicks is as follows: the analysis of investment opportunities strengthens the whole of Hicks's theory by exploring the nature of autonomous investment, and it strengthens one variant especially by providing a rationale for humps in autonomous investment. Unfortunately, the relation between the concepts of investment in the two analyses is not easy to clarify. It is clear that not only autonomous investment but also the amount of induced investment allowed for in Hicks's equilibrium line comes out of the stock of investment opportunities as defined by Gordon. There is, therefore, a rough correspondence between the rate of investment that would take place in equilibrium and the rate at which new investment opportunities get created.

I infer that the induced investment of the first part of Hicks's upswing, while output is rising from the lower limit to the equilibrium line, generally comes under the heading of exploiting the stock of investment opportunities, since the capacity created is needed to accommodate the long-run growth of the economy. The induced disinvestment of the downswing generally comes under the heading of an impaired (reduced) stock of opportunities, inasmuch as correct

---

48. Some would disagree with this as far as Schumpeter is concerned, on grounds that technological change—the basis for innovation—is external. Schumpeter himself did not look at it this way (*Business Cycles*, I, 8-9). Whatever the merits of the case, it will be convenient here to take Schumpeter at his word, since the contrast between him and Gordon is beyond question.

appraisal would reveal excess capacity, but to some extent impairment of incentives is involved. What Hicks calls depression (the period when output creeps along the lower limit) appears to have a counterpart in Gordon, but whereas for Hicks it is a period of working off excess capacity, for Gordon it is a period of accumulating investment opportunities. There is a common element in both these views, since failure to make replacements adds to the stock of investment opportunities in the sense defined, but Gordon adds something that is not in Hicks. For Hicks the equilibrium line is normally below the full employment ceiling; presumably for Gordon this is an exceptional case. The divergence over what is considered normal is one of the main differences between the two. If, however, output rises above equilibrium, the investment in excess of what would be made at equilibrium is the result, from Gordon's point of view, of incorrect appraisal of investment opportunities. It probably, but not necessarily, reduces the stock of opportunities. (Not necessarily, because if the investment is misdirected it would be of little or no use in equilibrium.)

The distinction between autonomous and induced investment, so prominent in Hicks's thought, does not figure in Gordon's analysis *per se,* but he has commented that "the rate at which . . . investment actually takes place depends upon how the cyclical inducements to invest operate in the industries affected, so that such 'autonomous' or 'structural' investment is also induced by the 'endogenous' variables in our system."[49] There is an echo of this idea in Hicks, inasmuch as autonomous investment may be depressed in the downswing. Nevertheless, Hicks makes autonomous investment far more independent of business conditions than Gordon believes appropriate. *A priori,* one is bound to side with Gordon. In reality, there are not simply two categories of investment, autonomous and induced, but rather a series of gradations between the two. Some investment is closely geared to the current business situation and the way it is changing, some is independent of it, but a great deal falls somewhere in between. It may be useful to start by assuming that all investment falls into one or the other of the two polar categories, but this is a simplification and a pretty drastic one at that.

Whereas the relation between Gordon and Hicks is complementary, the former strengthening the latter, they offer quite different hypotheses for the cause of deep depression. Hicks attributes deep depression to monetary factors—real forces alone are not likely to be enough. Gordon not only regards insufficient investment opportuni-

[49]. "Investment," p. 28.

ties as the cause of major depression but has built that hypothesis into his definition of major cycles.

Those who regard investment opportunities as the key to business fluctuations usually give a bow in Schumpeter's direction, but they differ from him on a fundamental point. For Schumpeter, a deficiency of investment opportunities is never to blame. It is true that innovating opportunities are limited: they tend to get depleted during prosperity; and this is part of the explanation of the downturn. But it is not a sufficient explanation: autodeflation and the competing-down process are essential. There is normally unemployment in equilibrium neighborhoods for both Hicks and Schumpeter for quite different reasons: for Hicks it is because investment opportunities in Gordon's sense are deficient; for Schumpeter it represents, paradoxically, a kind of disequilibrum. In Schumpeter's theory, only the inducement to exploit gets impaired. The innovation of prosperity opens up new economic space, creating investment opportunities for the succeeding three phases.

Gordon's major cycle is by no means the same as Schumpeter's Juglar, but the two are attempts to explain approximately the same phenomena. The relation between Gordon's minor cycle and Schumpeter's Kitchin is similar. Gordon does not employ the concept of a Kondratieff, and Schumpeter has no counterpart for hybrids.[50]

There is no necessary contradiction between the explanations of Schumpeter and Gordon. Both could operate simultaneously and could be combined into one theory with an infinite variety of emphases. It is a question for empirical investigation.

Conclusion

A synthetic framework or theory has just been sketched. It would be better to develop it fully and rigorously, since rigor is a valuable safeguard against error. But in view of the purposes of this study, such an undertaking hardly seems worth the space. I shall leave theory to the theorists and do no more with it than my task requires.

The synthesis is particularly weak at one point—the Kitchin or minor cycles. Under other circumstances, it would be advisable to go into them more fully and in particular to incorporate Metzler's

---

50. The three examples of hybrids suggested by Gordon—1907, 1937-38, and with qualifications 1921—in each case, with qualifications again for 1921, were outside Schumpeter's schema and not explicable in terms of his theory: "Investment," p. 31; Schumpeter, *Business Cycles*, I, 424-25, II, 786 and 1011-50.

theory of inventory cycles;[51] for Schumpeter, Hicks, and Gordon are not much help at this point. But for want of data, particularly with respect to inventories, I shall not be able to make much headway with short cycles.

This chapter has made no attempt to apportion emphasis in accordance with the importance of the factors in the real world. In particular, monetary factors have been slighted. This is partly because monetary influences are often external and therefore drop out of discussion of internal mechanisms. It is partly because little need be said. There is a monetary cycle in the synthesis, even though it sneaked in via Hicks.

Some twenty years ago, prior to publication of the three contributions discussed in this chapter, Gottfried Haberler reviewed business cycle theory as it then stood and developed a synthetic theory.[52] It is worth checking what has been done here against his synthesis to see if anything has been left out. Although much of Haberler's discussion is here only by implication, two topics alone have been apparently neglected. One of them, wage and price flexibility, will be dealt with in the next chapter. The other, maladjustments in the structure of production as cause of the downturn, actually figured in the discussion in two places. Schumpeter's competing-down process is in fact an analysis of causes and consequences of maladjustments. One type of hybrid cycle in Gordon's treatment, where the boom is choked off by shortage of capital, is another kind of maladjustment. Maladjustments might arise in other ways, for instance by the playing out of investment opportunities in a particular direction, such as house or railroad building; and since such a maladjustment would ordinarily coincide with a decline in the stock of investment opportunities, depression might follow even if the aggregate stock was not too low for full employment. Such possibilities must be kept in mind.

Haberler showed that when he wrote there was not so very much difference among business cycle theories. They were seldom contradictory; they often differed mainly in emphasis. The discussion here illustrates that his statement is still true, a statement that foreshadows the nature of the empirical problem—to discover where to put the emphasis.

---

51. Lloyd A. Metzler, "The Nature and Stability of Inventory Cycles," *Review of Economic Statistics*, XXIII (Aug. 1941), 113-29.

52. *Prosperity and Depression* (Geneva, 1937), hereafter referred to as *Prosperity*. A number of chapters were added in later editions, but these were in the nature of addenda.

3

PRICE AND WAGE FLEXIBILITY DURING CYCLICAL CONTRACTION

THE LITERATURE on the role of downward price flexibility on income and employment falls into two main divisions. One group deals with the effect of flexibility on the equilibrium level of national income. The other deals with its effects on a process of business cycle contraction. The two problems are distinct. Falling wages and prices could raise the equilibrium position to full employment and at the same time intensify or prolong a cyclical contraction already under way. They could raise the equilibrium level by increasing the value of the stock of money and government bonds, thereby raising the consumption function; and at the same time they could drive the economy ever further away from equilibrium by creating such unfavorable price expectations that spending of all kinds is postponed. This chapter is concerned with the second question, namely, the effects of flexibility on the path of cyclical contraction. Its purpose is to develop some tools needed to analyze the depression of the 1870's.

The theoretical literature on flexibility is not very helpful for explaining historical contractions.[1] This inadequacy has several origins

---

1. Among the more interesting writings are Haberler, *Prosperity* (3d ed.), pp. 395-405; Alfred C. Neal, *Industrial Concentration and Price Flexibility* (Washington, 1942), pp. 141-62; Alvin H. Hansen, *Fiscal Policy and Business Cycles* (New York, 1941), pp. 313-38 (hereafter cited as *Fiscal Policy*); Edward S. Mason, "Price Inflexibility," *Review of Economic Statistics*, XX (May 1938), 53-64; Kenneth E. Boulding, "In Defense of Monopoly," *Quarterly Journal of Economics*, LIX (Aug. 1945), 524-42; Gardiner C. Means, *Industrial Prices and Their Relative Inflexibility*, 74th Congress, 1st Session, Senate Doc. No. 13 (Washington, D. C., 1935); Gardiner C. Means in U. S. National Resources Planning Board, *The Structure of the American Economy, Part II* (Washington, D. C., 1940), pp. 13-15; and George W. Stocking and Myron W. Watkins, *Cartels or Competition?* (New York, 1948), pp. 240-54.

besides the inherent complexity of the subject. Writers have often investigated whether flexibility or inflexibility is the better anticyclical policy. If an author discovers that flexibility has both favorable and unfavorable repercussions, as is in fact the case, he concludes that reducing prices during depression has no clear advantage; and he does not trouble to work out its consequences under different conditions. Concentration on policy has sometimes made the discussion more polemical than dispassionate. Writers sometimes seek a clearcut conclusion rather than the drab complexity of truth.

The literature has often suffered from not distinguishing sharply between the monetary and physical aspects of cyclical contraction. An example will bring out the distinction. If the demand for capital goods is somewhat inelastic, a price cut in that industry will intensify the contraction of prices and aggregate money expenditures but, as will be shown below, will on balance expand output for the economy as a whole. Hence, the repercussions of both the intensified monetary contraction and the mitigated physical contraction must be analyzed before the results of cutting the prices of investment goods can be determined.

Depending on whether one is preoccupied with the monetary or production aspect, one can establish a general presumption that flexibility will either intensify or mitigate cyclical downswings. A presumption that flexibility is detrimental can be established by considering an economy resting in Keynesian underemployment equilibrium. If prices and wages are flexible, a deflation will commence that might go on indefinitely. Even if investment conditions now become favorable, revival may be postponed while the deflation lasts. An author starting with this presumption can easily find sophisticated arguments to strengthen it into a general conclusion. This appears to be what Boulding has done.

A presumption that flexibility will mitigate the contraction of output can be established in two ways. If all producing units and factors of production behaved like farmers and maintained output irrespective of what happened to price, the decline of output would be very small during cyclical contractions. This would be possible for most firms within wide limits if labor entered into overhead rather than marginal costs, as is the case for most labor in agriculture. The workers attached to a firm would participate in receipts (less cost of materials bought) on some prearranged basis. If, in addition, competition were perfect, real national income would hardly fall at all. Alternatively, if one assumes that the contraction of aggregate spending in money terms is given, then the lower prices are, the greater is the level of output at any given time. This reasoning is patently too simple, but it is possible to find sophisticated arguments to support the presumption and strengthen it into the conclusion that price cutting during contraction is beneficial. This appears to be what Means has done. In his first essay on flexibility Means put forward the presumption without recognizing the need for further analysis. In his later essay he made the argument more penetrating.

Even the eclectic discussions of flexibility such as Neal's[2] have not combined these two presumptions; but if one does so, one arrives at the expectation that flexibility would make a contraction more severe in monetary terms and less severe in terms of output. Such a result would not necessarily occur; for flexibility has many repercussions, some favorable and others unfavorable. The result in any concrete case would depend on particular circumstances, which might intensify favorable reactions and mitigate unfavorable ones, or vice versa. But of the four cases in American cyclical history that this discussion can be applied to, the two that had marked price-wage flexibility (1873-79 and 1920-21) were much more severe in monetary series than output series, and vice versa for the other two (1929-33 and 1937-38). This fact makes the combination of the two presumptions more interesting than pure theory would warrant.

The distinguishing features of the present study are the attempt to obtain results useful for historical analysis and the sharp distinction between monetary and production aspects of contractions. In addition, I shall attempt to be more nearly complete in covering all the complications involved. I shall also present a mathematical formula that so far as I know is original.

Precise definitions of wage and price flexibility are not needed for present purposes. This is fortunate, for no satisfactory definitions have yet been devised. By wage flexibility, I shall mean merely a tendency for money wages to fall in labor markets experiencing abnormal unemployment.[3] By price flexibility, I shall never mean prices of labor services and shall contrast two extreme cases: "on the one hand the

---

2. Boulding, Means, and Neal references are given in footnote 1 of this chapter.

3. Wage flexibility could be defined more precisely as a ratio in which the numerator is the percentage fall of wage rate (per some specified unit of time) and the denominator is the percentage of workers in the labor market for whom there are neither jobs nor job vacancies. For some purposes it might be better to define wage flexibility as the percentage fall of wages per unit of time. Both alternatives apply only to periods of declining or stationary demand for labor. In times of rising demand, rates are apt to go up even in competitive markets experiencing unemployment.

case of perfect competition . . . where prices are quite flexible and on the other hand a case where prices remain unchanged in the face of changes in demand and cost conditions."[4] That is, I am not necessarily concerned with the frequency and amplitude of price changes but rather with the response of price to changing conditions.

A great many different combinations of wage and price flexibility and inflexibility can be imagined, but I need to consider only three of them: (1) wage flexibility; (2) flexibility of the unit overhead-plus-profit margin; and (3) price flexibility in particular types of industries. All the theory needed for empirical application is covered by the three.

Wage Flexibility

The obvious starting point for a discussion of wage flexibility is Haberler's treatment, first analyzing the effects of wage reductions on (or via) a particular industry and later introducing indirect repercussions on other industries.[5] If the elasticity of demand for labor in a particular industry is greater than unity (implying that elasticity of demand for the product of the industry is greater still), wage reductions will increase (or mitigate the reduction of) not only output and employment but payrolls as well, so that cyclical contraction is mitigated. At the other extreme, if demand for labor in the industry is completely inelastic, there may be no increase in output or employment. If sales receipts fall but fall less than payrolls, part of the savings are likely to be used to increase liquidity, intensifying the deflation. Even under perfect competition, payrolls fall faster than sales receipts unless marginal prime costs are constant;[6] they fall faster yet under imperfect competition. (Hence, the freer the competition, the less likely are wage cuts to be deflationary.) Therefore, in the extreme case where the fall of wages does not increase employment or output at all, cyclical contraction is intensified.

Now assume the intermediate case where there is a fall in wages in one industry that increases output but decreases payrolls. What are the indirect effects? If part of the increased gross profits are hoarded, demand for other products will be reduced. This will partly or wholly offset the increase in the first industry. It is improbable that wage reductions will decrease output below what it would have been

---

4. Haberler, *Prosperity* (3d ed.), p. 492.
5. *Ibid.*, pp. 395-405.
6. If marginal prime costs are the same for any output whatsoever, price will equal average prime costs, and any reduction in wages will be entirely passed on to consumers in the form of lower prices. This is a most improbable case.

without the wage cuts. But even in such an unfavorable case, the increase in the real value of hoards (resulting from falling prices) will eventually reverse the tendency to hoard, thus bringing contraction to an end.[7] "If there are reasons to believe that even without a wage reduction contraction of MV will go on . . . it will certainly increase unemployment and prolong contraction if wages are not allowed to fall."[8]

Haberler's discussion is subject to one correction and a number of additions. (1) In discussing the repercussions of a wage-price cut on other industries, in one case he seems to ignore the effect of altered consumer expenditures for the product of the latter on their expenditures for the products of the former. In the favorable case where demand for labor in the industry is elastic (and therefore the demand for the product is still more elastic), the relative increase in aggregate expenditures is offset by a reduction in the money consumers have available to spend on other commodities. Hence, although wage reductions may increase output (apart from effects on investment), they will not mitigate the decline of aggregate spending merely because demand for the industry in question is elastic. My argument, however, is subject to a qualification. It does not apply to investment goods industries. If the demand for capital goods is elastic, the extra money will probably come from expansion of bank credit or idle balances.

(2) The preceding discussion has underrated the effects of wage cuts on investment. (a) Sagging wages and prices may inhibit investment by creating expectation of further price declines.[9] It must be conceded, however, that the Keynesians have overworked this point. Postponement of purchases implies that their urgency becomes ever greater. (b) The discussion above implies that the less profitable business is, the more quickly will contraction come to an end. In favor of this is the argument that higher profits (or lower losses) give greater scope to hoarding. But if revival depends on investment, and investment in turn is affected by current profits (which affect anticipations of future profits and provide a source of funds), then cutting profits is a two-edged sword. (c) Cutting profits may increase the number of bankruptcies. Failures increase the severity of contraction in two ways: they engender pessimism, and they reduce the flow of

---

7. Presumably, Haberler is thinking of both increased consumption and increased investment resulting from the accumulation of hoards.

8. Haberler, *Prosperity*, p. 405.

9. Haberler does, however, discuss this point elsewhere in his book.

money, both by leading to liquidation of debts to banks and others who are not likely to relend the proceeds during contraction and by tying up the firm's cash temporarily during liquidation proceedings. (d) Wage cuts may affect investment through the acceleration principle.[10] If lower wages result in greater output than would otherwise have been the case, consumption of capital may be reduced (i.e., investment may be larger than it otherwise would have been). (e) Lastly, wage cuts may affect business confidence, but in which direction it is not possible to foretell.

(3) In discussing the inducement to dishoard from a falling price level, the "money illusion" has so far been omitted. If consumers and businessmen believe in a normal level of prices, a decline below normal may induce more expenditures because they do not realize that a given percentage change of all prices and incomes does not alter the fundamental situation.

(4) In the intermediate case, demand for the wage-cutting industry's product is somewhat inelastic (i.e., greater than zero but less than one). It has already been stated that probably aggregate output will increase but aggregate spending decrease because the decline of payrolls in relation to sales increases hoarding. There is another reason for expecting aggregate spending to decline. Since aggregate output has increased, aggregate real income has also increased (or, rather, has not fallen as much as it would without the wage cut). On the usual assumption that an increase in income is divided between saving and consumption, aggregate spending will be less than it otherwise would have been. But this effect can only mitigate and cannot reverse the tendency for a wage cut to expand production; for it operates only insofar as total output does increase.

(5) If prices of other factors are rigid, a fall of wages will induce substitution of labor for other factors, increasing employment (but not output) and altering the distribution of income. (a) Aggregate workers' incomes may either rise or fall with resulting changes in aggregate spending in the same direction because of the workers' higher marginal propensity to consume. (b) Sometimes investment may increase in order to utilize methods involving a larger proportion of labor. But substitution effects would hardly be large during a cyclical contraction.[11]

10. This point is mentioned by Haberler in a footnote.
11. See James Tobin, "Money Wage Rates and Employment," in Seymour E. Harris, ed., *The New Economics* (New York, 1947), pp. 572-87, and Benjamin H. Higgins, "The Optimum Wage Rate," *Review of Economics and Statistics*, XXXI (May 1949), 131.

(6) In principle, a redistribution of income through falling wages takes place simultaneously in both directions, but in practice payrolls get affected sooner than dividends. Consequently, reduced spending by employees comes first and tends to reduce profits, thus nullifying the offsetting increase in consumption that otherwise would be expected from higher dividends.

(7) Under prevailing accounting practices, falling prices create inventory losses that are illusory. To the extent that decisions are governed by accounting profits rather than underlying reality, the inventory losses intensify the downswing. Presumably top managements in progressive firms have by now become sophisticated on this point. But sophistication cannot be assumed for the nineteenth century, and even today it is far from universal.

By now the discussion has covered all the important factors and some unimportant ones as well. All that remains is to summarize and draw conclusions. The starting point is the principle that with aggregate spending unchanged, wage cuts will increase output. What repercussions act in the direction of increasing spending, and what ones tend to reduce it? In the first category come the stimulus to investment from higher profits (2b above), reduction of bankruptcies (2c above), the money illusion (3 above), the increased value of hoards and government bonds in real terms, and greater investment as businessmen attempt to substitute labor for other factors (5b above). Operating to reduce aggregate spending are reduced investment caused by expectations of further wage and price cuts (2a above), increased hoarding made possible by redistribution of income, the lag between wages and dividends (6 above), and the illusion of inventory losses (7 above). There are two effects that may work in either direction: confidence may be affected one way or the other (2e above), and substitution of labor for other factors may alter the distribution of income either favorably or unfavorably to consumption (5a above). The net result of the above forces may be either an increase or a decrease of aggregate spending; if the latter, there may nevertheless be a net increase of output. If output increases, it may be increased still further (and spending either increased or prevented from falling so rapidly) by reduced consumption of capital (2d above); but the expansion of output will be hindered (and spending relatively reduced) by the tendency to save more out of a larger real income.

No general conclusion can be drawn that will apply to all cases. But only in very unusual cases would falling wages fail to increase output. This might occur if commodity prices were rigid and investment insensitive to current profits. The harmful effects of redistributing income would then be mitigated neither by increased value of hoards and the money illusion nor by greater investment. Falling wages might also result in lower output if prices were flexible and induced strong expectations of further falls and impaired confidence, leading to postponement of expenditures. Such a situation could not endure indefinitely, for the greater the price cuts, the more potent the money illusion and the increased value of hoards; and the longer expenditures are postponed, the more urgent they become.

Wage cuts could increase spending above what it otherwise would have been. Most economists are so impressed by two factors making for reduced spending—expectations of further declines and redistribution of income in favor of hoarding—that they would expect wage cuts to reduce spending on balance. If so, the presumption that wage-price cuts will mitigate the reduction of output but intensify monetary contraction stands up fairly well.

If wage cuts mitigate the reduction of output but intensify the reduction of spending, what will they do to the duration of the contraction phase of the business cycle? Haberler believes that if aggregate spending would contract anyway, wage cuts shorten the contraction phase by increasing the value of money. This is true save in the most exceptional cases. But if the contraction of aggregate spending has run its course, wage cuts are apt to prolong the contraction phase. Even if wage cuts have been neutral or somewhat favorable in their effects on aggregate spending while it was falling, a vigorous cyclical expansion is not likely to get under way in the face of continuing price deflation. Assume that contraction ultimately reaches an interval of Keynesian unemployment equilibrium. With stable wages and prices, there would be no further contraction (although the N.B.E.R. would not record a trough until the point of upturn was reached). But if wages and prices continue to fall, even though their net effect on aggregate spending is neutral, statistical series will record continued cyclical contraction. If wage cuts reduce aggregate spending (as seems likely), the situation is so much worse. Moreover, the effect of falling prices and wages in postponing investment is likely to be more potent at a stage of incipient expansion than earlier. As long as a vigorous contraction is under way, a good deal of such potential investment as can be postponed will be put off irrespective of whether the decline is confined to output or extends to prices as well. But expansion depends on induced investment—that is, on the kind of investment that is sensitive to the current business situation and the short-term outlook. If general flexibility prevails, the original forces making for contraction will die out sooner but will be replaced by the adverse effects of flexibility. The net result may be either to shorten or lengthen the contraction, depending on particular circumstances.

Overhead-Plus-Profit Margin

It is possible to deal with the question of unit overhead-plus-profit margins briefly. If prices and margins are reduced relative to costs, the forces at work for the most part are the same as for wage flexibility, but some are much changed in importance. Substitution of labor for other factors drops from the discussion altogether, inasmuch as changes of relative prices of factors are not involved except insofar as prices of capital goods fall relative to wages. Disastrous price expectations are unlikely because margins cannot be reduced without limit. Since the scope for price reductions is less when wages are rigid, the value of hoards cannot be much increased, nor is the money illusion important. The principal repercussions are through redistribution of income, which will increase consumption. Unfavorable effects are lowered profitability of investment and increased likelihood of bankruptcies.

Selective Cuts

The next question is the effect of price and wage flexibility in particular types of industries. It is sometimes urged that selective price cuts are particularly desirable in durable goods industries because they play a strategic role in business cycles. The counterargument says that demand for capital goods and durable consumer goods during cyclical contraction is probably inelastic.

Two qualifications need to be made to the last statement. First, it seems to be based primarily on the 1930's; in situations like 1921, when investment opportunities are more numerous, demand may have considerable elasticity. Moreover, "price cuts make new goods cheaper relative to old goods and thus encourage people to replace old goods with new. Competition between new goods and old goods is one of the most important kinds of competition in the economy."[12]

---

[12] Sumner H. Slichter, "The Economic Picture: More White Than Black," *New York Times Magazine*, XCVII (May 22, 1949), 58.

Second, even if demand is somewhat inelastic, small relative price cuts in capital goods industries expand output as a whole and employment as well and may even increase output in consumer goods industries. The formula for the elasticity that will leave output unchanged with a given price change is

$$e = \frac{a}{1 + a - A}$$

where e is elasticity, a is the marginal propensity to spend of the capital goods industries, and A is the marginal propensity to spend of the entire economy.[13]

If a and A are both 1/2, then e in the formula is also 1/2. If a and A are both 2/3, then e likewise is 2/3. (The formula holds only if A is less than 1.) For probable values of the two marginal propensities, the critical value of e is perceptibly less than one, and price reductions in the capital goods industries may do more good than harm. This would not be the case where price reductions resulted in bankruptcies and reduced inventories.

In general, selective price cuts for nondurable consumer goods have no effects other than the repercussions discussed in the section on wage flexibility. If demand is inelastic, the customers have more money to spend on other products, but those who receive their incomes from the industry in question have less. There is a small net effect: price cuts for consumer nondurables increase the value of a given real income. Consumers for the moment are better off than

[13]. I am grateful to Nicholas Georgescu-Roegen for helping me with the mathematics presented here. The formula can be proved as follows. Assume that money spent on capital goods comes entirely out of hoards so that consumption is not directly affected by changes in the amount of money invested. Where p and q stand for price and quantity respectively, point elasticity (e) is defined as

$$e = \frac{-p}{q} \cdot \frac{dq}{dp} \quad (1)$$

The problem is to find the value of e in terms of a and A for which

$$dq = \frac{-a}{1-A} (pdq + qdp) \quad (2)$$

The left side of (2) represents the increase in output in the capital goods industries. The righthand side represents the reduction in output in the rest of the economy, the expression in parentheses being the reduction of money incomes in the capital goods industries. Dividing (2) by qdp, and taking p as equal to 1, we get

$$\frac{p}{q} \cdot \frac{dq}{dp} = \frac{-a}{1-A} \left(\frac{p}{q} \cdot \frac{dq}{dp} + 1 \right) \quad (3)$$

Substituting (1) into (3) and solving for e, we get

$$e = \frac{a}{1 + a - A} \quad (4)$$

they otherwise would have been (apart from the considerations of the section on wage flexibility). They will divide their greater income between consumption and saving, so that their real expenditure will be greater but their money expenditure less than it otherwise would have been. If demand is inelastic, there is a minor tendency for spending to increase. Income is redistributed away from the industry in question. Since the redistributed income is now immediately available for spending instead of having to pass through the industry in question, the income velocity of money is increased. The principal example of this effect in practice is agriculture. In 1920-21 and 1929-33, the prices of farm products fell more rapidly than other prices. As demand for farm products is inelastic, the velocity effect presumably came into play.

Consumers' durable goods are in part like capital goods so that the formula and the attendant reasoning apply in part but only in part. To some extent, durable consumers' goods are purchased out of old savings and new loans, although for the most part they compete with other goods for the consumer's dollar.[14]

Selective margin cuts in an industry that offers especially large investment opportunities may reduce current profits if pushed too far, may hinder new investment, and may intensify and prolong the contraction. The chief example is the railroad rate wars of 1877. It may be objected that rates were merely a symptom of unfavorable investment possibilities and that the underlying causes would assert themselves in the long run. To some extent that is true (although to some extent the rate wars grew out of the short-run effects of the depression itself). My answer is that the present discussion is concerned purely with the short-run effects on the cyclical situation, not on the long-run investment outlook. If the rate wars had not occurred, investment in railroads would have looked more attractive and the contraction would have been shortened. Price increases in such an industry may have favorable effects; witness the rise of rents, absolute as well as relative, in 1920-21, which stimulated building construction.

14. Cf. Colin Clark, "A System of Equations Explaining the United States Trade Cycle, 1921 to 1941," *Econometrica*, XVII (April 1949), 99-100. Clark did not find it necessary to distinguish between consumers' durables and nondurables at all.

4

EXTERNAL EVENTS

The two preceding chapters have dealt with endogenous theory, i.e., the internal economic mechanism. In practice, the economy is continually buffeted by exogenous or external events. The pure theorist is properly concerned with the question whether in the absence of outside shocks the economy would behave cyclically, and he impounds them by saying *ceteris paribus,* but the historian needs to deal with them systematically.

External events are those the investigator does not undertake to explain. He takes them as given. Internal events are those whose causes he explores. An economist usually regards all non-economic factors as external, but not always. If his hypothesis traces business cycles via weather cycles to sunspots, he includes in his research the non-economic problem of what causes weather. On the other hand, he may regard some economic factors as external in order to narrow his problem. Division of labor dictates where one draws the line between internal and external events.

As an economist, I shall regard wars, variations in weather, and changes in policies by the government as external. Although the cyclical problem, strictly speaking, is worldwide, I shall narrow my problem to the United States and regard changes in economic conditions elsewhere as external. This means ignoring the fact that a change in the market for American exports may have resulted from a change in American imports caused by domestic circumstances. I shall not always adhere to these rules if the explanation of an external event is obvious.

To facilitate the historical parts of this study, the present chapter will set forth some theory needed to deal with two of the most important types of external events from the nineteenth century, viz., international trade and crop fluctuations.

International Trade

Early in the Civil War the United States in effect went off the gold standard. Specie payments were resumed on January 1, 1879. Fluctuations in foreign trade had quite different repercussions on domestic business during the two currency regimes.

Gold Standard.[1] Assume that foreign demand for American exports increases. *Ceteris paribus,* exports will go up both in price and volume, the division between the two depending on demand and supply elasticities. Initially the increased value of exports gets financed by the transfer of short-term capital.

Increased exports tend to stimulate the American economy by increasing American incomes. To the extent that the exports reduce inventories, the stimulus may be lost (except to the extent that inventory liquidation frees funds that get invested elsewhere or inventories are promptly restored through a rise in output). Such an offset is most likely when increased export demand arises from crop failure abroad, since output of farm products in the short run may be completely inelastic. Insofar as American money incomes go up, expenditures on consumption rise via the multiplier. Once more, the rise is divided between higher prices and higher output and employment. During most of the period 1865-97 American output had a good deal of elasticity in the intermediate run. The rise in exports and consumption stimulates investment with further multiplier effects and further stimulus to investment. The initial increase in exports tends to raise the gold supply and therefore the basis for expansion of bank credit to finance increased domestic business. Gold imports need not be involved, as the United States may merely retain a larger share of its own gold output. Prosperity in the United States stimulates greater immigration and larger imports of long-term capital. Thus, an initial increase in exports can under favorable circumstances initiate a cumulative expansion, which (provided that the coefficient of induced investment is high) may go on indefinitely, generating its own supply of money, labor, and capital, and limited only by its

---

1. As the theory of the gold standard mechanism is highly developed, only a condensed account is needed here. A work in pure theory would have to spell out the analysis in much greater rigor and detail.

inherent tendency to increase imports.[2] But ordinarily autonomous changes in export demand were not large enough relative to other forces in the economy to be so important.

The rise in real incomes in the United States tends to get spent in part on foreign products or on domestic products requiring imported materials. The rise in prices in the United States diverts spending from domestic goods and services to imports. Increased imports are a leakage and tend to brake the expansion of business via both income effects and the gold supply. The leakages may or may not be great enough to restore equilibrium in the balance of payments and stop or reverse the domestic expansion of business.

An autonomous decrease in demand for American exports works the same way but in the opposite direction. I shall generally regard changes in exports as autonomous.

An autonomous decrease in American demand for imports works the same as an increase in exports (and vice versa). But changes in imports were not often autonomous in the last part of the nineteenth century. They were either leakages, responding to changes in American incomes and prices, or the result of innovations that were part of the cyclical process.

Changes in the rate of net long-term capital imports may be either induced (cf. above) or autonomous. Assume that there is an autonomous increase in foreign purchases of American securities. Temporarily there may be a reverse flow of short-term capital. But normally the supply of gold, money, and capital increases, putting downward pressure on interest rates. It becomes easier to finance investment projects. Only rarely would capital imports increase (or capital exports decrease) at a time when there was a Keynesian liquidity trap.[3] Normally, increased capital imports imply greater investment by an amount less than the capital imports. From here on, the analysis is the same as for increased demand for American exports, with due allowance for the probability that dollar for dollar the latter is more stimulating. An autonomous decrease in foreign

---

2. It is possible that the expansion may generate a further increase in exports (or a decline in imports). Greater output may achieve economies of large-scale production, enabling the U. S. to compete more effectively against foreign products. E.g., the expansion may make profitable railroad investment that enables farmers in the interior to send grain to seaports economically.

3. An autonomous change in capital markets abroad might occur at any time, but would not have much effect on capital movements if there were a Keynesian liquidity trap in the U. S.

borrowing by the United States works in the same manner in the opposite direction.

In practice, it is difficult to tell to what extent an observed change in capital imports is autonomous and to what extent induced. Since capital with international mobility had a number of alternative places to go during the years 1879-97, it was bound to be sensitive to changes in American business conditions; but the flow to the United States was necessarily influenced also by shifts in the capital markets of the world as a whole.

Paper Standard. For clarity, it helps to start with the extreme case of freely fluctuating exchanges, postponing complications that arise because the United States between 1862 and 1879 was not completely off the gold standard. Assume that there is an autonomous increase in foreign demand for American exports. As foreigners attempt to purchase dollars, the dollar appreciates, making American exports more expensive to foreigners and imports cheaper for Americans. If the elasticities are perverse,[4] the appreciation may be destabilizing; but as I have no reason to think they were perverse during my period, I shall ignore this possibility. Appreciation of the dollar, then, limits the rise in foreign purchases of American goods and diverts American purchases to imports. Thus, the stimulus to the American economy tends to be lost. The same kind of reasoning applies to changes in demand for imports, whether autonomous or induced.

There are ways in which a change in demand for exports (or imports) may have a net effect. Increased export demand may stimulate more investment in export industries than it discourages in import-competing industries (or vice versa). Also, it may be financed by changes in short-term balances, hindering the appreciation of the dollar and resulting in a net stimulus to the United States. On the other hand, short-term capital movements may be destabilizing—an appreciation may lead speculators to accumulate dollars in the hope that they will appreciate still more. In this case, the net effect may be depressing for the United States. Since shifts in ownership of short-term capital do not affect the supply of dollars, they can influence American conditions only by changing their velocity. Foreigners as well as Americans are not likely to hold cash and forego the interest that could be earned. All in all, changes in markets for

---

4. Cf. Lloyd A. Metzler, "The Theory of International Trade," in Howard S. Ellis, ed., *A Survey of Contemporary Economics* (Philadelphia and Toronto, 1948), pp. 226-27.

exports and imports are not likely to have a discernible effect on history.

By the end of the Civil War, the paper dollar had depreciated about 50 percent. Many expected that the United States would resume gold payments at the prewar ratio—implying that the gold value of a paper dollar would double. There was always political support for resumption. Such expectations presumably prevented temporary weaknesses in the paper dollar from generating destabilizing speculation against the greenback. On the other hand, speculation that the dollar would appreciate could not have been attractive[5] until the latter part of the seventies, when it very likely helped make resumption of specie payments successful. But the main reason that short-term capital movements were not destabilizing was undoubtedly their lesser importance compared to the 1920's and 1930's, when hot money flows caused real trouble.

The United States was not completely off the gold standard in 1862-79. Gold continued to circulate in California, to serve as international reserves, to constitute a legal reserve for banks, and to be required for payment of tariff duties. To the extent that the United States continued to use gold, the paper dollar may not have insulated the American economy. I do not believe that these uses of gold were quantitatively important until shortly before resumption.

Now assume an autonomous inflow of long-term capital. The supply of money in the United States is not affected. If the foreign exchange is converted into paper dollars, the greenback appreciates, stimulating imports and diminishing exports. The supply of goods increases with a deflationary impact on prices. But if the borrowed foreign exchange gets spent abroad on investment goods for installation here, there may be no effect on the exchange rate and domestic prices. If long- and short-term capital are in joint demand, the capital from abroad may make possible investment projects that generate expansion of domestic bank credit, increased velocity, and higher prices in the short run (in the longer run, completion of the investment projects depresses prices). *A priori* one would expect that with a given exchange rate increased resources for Americans would be divided between domestic and foreign goods. I shall argue in Chapter 6 that capital imports between 1865 and 1873 made possible more railroad building than could have been financed out of domestic long-term capital sources, so that there was on balance little, if any, deflationary

5. That is, political support for resumption was not strong enough to bet on or weak enough to bet against.

impact. After 1873, the flow of capital reversed. Any inflationary effects were then swamped by the increased output made possible by the railroad investment prior to 1873.

In sum, the paper currency insulated the American economy from international influences. Nevertheless, increased capital imports before 1873 and a reduced flow later accentuated the appearance of a major expansion followed by a major depression.

Crop Conditions

Crop conditions affected business as a whole primarily through international trade when the United States was on the gold standard. In 1879 and 1891, good crops in America coincided with poor crops elsewhere to give the United States a powerful stimulus. Prior to 1879, the paper currency tended to offset any effect of crop conditions on business generally via international trade.

In a closed economy, crop conditions would have minor importance. Assume that crop conditions are such as to increase farmers' incomes.[6] Farmers have more income to spend on industrial products, but other consumers have less. Some net stimulus or depressant may come because farmers' marginal propensity to consume may differ from that of the rest of the country; and as farmers allocate their spending differently from others, the direction of investment (and possibly its total) gets changed. In a closed economy, there is no reason to expect psychology to be influenced one way or the other.

In the United States of the latter third of the nineteenth century, the effect of crop conditions was somewhat greater than the last paragraph indicates, quite aside from the mechanical effects of crops via international trade. The United States was not a closed economy, and business had become used to the idea that good crops were good for business.[7] Hence, good crops induced favorable expectations. Moreover, agricultural products were a large part of the railroads' freight, especially in areas where new investment was most active. Good crops were good for the most important form of investment. Good crops probably stimulated farmers to borrow and spend before they received their higher incomes.

6. Presumably this would happen when crops were poor, inasmuch as demand for farm products is inelastic.

7. Strictly speaking, good crops were good for business only under gold standard conditions. But it is doubtful if businessmen of the greenback era understood that this did not hold under a paper currency.

Other things being equal, good crops depress prices of farm products and lead to inventory investment. If farmers simply store part of their output, there is little short-run effect on business—it is as if the produce added to stocks were produced in a subsequent year. If farmers borrow money on their increased stocks or if others invest idle or newly created money in inventories, business is stimulated.

To conclude, good crops may generally be assumed to be good for business. But their importance was not apt to be great except when they coincided with poor crops in Europe under the gold standard.

5

LONG-WAVE DEPRESSION

ECONOMIC LITERATURE often regards the last quarter of the nineteenth century as a period of long-wave depression. As Chart 2 shows, prices fell during most of the thirty-two years from the end of the Civil War to the upturn of 1897. The hardship that deflation works on debtors, numerous in a country where agriculture is important, alone would create a feeling of depression and generate political agitation. In addition, there were three protracted cyclical depressions. The long-wave depression is usually dated from 1873 to 1897, beginning with a cyclical peak, ending with a cyclical trough, coinciding with falling prices in the rest of the world. If to avoid distortion one compares the thirty-two years from 1865 to 1897 with the succeeding thirty-two, the depressions of 1873-79, 1882-85, and 1893-97 appear more protracted and troublesome than the sharp but short depressions of 1907-8 and 1920-21 and the abortive depression (if it deserves the name) of 1913-14.

The problem is to explain the twin facts of falling prices and unusually severe depressions. Some supplementary facts must be noted. Falling prices were accompanied by falling interest rates. (See Table 1 and Charts 3 and 8.) The rate on prime commercial paper did not exhibit a falling trend throughout the period. Instead, it fell drastically during the seventies—from an annual average of more than 10 percent in 1873 to less than 5 percent in 1878—and thereafter, if anything, tended to rise. Perhaps speculation that the United States would resume the gold standard at an appreciated value abnormally lowered short rates during the cyclical depression; and higher rates in the nineties resulted from the silver troubles. Municipal bond yields display a pattern much like interest on prime commercial paper.

CHART 2. Prices and Wages, 1865-97

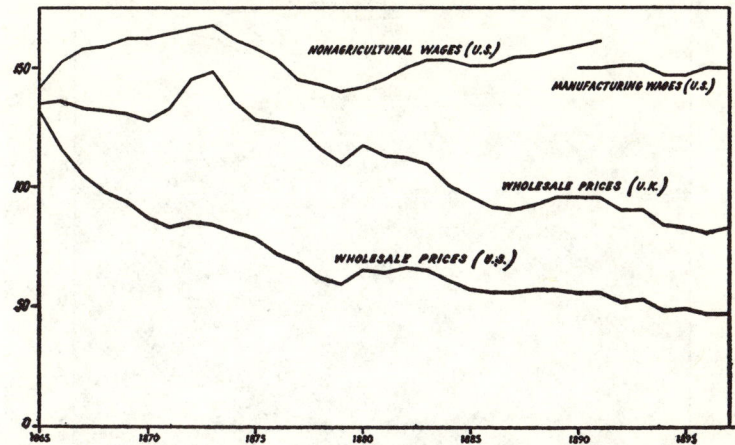

SOURCES: Nonagricultural wages (U.S.), *Historical Statistics of the U.S.*, p. 66; wholesale prices (U.S.), *ibid.*, p. 234; wholesale prices (U.K.), Walter T. Layton and Geoffrey Crowther, *An Introduction to the Study of Prices* (London, 1935), p. 229.

Another feature was retardation in the rate of decline in prices and interest rates and in the rate of increase of aggregate output. Table 1 shows the rate of change of Kuznets' overlapping decade estimates of real GNP and of a number of other series that I have put in the form of decade averages to make them comparable. The increase in real GNP in 1874-83 over 1869-78 was 44 percent; the rate of increase declined with each successive estimate to a low of 16 percent in 1889-98.[1] Similarly, the decline in prices, which was heaviest in 1874-83, also exhibited retardation (the apparent exception in 1889-98 was due to inclusion of the severe depression of the nineties, which distorts the story told by the decade averages). Railroad bond yields also exhibit retardation in the rate of decline.

Some doubts may be raised about whether there really was retardation in aggregate output at the beginning of our period. The 1869 census of manufacturers failed to achieve complete coverage. Kuznets believes that undercoverage calls for a maximum upward adjustment in his estimates of national product of 4 percent for 1869-78 and 2

[1]. The retardation shown in the final estimate (i.e., 1889-98 as compared with 1884-93) presumably is misleading, merely reflecting the fact that 1894-98 was much more depressed than 1884-88.

64   AMERICAN BUSINESS CYCLES

CHART 3. Interest Rates, 1865-97 (seasonally adjusted data).

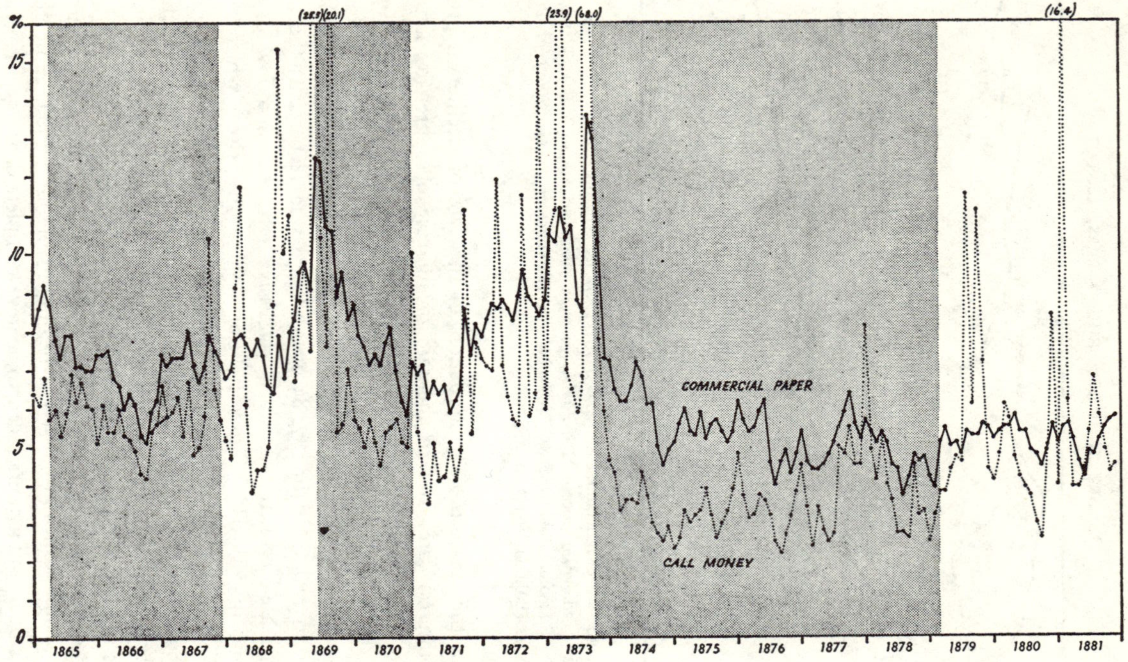

Shaded areas are business cycle contractions (N.B.E.R. dates).
SOURCES: Call money rates, N.B.E.R., series 13.01; commercial paper rates, *Historical Statistics of the U. S.*, pp. 346-47.

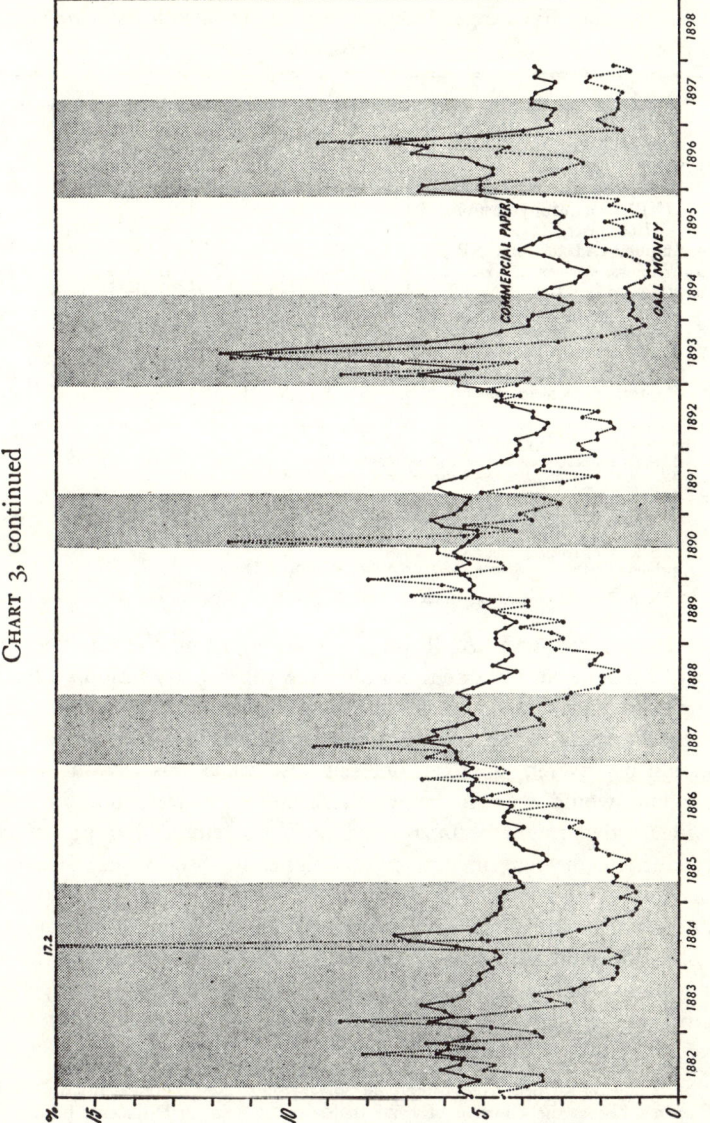

Chart 3, continued

TABLE 1. Rate of Change of Output, Prices, and Interest Rates, 1869-1913, by Percentage

	1869–1878	1874–1883	1879–1888	1884–1893	1889–1898	1894–1903	1899–1908	1904–1913
1. GNP, 1929 prices	—	+44%	+31%	+19%	+16%	+23%	+25%	+21%
2. GNP, adjusted 1929 prices	—	+41	+29	+19	+16	+23	+25	+21
3. NNP per gainfully occupied, 1929 prices	—	+26	+13	+ 1	+ 2	+11	+12	+ 7
4. Implicit deflator for GNP	—	−12	− 8	− 7	− 6	0	+ 8	+12
5. Wholesale prices, BLS	—	−14	−11	− 7	− 8	+ 1	+14	+10
6. Railroad bond yields	—	−17	−16	− 8	− 6	− 7	+ 3	+ 9
7. Crop production	—	+22	+16	+ 9	+11	+14	+10	+ 6
8. Manufacturing	—	+30	+34	+27	+19	+27	+32	+26
9. Transportation and communication	—	+32	+37	+37	+24	+28	+40	+32
10. Railroad capital formation	—	+ 9	+26	+ 5	−22	−32	+92	+55

SOURCES FOR UNDERLYING DATA:
  1. Simon Kuznets, *National Product Since 1869*, p. 119.
  2. Same as 1 except that 1869-78 was increased 4 percent, 1874-83 2 percent.
  3. *Ibid.*, p. 120.
  4. *Ibid.*, p. 119, col (4) divided by col. (9).
  5. *Historical Statistics of the U. S., 1789-1945*, pp. 233-34.
  6. *Ibid.*, p. 348.
  7. U. S. D. A. Technical Bulletin 703, p. 126.
  8. Edwin Frickey, *Production in the United States, 1860-1914*, p. 54.
  9. *Ibid.*, p. 117.
  10. N. B. E. R. Occasional Paper 43, pp. 60-61, col. (4) (first decade is 1870-78 with 1874 weighted double).

percent for 1874-83.[2] As Table 1 shows, adjusting the estimates upward by these maxima does not alter the general conclusion. Clearly, however, any such estimate of the maximum error is little more than a guess. If the nature of the error is failure to cover all that should be covered, how can one tell how much was left out? Such a doubt would scarcely be worth raising if it were not for other evidence that might be interpreted as contradictory. Except for crop production, the rate of increase was higher in 1879-88 than 1874-83 in the important sectors of the economy for which there is fairly good information—manufacturing, transportation and communication, and railroad capital formation. Building construction could not be included in Table 1 for lack of estimates worth putting in comparable form, but enough is known about building to be certain that for it, too, the rate of increase in 1879-88 was greater than for 1874-83.[3]

  2. Simon S. Kuznets, *National Product Since 1869* (New York, 1946), pp. 60-61. I do not discuss the omission of hand trades and custom establishments because the adjustment called for would have at most a negligible effect on comparisons of one estimate to the next.
  3. The years 1874-78 are of course common to the decades of 1869-78 and 1874-83 but not 1879-88. Since they were years of little building construction, whereas 1884-88 was a period of active building, the rate of increase for 1879-88 must have been high. The years 1879-83, coming at the beginning of the upswing in

There are other components of GNP, but available information about them is so scanty that the exceedingly high rate of increase of GNP in 1874-83 must be discounted. Nevertheless, in view of the behavior of crop production, a substantial part of the nation's output, the evidence is inconsistent with a rate of increase in 1874-83 lower than in 1879-88. Moreover, the sectors under discussion—manufacturing, transportation and communication, railroad capital formation, and building construction—are all distorted because the years 1874-78 were more depressed than 1884-88. Retardation in the rate of change of output, as well as in prices and long-term interest rates, is well established.

Statistics on unemployment are virtually nonexistent for the period, so that one can do little more than guess at what times full employment prevailed, under whatever definition is chosen for that phrase. Nevertheless, with the single exception of 1895, it seems certain that cyclical upswings achieved a reasonable approximation to full employment. In other words, depression was not chronic, simply more frequent.

The picture of the United States during 1873-97 resembled in main outline that for the rest of the industrial world, particularly England. Chart 2 shows that the index of wholesale prices in the United Kingdom had its peak in 1873 rather than 1865 but otherwise behaved much the same as in America.[4] Although the timing was somewhat different, the United Kingdom also suffered severe depressions in the seventies, eighties, and nineties. Rates of interest and profit

---

building, could not have been high in comparison with 1869-73, which include a building peak. In fact, it is not unlikely that the rate of increase in 1874-83 was zero, or even negative.

4. Brown and Ozga find "reason to believe that the downward trend of 1873-96 actually set in from the end of the American Civil War, the boom following the war of 1870 being only an interruption of a process already under way. . ." (E. H. Phelps Brown and S. A. Ozga, "Economic Growth and the Price Level," *Economic Journal*, LXV [March 1955], 1, n. 6). They show that the peak in the yield of consols and the troughs relative to trend in real wages and in terms of trade expressed as volume of imports per unit of British labor came in the middle sixties and analyze the period on the basis of these four series. They conclude that the gold supply in the long run made very little difference.

They unfortunately use the misleading term "secondary secular fluctuations," which they borrow from Kuznets, to describe the movements they are interested in. The secondary secular movements studied by Kuznets and Burns (whose work is also mentioned by Brown and Ozga) had phases of only ten years rather than the phases of twenty to thirty years that Brown and Ozga discuss (Simon S. Kuznets, *Secular Movements in Production and Prices* [Boston and New York, 1930], chap. 4, and Arthur F. Burns, *Production Trends in the U.S. since 1870* [New York, 1934], chap. 5). Cf. my appendix on twenty-year cycles.

margins fell. Yet real wages rose rapidly, and unemployment on the average, taking good years and bad together, was not abnormally large.[5] Because England's foreign trade and foreign lending were great, the explanation of her "Great Depression" necessarily runs in terms of the entire world economy, including America. The problem of this chapter is therefore part of a puzzle that has been under discussion by professional economists for almost three quarters of a century.

From the very beginning, explanations have been of two kinds—monetary and real. The monetary explanations originally went back to the lag in gold production prior to the upsurge of the nineties. It was inferred that the money supply was not growing rapidly enough, so that prices fell; and when the money supply began to grow more rapidly, prices rose. The real explanations have run in terms of overproduction, idle capital, and lack of investment opportunities. The two kinds of explanations are not mutually exclusive, and differences of opinion have mainly been on emphasis. Adherents of the monetary type usually discussed the money supply in relation to the growth of output; and lurking behind the real explanations is generally some concession to monetary influences. This does not imply that the differences are of little importance. On the contrary, the relative strength of monetary and real factors is a problem of great significance.

The Money Supply

However strange it may seem to turn to as staunch an advocate of real factors as Hicks for a monetary explanation, he has endeavored to rescue the monetary explanation for the long-wave depression in England from the attack of Rostow.[6] The latter had pointed out that interest rates were higher in the period of rapidly increasing gold supplies of the 1850's and 1860's than during the 1870's and 1880's when England was supposed to be suffering from lack of gold. Since a plentiful gold supply would presumably operate on prices by depressing the interest rate and vice versa, Rostow ruled out a monetary explanation entirely and explained the "Great Depression" in real terms. Although Hicks accepted the importance of the real forces, he nevertheless argued that monetary factors were operating in the same direction.

---

5. Brown and Ozga, "Economic Growth"; Rostow, *British Economy,* pp. 48 and 58-59.

6. Hicks, *Contribution,* p. 154n; Rostow, *British Economy,* pp. 145-60.

Hicks assumes a liquidity function that, with the money supply and monetary system given, is highly elastic at low levels of national income but highly inelastic in its upper reaches. An increase in the money supply relative to the investment function means that the liquidity function has shifted to the right. If the economy was in equilibrium to begin with, interest rates tend to fall to the point appropriate to the level of national income. Investment accordingly rises, and consequently national income rises too. But because the monetary system has a good deal of play in it in the short run, interest rates are slow to react.

In the 'fifties and 'sixties, when the gold supply was increasing, the L-curve would be moving to the right, but would remain inelastic. The rightward movement would nevertheless facilitate short-run expansion of credit; with the new gold coming so frequently to their rescue banks would be inclined to take risks. A strongly marked monetary cobweb, with high interest rates at the top of the boom, would be then what we should expect. Later on, when the supply of gold ceased to expand, relatively to the normal demand for it, expansions away from the L-curve would be more difficult. The monetary booms would therefore be weaker, and the interest rate would rise much less.

This argument applies, in the first place, to short-term rates of interest, which were still of great importance; but in view of the known relation between short and long rates, we should expect to find that the occasionally very high short rates in the first period would keep up the long rate in that period; while the disappearance of these acute stringencies in the second period would result in a gradual fall of the long rate.[7]

In other words, the money supply operates on the equilibrium rate, whereas observed historical rates represent not the equilibrium rate but fluctuations about it; and Hicks believes that in times when the equilibrium rate is low, the average of observed rates is high on account of the extremely high rates that prevail during the boom, and vice versa when the equilibrium rate is high.

Thus, Rostow's criticism has destroyed the older monetary hypotheses, based on the quantity theory, but not Hicks's hypothesis, which is subtle and ingenious. Even *a priori*, however, Hicks is not entirely convincing. If the cobweb about low equilibrium rates is biased in the upward direction, it must be biased enough not merely to offset in the statistical record the lower equilibrium rate but to

---

7. Hicks, *Contribution*, p. 154n.

more than offset it. For observed rates to move in the opposite direction from equilibrium rates is possible, but is it likely?

Hicks and Rostow were thinking primarily of the English situation. How can their reasoning be applied to American experience? The Hicks hypothesis requires that short-term rates rise relatively little during the booms that occur during periods of falling prices. This was the case in the early 1880's (see Chart 3). But inasmuch as the circumstance could be completely explained by real factors such as investment opportunities, the failure to disprove the Hicksian hypothesis does little to increase confidence in it. The short-term rates that prevailed in 1890, 1893, and 1896 were intermediate between the high peaks of 1869 and 1873 and the low peaks of 1882 and 1887. Since external events clearly tended to raise rates from 1890 on, Hicks's hypothesis again is not disproved, but this too does not increase confidence in it.

The most interesting case is the period from 1865 to 1873, when wholesale prices and interest rates tended in opposite directions, prices going down and interest rates up.[8] Although information is inadequate, the money supply apparently was not increasing as fast as output. The case appears to tell in favor of the old-fashioned quantity theory and against Hicks and Rostow. An inadequate money supply operated by driving up interest rates and driving down prices. The case is immune to Rostow's criticism and contradicts the hypothesis of Hicks.

But the case does not demonstrate that monetary forces are supreme. For it was real factors that brought about increased output, an investment boom, and rising employment. Like much of the other evidence, the case indicates that both kinds of forces can be powerful; and when they are working at cross purposes, the result is a kind of compromise. Even during the downswing of the seventies, when investment as well as monetary conditions had turned unfavorable, real forces asserted themselves in the form of increasing output.

---

8. The facts are actually a bit more complicated than this. From August 1871 to February 1873, wholesale prices rose and at the cyclical peak of October 1873 were still as high as at the preceding trough in December 1870. Since wholesale prices normally rise in the course of a cyclical upswing, this hardly counts against the assertion of a falling trend. The peak in railroad bond yields came at the end of 1869, but the small decline thereafter may be ascribed to a lower evaluation of the risk factor during the boom of the early seventies. Commercial paper rates reached extremely high levels just before the end of the Civil War inflation for obvious reasons. It took until October 1866 for them to reach the low of 5.1%. From then on the trend was irregularly upward to the peak of 13.6 in September 1873, seasonally adjusted. (See Chart 3.)

Other Monetary Aspects

The discussion so far has omitted a number of relationships of a mixed character that can be thought of in part as monetary. Falling prices increase the real burden of interest and principal payments on debtors and the real return to creditors.[9] The contractual interest rate understates the real interest rate. If creditors and debtors are aware of the falling trend of prices and expect it to continue, the market rate will be depressed because investors will have a greater preference for money and bonds relative to other kinds of assets, and potential borrowers a reduced preference. This could not be a complete explanation of the long-wave depression, since something else would have to initiate the regime of falling prices; but once prices had fallen for several years, this consideration might tend to depress interest rates, reduce investment,[10] and increase cash holdings, helping to perpetuate falling prices and declining interest rates. Such a vicious cycle by itself could hardly keep prices and interest rates falling for over two decades, but it could be a supplementary factor.

Three tests of the hypothesis suggest themselves. (1) If true, one would expect to find in contemporary financial literature statements that the attractiveness of bonds was altered by the behavior of prices. I have not noticed any such statements. But this is not necessarily decisive. Aside from possible shortcomings of my research, this consideration need not have been discussed in print to have influenced decisions of investors. (2) If the hypothesis were correct, one would expect to find that the yield on stocks would increase compared to bonds. Available statistics do not render a clear verdict. From 1873 on, the yield on stocks was higher than in 1871 and 1872. Unfortunately, the series on stock yields does not go back further. Moreover, the hypothesis implies that the yield on stocks would decline relative to that on bonds in the period of rising prices and interest rates that began just before the turn of the century, but this did not occur. The statistics would in any event be affected by changes in the risk factor. The risk on both stocks and bonds was presumably

---

9. For a recent discussion of this theoretical point, see Fellner, *Trends,* pp. 171-73.
10. The point discussed is independent of the initial cause of falling prices, but generally such is not the case. Usually, falling prices are merely part of the mechanism whereby something fundamental influences investment and other variables. E.g., if prices fall because demand declines, investment gets curtailed; but the fundamental reason for restriction of investment is declining demand rather than falling prices. If prices fall because costs decline, investment increases; but it increases not because prices decline but because opportunities to reduce costs have created opportunities for profitable investment.

declining during this period (aside from the behavior of prices), but did it decline in equal degree? I would guess that the risk on stocks declined more than on bonds;[11] if so, the figures seem to favor the hypothesis. (3) If the hypothesis were true, one would expect to find that the velocity of money was declining relatively rapidly. Statistical research, unfortunately, has not progressed far enough to make possible a convincing test. In sum, although one cannot disprove the hypothesis, there is little reason to place confidence in it.

The reduction of the federal debt by $1.8 billion between 1866 and 1893 was deflationary for two reasons.[12] Taxes at that time were almost entirely on consumption, so that debt retirement in effect increased the proportion of national income saved. In Keynesian terms, the drag on consumption reduced the schedule of the marginal efficiency of capital at the same time that the relative supply of savings was going up. Both influences worked in the direction of reducing interest rates as well as prices and output.

Debt reduction induced retirement of national bank notes, which were secured by government bonds. This latter influence would tend to raise interest rates instead of lowering them; and it could be an additional deflationary force when the economy was suffering from a shortage of money, i.e., during the period from 1865 to 1873 and during the recurring periods of money stringency from 1890 on. Since the number of national bank notes outstanding increased between 1865 and 1873, the retirement of debt during this period did not reduce the volume of bank notes except in the sense that they might otherwise have increased more rapidly. Since retirement of federal debt stopped in 1893, no further effect was felt thereafter.

Another kind of monetary disturbance was the silver purchase policy with its threat to the gold standard. The silver problem was a relatively minor factor in the troubles of 1893, but it intensified the depression by weakening confidence and encouraging foreigners to withdraw capital, reducing bank reserves at a critical moment. In 1896 the silver scare once again served to intensify contraction, creating an artificial shortage of credit at a time of cyclical downswing when funds ordinarily are plentiful.

In 1875 Congress passed the Resumption Act, and early in 1877 the Secretary of the Treasury began active steps to make resumption successful. Although the resumption policy did not cause deflation,

---

11. Fellner, *Trends*, p. 253, suggests the opposite view.
12. Seymour E. Harris, *The National Debt and the New Economics* (New York, 1947), pp. 263-64.

if the United States had been on the gold standard at the exchange rate existing in 1873[13] much of the monetary deflation of the last two years prior to resumption would have been avoided; the recovery of physical output, which probably began no later than 1877, would have been vigorous; the date of the cyclical upturn, using N.B.E.R. methods, would have come two years earlier; and the depression of the seventies would never have come to be regarded as outstanding in the history of cycles. But this is a backhanded kind of argument at best. It indicates the results of another kind of policy but does not explain what caused the deflation that actually took place.[14]

There were three banking panics, two of them severe. This raises the question of what contribution, if any, the weaknesses of the American banking structure made to the depression. No doubt the country would have been better off if the banks had been sound. Moreover, during the past century there was a gradual improvement in banking practices. Yet the difference in this respect between the third of a century preceding 1897 and the prosperous period following it must not be overdone. The panic of 1907 and the troubles of the early thirties demonstrated that the traditional weaknesses remained. Nor can much importance be attached to the advent of the Federal Reserve System in 1914; the deflationary policy pursued after the downturn of 1920 was a pretty close substitute for a panic.

Shortage of Investment Opportunities

According to Hansen, "In the long sweep of technological and innovational developments the decade of the [nineteen] thirties is ... in many respects not unlike the fourth quarter of the nineteenth century, with its deep depressions of the seventies and nineties."[15] "The declining role of the railroad was, indeed, the most significant single fact for this period and offers the most convincing explanation for the chronic hard times, particularly of the decade of the nineties."[16] "New railroad mileage experienced a rapidly rising trend from the middle forties to the decade of the seventies, and thereafter flattened out with, however, a major spurt in the middle eighties, and eventually

---

13. The greenback appreciated at least 10% between 1873 and 1879.
14. One could advance a hypothesis that businessmen's anticipations were adversely affected by knowledge that there would be more deflation or that their beloved gold standard would not be regained, but it would be hard to support it with evidence.
15. *Fiscal Policy*, pp. 39-40.
16. *Ibid.*, p. 39n.

in the nineties sharply declined."[17] "The mere slowing down in the *rate* of growth caused an absolute decline in the volume of new investment required in the plant and equipment of subsidiary industries, such as iron and steel, which manufactured the materials that went into railroad construction."[18]

Thus, declining investment opportunities in railroads together with acceleration principle effects on related industries can be used to explain the long-wave depression. To this should be added the building cycle, which can account for the fact that the depression of the eighties was relatively mild.[19] Lack of investment opportunities can also explain declining long-term interest rates.

The sentences quoted from Hansen were written before World War II, not many years after the debut of Keynesian theory. For present purposes, the significance of the *General Theory*[20] lay in showing why the classical equilibrators might not operate to produce full employment. Keynes's model was illuminating for the short run and, indeed, for problems of a limited number of years, such as the eighteen seventies, the eighteen nineties and the nineteen thirties. I therefore shall discuss Hansen's interpretation of individual depressions in succeeding chapters without going into the theory on which it rests, and there is no need to repeat what will then be said. Separate discussion is needed, however, because a period of twenty or thirty years is too long to be dealt with in terms of a static, short-run model.

Two intermingled strands of discussion growing out of Keynes's model need to be noted and applied to our problem. The Harrod-Domar kind of model put Keynesian theory into dynamic form in an attempt to deal with the problem of economic growth. In the meantime, defenders of the classical faith were trying to rehabilitate the equilibrators and find new ones. In general, the Keynesian model has stood up pretty well for short-run purposes; that is, nobody has been able to find equilibrators that rule out the possibility that underemployment equilibrium may persist for several years. More recent work has turned to the problem of introducing equilibrators into the dynamic growth models. This is necessary because the requirements for stability in the growth models are much too rigid to explain economic history. On the one hand, lapses from full employment have

17. *Ibid.*, p. 39.
18. *Ibid.*, p. 40 (Hansen's italics).
19. Alvin H. Hansen, *Business Cycles and National Income* (New York, 1951), p. 42.
20. John M. Keynes, *The General Theory of Employment, Interest and Money* (London and New York, 1936).

proved temporary; on the other hand, the degree of inflation experienced in peacetime has never been large. An account of the relatively unsatisfactory performance of the American economy between 1873 and 1897 must be within a framework that explains why capitalism in general has worked pretty well.

The next task, then, is to reinterpret Hansen's remarks in terms of dynamic growth theory, paying due attention to equilibrators. Doing so departs from what Hansen himself has written, and he must be absolved at the outset of responsibility for the hypotheses about to be discussed. It will be convenient to use Hicks's theory, which combines a growth model with cyclical analysis,[21] as a starting point and bring in the equilibrators subsequently.

Assume that the average rate of growth of the labor force is given. Assume also that from sometime in the forties until sometime not long after the Civil War, autonomous investment in Hicks's sense grew at an average rate sufficient to keep equilibrium output in the neighborhood of full employment output. Consequently, times were generally prosperous, prices stable, and long-term interest rates high. Cyclical disturbances of the period can be attributed to fluctuations in the rate of growth of autonomous investment, international influences, exogenous events such as crop conditions, and monetary and banking difficulties.

Assume, now, that the average rate of growth of autonomous investment began to taper off in the early seventies, so that until the end of the century the path of equilibrium output lay chronically below the path of full employment output, with the divergence tending to become wider. Consequently, each depression became more severe in terms of output than the preceding. Prices and interest rates tended to decline. Autonomous investment did not increase at a constant rate but was subject to humps and slumps; this explains why the downswing of 1888 did not result in deep depression. Either the coefficient of induced investment or humps in autonomous investment were high enough so that upswings ordinarily led to full employment. Monetary factors and external events can be thrown in to complete the explanation.

Without incurring responsibility for this explanation, Hansen and Hicks have provided a hypothesis that accounts for a number of diverse facts—an abnormal number of depression years together with

21. Hicks, *Contribution*.

intervals of prosperity, retardation in the rate of growth of output,[22] and declining prices and long-term interest rates. It does not account for retardation in the rate of decline of prices and interest rates.

Now the analysis must be complicated by introducing some omitted factors, including possible equilibrators. Up to this point it has been assumed that the growth of population was given. But immigration (and probably birth rates as well) fluctuated with business conditions; and although the relative importance of conditions in the United States and conditions abroad is not entirely clear, the American situation was significant.[23] Economic opportunity was a prime motive for migration; and the fact that emigration occurred in waves from certain countries during certain periods instead of being spread uniformly over time and space indicates that information from previous migrants on conditions in the new world had considerable influence. This factor would be even more important over a period of a quarter of a century than during the span of a business cycle.

The analysis must be modified to assume that the labor force tended to adapt itself to economic opportunities. The new assumption is a two-edged sword. In so far as the labor force adapts itself to economic opportunities, there is an equilibrating force that adapts the path of full employment output to the path of equilibrium. In so far as investment opportunities depend on the growth of population, there is another equilibrating force that tends to adapt the equilibrium path to the full employment path. But, paradoxically, the sum of two equilibrators may be disequilibrating. For if the two paths have diverged, a reduction in the rate of growth of population lowers both paths; and whether the net result is equilibrating or disequilibrating depends on which path is depressed more.

For the very long run and for very large changes in growth rates, adaptation of the labor force to economic opportunities may constitute a fundamental reason why the American economy succeeded. But in a period of a quarter century, nearly half of it reasonably prosperous,

22. Or, what comes to nearly the same thing, the fact that the decline in output was greater in the second depression than in the first and greater still in the third.
23. Harry Jerome, *Migration and Business Cycles* (New York, 1926), p. 208, concluded that conditions in the United States dominated cyclical fluctuations in migration. Brinley Thomas, *Migration and Economic Growth* (Cambridge, Eng., 1954), p. 84, noted that Jerome's finding was limited to short cycles and inquired whether the conclusion also held for twenty-year cycles. He concluded that, prior to 1871, conditions in the old world predominated, but the year named marked a change (pp. 92 ff.). Thereafter, immigration lagged behind business conditions in the U.S. rather than led them.

marginal adjustments in the rate of immigration need not have been equilibrating.

In the pre-Keynesian economics, one of the principal equilibrators ensuring full employment was the rate of interest, which was supposed to bring saving and investment into balance. Keynes showed the possibility of a liquidity trap: with the propensity to save insensitive to interest rates, the market rate may be unable to fall low enough to bring about full employment. Antistagnationists argued that in the long run people would not go on saving in the absence of opportunities for profitable investment.[24]

This encounters a theoretical objection that will be taken up in two stages. First, consider a situation of static underemployment equilibrium. Aside from changes in wage rates, which will be discussed later, there is no reason why interest rates should fall in order to restore full employment unless something is being done to increase the money supply. The equilibrium is stable, with savers investing their savings at remunerative rates. Second, in a dynamic growth process, investment may be steadily increasing, aided by an increasing supply of money. But if investment is not growing rapidly enough to provide jobs for all the new workers entering the labor market, there is no reason (aside from the impact of the new workers on wages) why the rate of interest should fall to restore full employment.

Hence, even in the absence of a liquidity trap, the rate of interest will not adjust to compensate for a tapering off in the rate of growth of investment opportunities relative to the rate of growth of the labor force. Saying this, however, brings in the money supply by the back door. For, unless a liquidity trap existed (which is doubtful for the period in question), a more rapid increase in the money supply would have depressed interest rates and increased investment and employment.

In pre-Keynesian economics, falling wage rates were expected to correct unemployment. Although wage rates too high relative to prices can unquestionably cause unemployment, Keynes showed reasons for doubting whether falling wages could correct unemployment caused by a marginal efficiency of capital too low relative to the propensity to save. Defenders of classical economics have tried to revive the argument.

Chapter 3 distinguished the effects of price and wage flexibility on the equilibrium position from their effects on a dynamic process of

---

24. The argument requires definitions (such as Schumpeter's) under which saving and investment are not necessarily equal.

cyclical contraction. That chapter dealt with the dynamic problem, whereas this one is concerned with the equilibrium position. The discussion in the literature is extensive and complex, but the best the neo-classicists have been able to come up with is the so-called Pigou effect—falling wages and prices increase the real value of currency, bank deposits, and government bonds, and thereby increase the propensity to spend.

Now, even if every person had only one dollar, an infinite increase in the purchasing power of that dollar (as a result of prices approaching zero) would lead him to consume more than his income. The increase in the purchasing power of money in the last third of the nineteenth century was substantial, although not infinite. The BLS wholesale price index declined more than 50 percent. Probably this overstates the case (cf. lines 4 and 5 of Table 1), but it indicates roughly the order of magnitude. To some extent, it was vitiated by the retirement of government debt.

No decisive test of the Pigou effect appears possible, but it seems reasonable to suppose that it would stimulate consumption more than investment. Kuznets' figures show a decline of the percentage of net national product consumed from 88 percent in 1869-78 to 86 percent in 1889-98, just the opposite of what one would expect from the Pigou effect.

Even according to Keynes, a fall in prices and wages has a stimulating effect via the interest rate. Since prices and interest rates fell together, there may have been some equilibrating force from this source, offset in part perhaps by the effect of falling prices on the real return to investors. The increase in the proportion of NNP invested is consistent with this hypothesis.

Another possible equilibrator is the division of the labor force between agriculture and industry. In principle, any tendency toward chronic unemployment in a country whose rural areas are sparsely settled can be corrected by absorbing more workers into farming. The combination of high overhead costs and atomistic competition means that agriculture does not react to adverse demand conditions by cutting inputs and outputs. Now, this sort of equilibrator certainly operated in the United States over the long run. With the number of workers in both agricultural pursuits and nonagricultural pursuits growing, the latter more rapidly than the former, and with a good deal of geographical migration and shifts of workers between industries, surely the number of workers outside farming tended to adjust itself to the number of jobs available. This is perhaps the most important single reason for thinking the United States could not have had chronic unemployment for long years at a time during the nineteenth century. The existence of this equilibrator does not throw doubt on the shortage of investment opportunities hypothesis: a tapering off in the growth rate of investment opportunities in conjunction with the equilibrator would mean recurrence of severe depressions as the mechanism for inducing workers in larger numbers to enter agriculture rather than industry, with the former exhibiting symptoms of distress comparable in degree (although different in kind) to those of the latter.

The equilibrator does, however, provide an indirect test of the hypothesis. For tapering in the growth of investment opportunities together with the equilibrator implies that relatively more workers would enter agriculture. Specifically, it implies that the percentage of the increment of the work force going into nonagricultural pursuits should decline. That is, if W is the total number of workers and I is the number of workers in nonagricultural pursuits, then the ratio $\frac{\Delta I}{\Delta W}$ should decline. The statistics indicate that 61 percent of the increase in the work force between 1870 and 1880 went into nonagricultural pursuits. For 1880-90 the percentage rose to 77 percent, and for 1890-1900 it went even higher to 83 percent.[25] This much of the evidence tends to contradict the hypothesis. It must be modified by two considerations: the percentage for 1860-70 was 73 percent higher than that for the following decade; and there was undercoverage in the 1870 census, particularly in the South, a correction for which has been made in the figures given. Since the correction may itself be in error and errors are especially serious where first differences are taken, any computation involving 1870 is suspect. For what it is worth, the ratio for 1860-80 is 65 percent, considerably lower than for the two succeeding decades. On the whole the test is unfavorable to the hypothesis.

Consideration of capital imports must be divided into two parts, the first being the period when the United States was not on the gold standard. Although in pure theory there are reasons for arguing that capital imports are deflationary under paper standard conditions, I believe that in the period 1865-78 their fluctuations had little net effect in either an inflationary or a deflationary direction. After the United

25. U. S. Bureau of the Census, *Historical Statistics of the United States, 1789-1945* (Washington, D. C., 1949), p. 63.

States returned to the gold standard in 1879, capital imports tended to be inflationary. Since declining investment opportunities would tend to reduce capital imports, the effect would be disequilibrating. There are, therefore, no grounds for doubting the hypothesis on this score.[26]

Schumpeter

In Chapter 2, I suggested abandoning Schumpeter's four-phase Kondratieff (with depression dated 1869-83 and revival 1884-97) in favor of a two-phase Kondratieff, the recession phase (1869-97) of which roughly coincides with the era of falling prices. This revision has a number of advantages.

In the first place, there is no conflict with the hypothesis of a tapering off in the growth of investment opportunities. In Schumpeter's view, chronic insufficiency of investment opportunities leading to chronic unemployment is impossible, but a tapering off in the rate of growth of investment opportunities is not only possible but is an essential part of the recession phase.

In the second place, the two-phase Kondratieff fits Kuznets' figures on the growth of output. In Schumpeter's model, recession is the period of reaping the harvest from the innovations made during prosperity. In other words, output (especially of consumers' goods) rises most in recession (and revival), least in depression.[27] Table 1 shows the largest increase in real consumption and real GNP in 1874-83, a decade that falls in the depression phase of Schumpeter's four-phase Kondratieff but the recession phase of my two-phase Kondratieff. As time went by, the depression effects of the recession phase more and more affected output, so that its rate of increase declined or, in other words, the severity of depressions increased.

26. This paragraph suggests a test: if long-wave depression resulted from retarded growth in investment opportunities, one would expect that capital imports would grow at a retarded rate or even decline. Two considerations unfortunately render the test unfeasible: numerous external events and unreliability of statistics of capital movements.

27. More precisely, output of consumers' goods increases most in recession and revival, whereas output of producers' goods increases most in revival and prosperity. Total output increases through all four phases with the partial exception of depression. The growth of consumers' output in recession tends to be enough greater than the decline in output of producers' goods to cause a greater increase in total output in recession than prosperity because it is in recession that the results of technological innovation come to fruition; but this tendency for total output to increase more rapidly in recession may be offset by changes in employment. Consequently, there is no clearcut expectation for the behavior of total output in recession compared to prosperity (Schumpeter, *Business Cycles*, II, 500-4).

In the third place, the two-phase formulation fits Schumpeter's own diagnosis of the nature of the crisis of 1893 as the culmination of readjustments, need for which had been accumulating for a long time.[28] His diagnosis contradicts his four-phase model, since recession, not revival, is the phase when needs for readjustments accumulate.

In the fourth place, the two-phase hypothesis fits the behavior of prices and interest rates, both of which are expected to fall in recession but rise in revival. Their actual behavior contradicted Schumpeter's hypothesis with respect to revival, a circumstance that Schumpeter explained away none too successfully.

Conclusion

Following Rostow, the preceding discussion has rejected older explanations based on inadequate growth of the money supply, because they are inconsistent with the behavior of interest rates. It has also rejected Hicks's variant of the monetary explanation, though on somewhat tenuous grounds. Nevertheless, a number of monetary or quasi-monetary influences of an adverse nature have been noted: the silver policy of the nineties, retirement of the federal debt, the effect of falling prices on the real interest rate, the weak banking structure, the return to the gold standard. On the real side, a revised version of Schumpeter's theory incorporating the analyses of Hansen and Hicks fits the facts well,[29] except that doubt is thrown on the

---

28. *Business Cycles*, I, 388-89.

29. Brown and Ozga, "Economic Growth," discuss the entire period since 1790 and concentrate on the United Kingdom. To them, twenty- to thirty-year phases of rising prices are periods in which the industrial capacity of the world is rising particularly rapidly, whereas the phases of falling prices are periods when industrial capacity rises more slowly. They make no attempt to explain the historical reasons for alternating periods of rapid and slow growth in industrial capacity; thus their hypothesis is incomplete, avoiding the fundamental question but throwing light on some secondary problems. They find that British wages rose most rapidly in periods of falling prices. Up to this point, their alternating phases incorporate essential features of Schumpeterian prosperity and recession—during prosperity, expansion of capacity generates rising prices; during recession consumers reap the harvest of the previous investment—and their analysis differs from Schumpeterian prosperity and recession primarily in what it leaves out.

The contribution of Brown and Ozga to the problem lies mainly in their analysis of the interaction between the industrial and raw material sectors of the world economy. They find that world output of raw materials rose at approximately a constant rate irrespective of whether prices were rising or falling. Rising prices resulted from the fact that industrial capacity—and therefore demand for raw materials—was growing more rapidly than the supply of raw materials, and vice versa for falling prices. This implies some significant differences from Schumpeterian analysis

hypothesis of retarded growth of investment opportunities by the increasing tendency for the increment in the work force to go into nonagricultural pursuits.

The issues evidently are far from settled. This discussion indicates that real and monetary factors combined to produce the observed result. Since hardly anybody doubts that both kinds of forces have some significance in the real world, the question is which was more important. I am inclined to regard both as powerful but to emphasize the real factors, the more so since one important monetary factor—the silver problem—was the result as well as a cause of the relatively unsatisfactory performance of the economy.

—e.g., for Brown and Ozga, recession (if I may use the term) was a period in which British consumers reaped the harvest of previous investment not because output was increasing more rapidly but because the terms of trade improved for industrial nations vis-a-vis raw material producers. It is not necessary to discuss the merits of Brown and Ozga's hypothesis here. For the one period and one country that I analyze, I do not see that their findings contradict mine.

6

THE CYCLES OF 1865-79

THE AMERICAN DEPRESSION of the 1870's is famous as the longest cyclical contraction in American history; yet the literature on it is limited.[1] Although the United States was insulated from international influences by a paper currency, its experience diverged no further from that of Great Britain, France, and Germany than might have been expected under gold standard conditions.[2] In Britain, the contraction was even longer, beginning a year earlier and ending a few months later. France experienced a downturn almost simultaneously with the United States in 1873 and an upturn in 1879 half a year later; but in France there was an additional cycle in the seventies (an upturn in 1876 and a downturn in 1878). Germany's upturn in 1879 almost coincided with the upturn in the United States. In the sixties there was more divergence, the crisis of 1866 being specifically British.

  1. The *Review of Economic Statistics* published a lengthy factual account in 1920, but it is devoid of cyclical analysis and rendered out of date by recent statistical research: Warren M. Persons, Pierson M. Tuttle, and Edwin Frickey, "Business and Financial Conditions Following the Civil War in the United States," *Review of Economic Statistics*, Supplement, II (July 1920). Schumpeter has given his interpretation of the period but not a connected history (*Business Cycles*, I, 335-40). Auble has dealt with the depression of the 1870's in his doctoral thesis, which was not published: Arthur G. Auble, "The Depressions of 1873 and 1882 in the United States," Harvard University, 1949. Another dissertation, this one mimeoprinted, is Ernest R. McCartney, "Crisis of 1873," University of Nebraska, 1932. Mitchell's book is primarily a collection of statistics; he never completed the analysis for which the statistics were intended: Wesley C. Mitchell, *Gold, Prices and Wages Under the Greenback Standard* (Berkeley, Calif., 1908). Save for isolated references and studies of particular problems—e.g., Samuel Rezneck, "Distress, Relief, and Discontent in the United States during the Depression of 1873-78," *Journal of Political Economy*, XXXVIII (Dec. 1950), 494-512—this completes the roster of noteworthy attempts to deal with this chapter of cyclical history.

  2. Arthur F. Burns and Wesley C. Mitchell, *Measuring Business Cycles* (New York, 1946), pp. 78-79.

The period 1865-79 forms a natural unit for study. It roughly encompasses both a major business cycle and what Isard calls a transport-building cycle. Because it comprises the era, exclusive of the Civil War, in which the United States had an inconvertible paper currency, cyclical influences from international trade were different from those in the years before and after.

Major cycles are defined as consisting of (1) upswings in which long-term investment opportunities are favorable so that downward spirals are minor and (2) downswings in which long-term investment opportunities have become seriously impaired so that cumulative expansions are weak and rare.[3] On the hypothesis that long-term investment opportunities were favorable from 1865 to 1873, became seriously impaired in the latter year, and did not recover until about 1879, the period 1865-79 forms a major cycle.[4] Business was generally prosperous from the end of the Civil War through the boom of the early seventies (except for two recessions) and was decidedly depressed from the panic of 1873 until 1879. The hypothesis will be on trial throughout this chapter, but some evidence of a general nature is best discussed at once.

In 1865 the stage was set for a burst of investment activity. During the latter half of the nineteenth century, railroad building was one of the most important forms of investment. Yet, on account of depression and strife, by the close of the Civil War it had been nearly a decade since any considerable railroad building had been done. Meanwhile, population was growing rapidly. The area west of the Mississippi, hitherto virtually untouched by the railroads, was ripe for development. A modern investor might have shuddered at the risks involved in building through the sparsely populated West, but in those days of rampant free enterprise, bonds could generally be sold at home or abroad, provided that the interest rate was high

---

3. See the discussion of Gordon in Chap. 2 (Robert A. Gordon, "Investment Behavior and Business Cycles," *Review of Economics and Statistics*, XXXVII [Feb. 1955], 23-34).

4. This formulation differs only in detail from the findings of Hansen and Isard. Hansen dates major depressions 1864, 1873, and 1883 (presumably the years mentioned are the peaks of the preceding prosperities), which implies a major cycle, counting from trough to trough, from sometime after the Civil War, say 1867, until the end of the depression of the seventies, say 1878 or 1879 (*Fiscal Policy*, pp. 23-24). Isard found troughs in the seven series that interested him scattered in the early 1860's and again in the years 1875-79 (Walter Isard, "A Neglected Cycle: The Transport-Building Cycle," *Review of Economic Statistics*, XXIV [Nov. 1942], 149-58). Schumpeter, on the other hand, dated a Juglar cycle from the beginning of 1870 to the middle of 1879 (*Business Cycles*, I, 396).

enough. The government often subsidized railroad building. The network east of the Mississippi needed to be filled in. Under such favorable conditions, investment rose to a climax in the early seventies, then collapsed (see Chart 4).

Conditions were also favorable for investment in housing. There is evidence of a housing shortage at the end of the Civil War,[5] and the close of hostilities greatly accelerated immigration. Hence it is hardly surprising that the building cycle also rose to a peak in the early seventies (Chart 4).

It may be concluded that the long-term outlook for investment was favorable in the fields of railroad and housing construction (and very likely in other kinds of construction too). Terborgh has discounted the importance of single great industries, pointing out that steam railroads accounted for only one eighth of total investment in the decade of the 1870's; and Burns and Mitchell reached negative conclusions on the effect of long building cycles on business cycles.[6] Stronger support is needed for the hypothesis of a major cycle.

Hansen has replied to Terborgh that the latter has neglected "the leverage effect of the multiplier and the acceleration principle."[7] The railroads in their expansion may have stimulated investment in the higher stages of production, e.g. steel. More important still, transportation costs were reduced not only by the building of the new roads but also by the consolidation of the old. The formation of such networks as the Pennsylvania, the New York Central, the Philadelphia and Reading, the Chicago, Burlington and Quincy, the Chicago and Northwestern, and the Milwaukee and St. Paul reduced the inconveniences of frequent tieups and delays, the cost of numerous interchanges of freight in long hauls, the diversity of railroad practices, and the irresponsibility of carriers.[8] Reductions in transportation costs in the new territories opened up in the West and in the areas already served by railroads in the East presumably stimulated investments not related to railroads. This was particularly the case for housing, for the railroads may be regarded as instrumental in sucking a great

5. David A. Wells, *Report of the U.S. Special Commissioner of Revenue*, 41st Congress, 2d Session, House Ex. Doc. No. 27 (Washington, D. C., 1869), pp. xxiii-iv; London *Economist*, XCV (May 25, 1867), 586: "all over the country there is positive distress for house room."

6. George Terborgh, *The Bogey of Economic Maturity* (Chicago, 1945), p. 84; Burns and Mitchell, *Measuring*, pp. 418-27.

7. Alvin H. Hansen, *Economic Policy and Full Employment* (New York, 1947), p. 303.

8. Walter Isard, "The Economic Dynamics of Transport Technology," unpub. Ph.D. dissertation, Harvard University, 1943, pp. 61-63.

86 AMERICAN BUSINESS CYCLES

CHART 4. Construction and Immigration, 1865-97

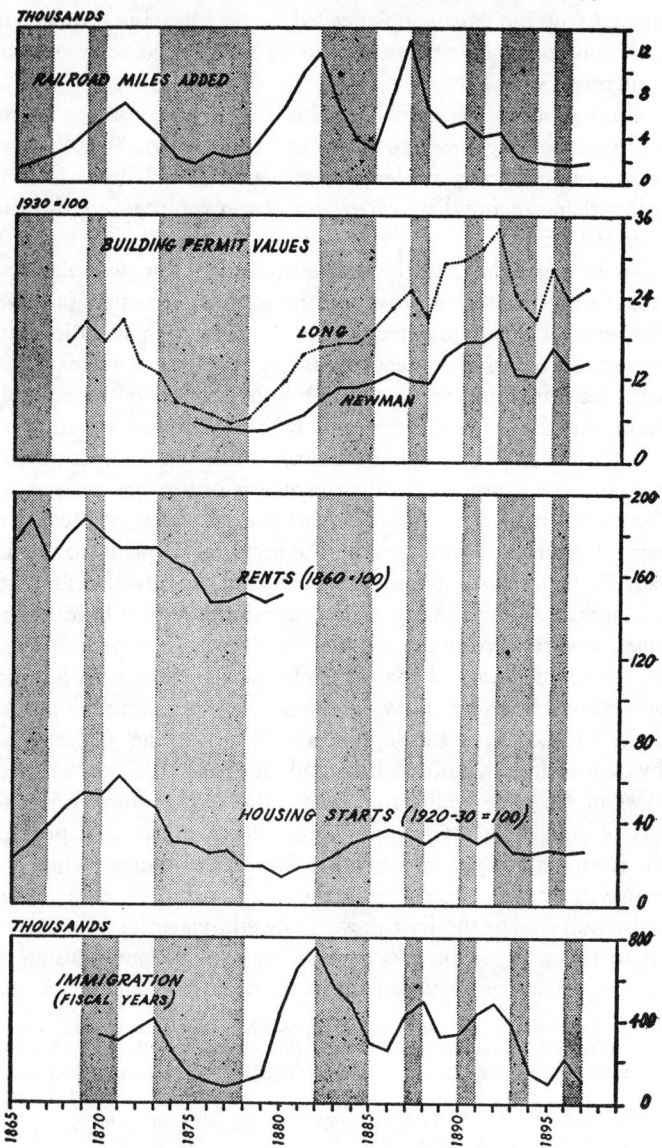

Shaded areas are business cycle contractions (N.B.E.R. dates).
SOURCES: Railroad miles added, *Historical Statistics of the U.S.,* p. 200 (first differences of col. 1) and A. P. Andrew, *Statistics for the United States, 1867-1909.* (Washington, 1910), p. 12; rents, *Historical Statistics of the U.S.,* p. 236;

wave of immigrants into the country and relocating the existing population. But it was also true for manufacturing, which now found new advantageous sites and the opportunity of producing for wider markets.[9] It may tentatively be concluded that the long-term investment outlook was generally favorable in the latter sixties.

The effect of international trade on business cycles in this period is not clear. The inconvertible paper standard in effect allowed exchange rates to fluctuate freely. The Civil War had partly been financed by printing several hundred million dollars' worth of paper money popularly called "greenbacks." Inflation forced the government to abandon the gold standard, since it could not maintain convertibility between gold and dollars. Nevertheless, it continued to require that import duties be paid in gold. Such gold as the banks held could continue to be counted as part of their reserves. The Pacific Coast never abandoned the gold standard. About $25 million of gold remained in active circulation there. Officially, the exchange rate between the dollar and foreign gold currencies such as the English pound sterling remained unchanged. But as gold could be bought for greenbacks only at a premium that varied from one transaction to the next, the exchange rate in reality fluctuated freely. (See Chart 5.)

Increased demand for the exports of a gold standard country—say, because harvests are poor abroad—tends to increase prices and incomes both because prices and incomes in the export trades go up, with multiplier effects, and because gold imports are increased (or exports decreased), thus increasing the money supply and bank reserves. Eventually, increased incomes and prices mean more imports and less exports, bringing trade back into balance; but in the meantime, an expansive impulse has been imparted which will accelerate a concomitant cyclical expansion or retard a cyclical contraction.

Under freely fluctuating exchanges, increased demand for exports merely increases the exchange rate or, in this case, lowers the gold premium. There is no significant way that the domestic money supply or aggregate income can be affected. Except for capital transactions, the business cycles of the domestic economy are largely isolated from

9. *Ibid.*, pp. 65-67. See also pp. 22-27. This kind of argument is part of Schumpeter's theory of the cycle.

---

housing starts, *ibid.*, p. 173, col. 74; building permit values, *ibid.*, p. 173, cols. 77 and 78; immigration, Simon Kuznets and Ernest Rubin, *Immigration and the Foreign Born*, N.B.E.R., Occasional Paper 46 (New York, 1954), p. 95 (arrivals minus departures; fiscal years).

88 AMERICAN BUSINESS CYCLES

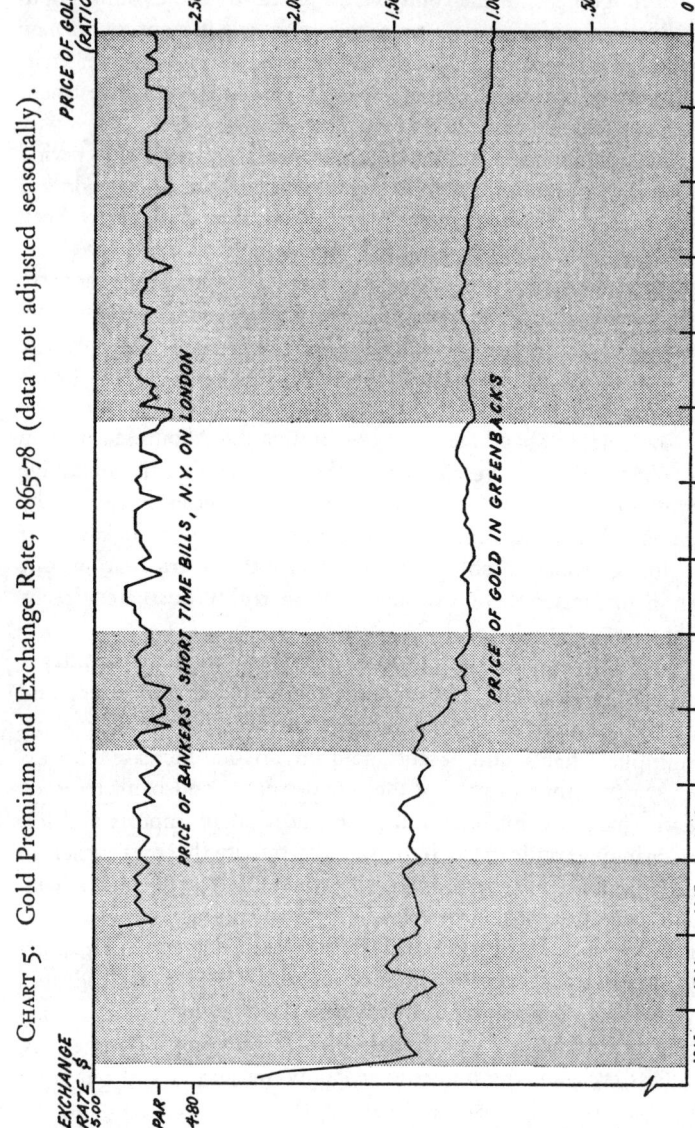

CHART 5. Gold Premium and Exchange Rate, 1865–78 (data not adjusted seasonally).

Shaded areas are business cycle contractions (N.B.E.R. dates).
SOURCES: Exchange rate, Persons, Tuttle, and Frickey, *Review of Economic Statistics*, Supplement, II (July 1920), 54; gold premium, W. C. Mitchell, *Gold, Prices and Wages*, pp. 6-12.

international trade. This conclusion must be qualified because the United States retained the use of gold for some purposes during the greenback era, particularly for international trade. To the extent that Americans were willing to absorb gold, increased exports could be expansionary; and to the extent that they were willing to give up gold, increased imports could be deflationary. But as far as can be told, annual fluctuations in the United States gold stock were small.[10] Evidently the paper currency greatly blunted the effect of international trade in goods and services on business cycles.

Capital transactions are a different matter.[11] With freely fluctuating exchanges, capital imports are deflationary. The supply of goods in the domestic economy is increased, either because the capital imports are spent abroad or because they lower the gold premium, increasing imports of goods and services and decreasing exports. At the same time, the supply of money is unchanged. Therefore, there is downward pressure on prices. In a similar manner, it can be shown that capital exports are inflationary. All this is subject to qualification for the limited monetary role of gold during the greenback era.

No figures are available on short-term capital movements. Between 1865 and 1873, the United States imported long-term capital. With the onset of depression, capital imports ceased and repayments began. But the deflationary effects in the first period were largely postponed, because the capital imports were used mainly to finance railroad building. As the capital market in the United States was still in an embryonic stage, without capital imports railroad construction would have been cut down by a corresponding amount, so that the imported capital for the time being increased demand as well as supply. In the longer run, the railroads could have been financed out of domestic funds. By using up investment opportunities so fast, the capital movement accentuated the depression of the seventies. By then, however, repayments had become substantial, with inflationary effects. Accordingly, no large net cyclical influence need be ascribed to long-term international capital transactions.

Largely cut off from foreign influences, wholesale prices fell every year except one between 1865 and 1879, the total decline amounting to 55 percent; or, to get away from the precipitate decline

---

10. U. S. Bureau of the Census, *Statistical Abstract of the United States, 1922* (Washington, D. C., 1923), p. 512; *Historical Statistics of the United States, 1789-1945* (Washington, D. C., 1949), pp. 275-76.

11. This paragraph summarizes the theoretical discussion in Haberler, *Prosperity* (3d ed.), pp. 446-51.

immediately after the Civil War, they fell 45 percent from 1867 to 1879. (See Chart 2.) For agricultural products, the chief reason is not far to seek. Under the influence of a population increase of 32 percent, the opening up of new areas by the railroads, release of a million soldiers from the Civil War, reconstruction of the South, and some mechanization, agricultural output doubled between 1866 and 1878. (See Chart 6.) Had the United States been on the gold standard, international trade would have put a floor under farm prices. With a paper currency, most of the impact of the enormous increase of output fell on the domestic economy. The twofold result was a fall of domestic prices and a fall in the gold premium as foreigners sought to buy cheap American products. The gold premium, which was 103 percent in 1864 and 41 percent in 1866, disappeared entirely by the end of 1878 (Chart 5).

While the steady increase in output indicated that low prices were profitable to many farmers who could obtain cheap land, hardship for some was inevitable. Farms that were marginal in 1865 became submarginal as time went on. Those with heavy debt loads were hard hit; the liquidation wringer they were forced through added to the depression of the seventies. Even before the depression, farm troubles were expressing themselves in agitation against the railroads; and there is evidence of a fall in farm wage rates in the face of a tendency for other wages to show the normal cyclical rise.[12] In the seventies the rapid growth of the Grangers gave further expression to agricultural troubles.

The fall of agricultural prices dominated the wholesale price index because (1) farm products enter directly into computation of the index, (2) they serve as raw materials for other industries (for instance, cotton textile prices fell because the price of cotton fell), and (3) falling agricultural prices depressed the gold premium, making imports cheaper. But there were other reasons why nonagricultural prices fell. The cyclical cumulative contraction following 1873 reduced wage rates as well as demand. Between 1865 and 1869, the currency supply contracted. There were also important technological improvements. Transport costs fell. The iron and steel industry, which started using the Bessemer process at the end of the war, made gains at the expense of England in spite of the appreciation of the greenback.

12. Frank D. Graham, "International Trade Under Depreciated Paper. The United States, 1862-79," *Quarterly Journal of Economics*, XXXVI (Feb. 1922), 271. The statistics for farm wages are even less reliable than the general run of statistics for this era. Presumably they indicate not necessarily that farm wages in general fell but only that they fell in certain localities.

CHART 6. Agriculture, 1869-97 (semi-logarithmic scale).

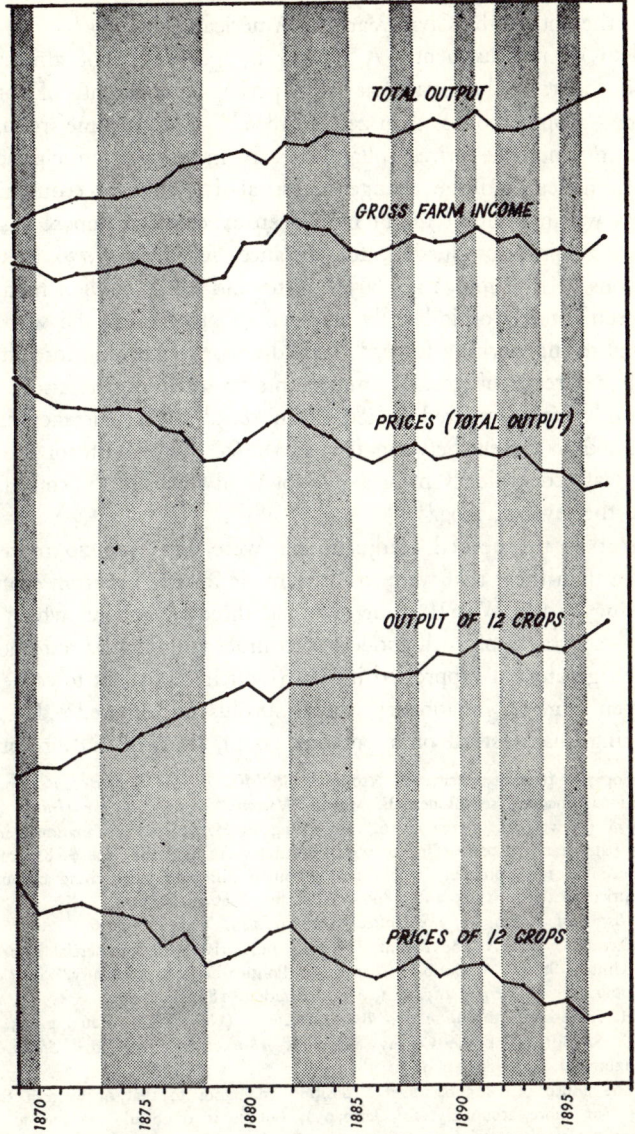

Shaded areas are business cycle contractions (N.B.E.R. dates).
SOURCE: Frederick Strauss and Louis H. Bean, *Gross Farm Income and Indices of Farm Production in the United States, 1869-1937*, U. S. Department of Agriculture, Technical Bulletin No. 703 (Dec. 1940), pp. 24, 126, 130, 142, and 144.

The Post Civil War Recession

At the end of the Civil War, the American economy faced a great problem of readjustment. A federal budget deficit of almost one billion dollars in the fiscal year 1865—perhaps one seventh of national income—dropped to less than zero in 1866.[13] The wartime speculative boom in wholesale prices collapsed early in 1865 in anticipation of sound finance, and the change necessitated a shift of economic resources which by itself might have been expected to impose a severe strain. Pig-iron production, for instance, fell from 1,136 thousand long tons in 1864 to 932 in 1865.[14] One and a half million men who had been directly or indirectly engaged in prosecuting the war were released to the working force.[15] In addition, the working force had to absorb a stream of 300,000 immigrants in each of the fiscal years 1866 and 1867, compared to 180,000 in 1865.[16] The currency supply contracted 30 percent between 1865 and 1869. The South for the time being was economically prostrate. Not until 1878 did the cotton crop regain the level of 1860.[17]

Great as the needed readjustments were, they are no more impressive than those that were so easily made in the American economy following World War II. But 1945 had three advantages which 1865 lacked—shortages of such modern consumer durables as automobiles and refrigerators, a suppressed inflation which was about to come into the open, and an inflationary export surplus to Europe.[18] It is not surprising that instead of a postwar boom, the N.B.E.R. records a

13. For the federal deficit, see *Historical Statistics of the United States*, p. 297. For national income, see Robert F. Martin, *National Income in the United States, 1799-1938* (New York, 1939), p. 6. According to Martin, realized national income in 1869 (the nearest date to 1865 for which estimates can be made) was $6,827 million. The figure for 1865 probably would not be much different, since rising output and falling prices between 1865 and 1869 tended to offset each other.

14. *Historical Statistics of the United States*, p. 149.

15. David A. Wells, "The Recent Financial, Industrial and Commercial Experience of the United States: A Curious Chapter in Politico-Economic History," in *Cobden Club Essays, Second Series, 1871-2* (2d ed.; London, 1872), p. 491.

16. Harry Jerome, *Migration and Business Cycles* (New York, 1926), p. 35.

17. U. S. Bureau of the Census, *Statistical Abstract of the United States, 1882* (Washington, D. C., 1883), p. 123.

18. The South in 1865 occupied a position analogous to that of western Europe in 1945 (or more accurately, to Germany), but it is doubtful if there was any significant net movement of capital into the South such as might have supported an interregional export surplus for the North. See E. Merton Coulter, *The South During Reconstruction, 1865-1877* (Baton Rouge, La., 1947), *passim*, esp. pp. 10, 20, 148-51, 154, 190-92 and 197.

CHART 7. Output, 1865-97 (semi-logarithmic scale).

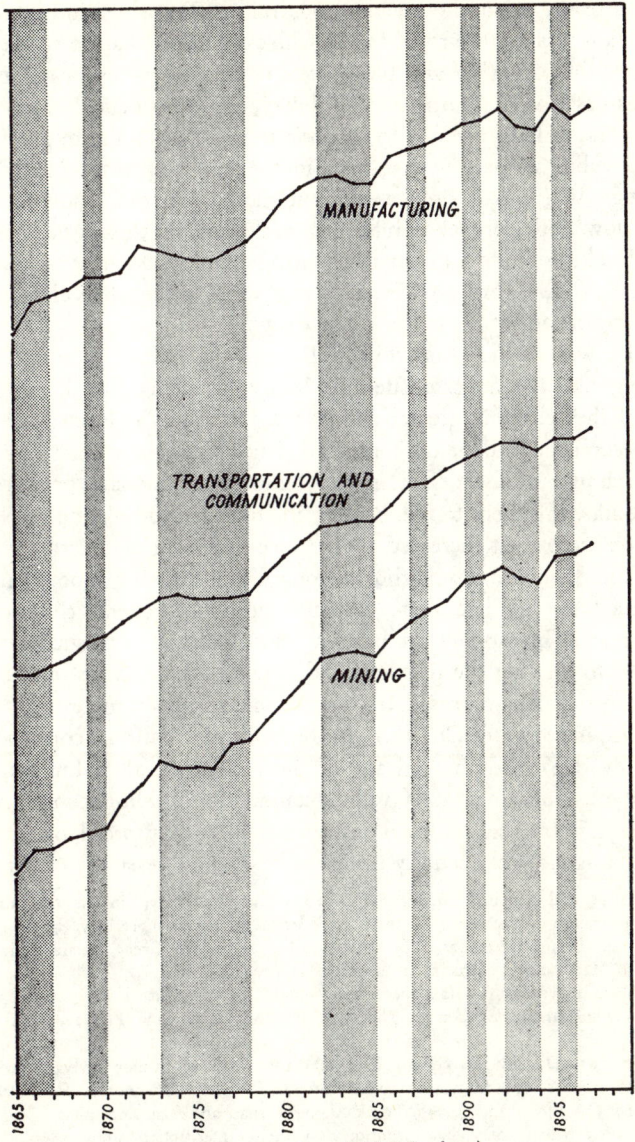

Shaded areas are business cycle contractions (N.B.E.R. dates).
SOURCES: Manufacturing, Frickey, *Production in the United States*, p. 54; transportation and communication, *ibid.*, p. 117; mining, Persons, *Forecasting Business Cycles*, p. 170.

cyclical contraction from April 1865 to December 1867.[19] Rather, it is surprising that the reaction was mild. The chief indication of depression was a more rapid fall in wholesale prices than in succeeding years.[20] Only in 1867 was the process of cumulative cyclical contraction, as described in business cycle theory, clearly evident.[21] Liabilities of business failures reached $97 million in that year, a figure moderately heavy but 20 percent less than in the boom of 1872; New York clearings, which had risen 20 percent in 1866, in the following year fell below 1865, probably reflecting a decline in the stock market; and Frickey's index of manufacturing production rose less than trend.[22] (Cf. Chart 7.) Here is one more piece of evidence that reconversion adjustments are made easily.

Why was the reaction mild? Balancing the federal budget had nothing like the adverse effect a similar balancing had in 1937, in spite of the relatively greater gap closed. In 1937, the level of activity had become dependent on continued deficit financing. In fiscal 1866 disappearance of the deficit merely removed inflationary pressure on prices, allowing them to fall, because the basis for speculation collapsed and because output increased. The price decline meant hardship and even liquidation for some, but as long as the existing money supply continued to circulate there was no cause for general contraction.

Increased investment in building and railroad construction contributed to making the reaction mild. According to one estimate, railroad construction increased from 1,177 miles in 1865 to 1,716 in 1866 and 2,249 in 1867 (see Chart 4). In the latter year, railroad construction was only one third the mileage of the peak year, 1871, but indirect effects must also be taken into account. In building construction, indirect effects from railroad investment were reinforced by a postwar shortage, so that activity rose in spite of the recession. And many

19. Burns and Mitchell, *Measuring,* p. 78. The dates given in the text are the peak and trough respectively. France's experience was almost precisely the reverse—an expansion from December 1865 to November 1867. In Great Britain there was a peak in March 1866, a trough in March 1868 (pp. 78-79).

20. More precisely, the fall was more rapid than that of a straight-line trend fitted to wholesale price data for 1866-80. Persons, Tuttle, and Frickey, "Business," p. 28.

21. In fact, Donald W. Gilbert held that there was a "minor revival" in 1866 ("Business Cycles and Municipal Expenditures," *Review of Economic Statistics,* XV [Aug. 1933], 140); and Isaiah Frank thought that an expansion phase began in August 1865 which may have continued without interruption until 1869 (Burns and Mitchell, *Measuring,* p. 111, n. 67).

22. Persons, Tuttle, and Frickey, "Business," p. 39; Edwin Frickey, *Production in the United States, 1860-1914* (Cambridge, Mass., 1947), pp. 54 and 60. The index of manufacturing rose more than trend in 1866.

of those added to the working force did not seek jobs in industry but went into agriculture, making use of the Homestead Act of 1862 or otherwise acquiring cheap land.

At the end of the Civil War, the government instituted a deliberate policy of currency contraction aimed at restoring the gold standard at the prewar value of the dollar. Unluckily, the results of this interesting experiment cannot be properly assessed. There are no reliable figures on the deposits of state banks, so that the behavior of the total supply of money is not clear. And the apparent decline of 30 percent in currency in circulation between 1865 and 1869 is misleading.[23] Nevertheless, the question is so interesting that consideration of some details is warranted.

"Currency in circulation" in this context is the sum of state and local banknotes, greenbacks (U. S. notes), subsidiary silver, fractional currency, gold coins and certificates, and interest-bearing legal tender notes of the United States government. A considerable part of the total did not circulate from hand to hand. In particular, currency held by banks is included in the total. Gold was used almost entirely for custom duties, interest on the government debt, settlement of international balances, and hoarding.[24] Interest-bearing legal tender notes circulated very little but did contribute to bank reserves. Consequently, "currency in circulation" in this context means not only currency in the hands of the public but also actual or potential bank reserves. It is a meaningful total because its decline either reduced the money supply directly or reduced bank reserves, tending to restrict the volume of bank deposits.

At the end of the Civil War, the currency supply was redundant in the sense that (1) the banks had excess reserves and (2) an unusual proportion of business during the war had been done on a cash basis.[25] Contraction was therefore possible without necessarily reducing aggregate demand (i.e., money supply times its average velocity).

23. *Historical Statistics of the United States,* p. 274.
24. Patterson excluded gold from his itemization of currency on grounds that it was either hoarded or traded as a commodity. Robert T. Patterson, *Federal Debt-Management Policies, 1865-1879* (Durham, N. C., 1954), pp. 150-51. Neither reason for exclusion is valid. The question of what constitutes currency must be distinguished from what is done with it: hoarded currency is nevertheless currency. And it is misleading to say that gold was traded as a commodity, since the three principal uses for it (as given by Patterson on p. 149) were essentially monetary uses.
25. *Ibid.,* p. 169. Patterson appeared to feel that the money supply was redundant in another sense, namely, that prices were high. This attitude was evidently colored by his stanch belief that specie payments should have been resumed promptly, coupled with his realization that resumption could not be attained without bringing prices down. Such considerations are irrelevant for present purposes.

To the extent that aggregate demand would have declined anyway (because the forces previously discussed would have brought about a cyclical decline) some further contraction could have taken place without having much deflationary impact. One who wanted to minimize the effects of monetary policy during these years could argue that Congressional action in 1867 and early 1868 to end currency contraction came just in time to permit cyclical upswing to begin from the trough of December 1867. Three circumstances count against such an easy interpretation. In the first place, Secretary of the Treasury McCulloch, whose policy was to contract the currency even at the expense of contraction of business, continued in office until March of 1869. In the second place, total currency in circulation (as defined above) was lower on every successive June 30 through 1869. In the third place, interest rates continued to rule high. It looks as if cyclical expansion not only commenced but continued for eighteen months in the face of a decline in the monetary base. If so, the incident would count heavily against the hypothesis that an expanding money supply is a necessary condition for an expanding economy.[26] It is unfortunate that the facts cannot be better established.

1867-73

Under the influence of railroad and building construction, cyclical expansion commenced at the beginning of 1868 and continued, according to the N.B.E.R., until June of 1869. After that, a mild contraction began. What started recession in the face of a 50 percent increase in railroad miles built must be a matter of speculation. Possibly it originated in financial difficulties. In June, there was a marked money stringency, the call loan rate reaching 44 percent and never falling below 16 percent (see Chart 3). This was no worse than November of the preceding year, but as call loan money financed the stock market, stock prices declined. The economy had become somewhat vulnerable to contractive forces.

In September, there was a short-lived panic when Jay Gould and Jim Fisk attempted to corner the gold market. They failed, but they temporarily ran the price of gold up from 132 to 162, demoralizing import and export markets and throwing the commercial world into

---

26. Due allowance must be made for the flexibility of prices in the period 1865-69, which in my judgment was considerably greater than nowadays. Present institutional arrangements, including labor unions, make an expanding money supply indispensable for cyclical expansion.

confusion.[27] Although the *Commercial and Financial Chronicle* observed no lasting damage to business, such a panic could have contributed to the mild recession that followed by discouraging inventory accumulation. In the minor business cycles since World War I, fluctuations in inventory investment played a large role. Inventory accumulation was relatively more than twice as large in the decade 1869-78 as in 1919-28.[28] Although these figures do not gauge the relative importance for cycles of inventory changes in the two periods, they indicate that actual decumulation of inventories would not have been necessary to start a general contraction in 1869. Cessation of accumulation would shut off an important avenue for the use of funds. With a declining stock market, the funds might be hoarded long enough to initiate contraction. The fact that the panic came after the cyclical peak does not damage the above hypothesis, for the peak in commercial paper rates coincided with the peak of the cycle.

Contraction was necessarily mild as it was bucking against expansion in construction. In fact, the acceleration in additions to railroad miles in operation was greatest in 1869 and 1870. The housing index, however, declined in 1870, although it was to reach a peak in 1871. The annual index of manufacturing did not increase in 1870, but neither did it decline (Chart 7). The sharp increase in railroad earnings came to a temporary halt. Imports declined for a time. By the beginning of 1871, the *Chronicle* was casually saying, "business is stagnant" but with no implication that anything was seriously awry.[29]

The trough came in December 1870, and by the second quarter of 1871, expansion was plainly under way again. Business flourished until the fall of 1873. Frickey's index of manufacturing rose 20 percent between 1870 and 1873, and his production index for transportation and communication increased even more (Chart 7). Wholesale prices, reversing their downward trend, rose sharply from August 1871 until the spring of 1873 (Chart 2). Oddly enough, wage rates,

---

27. Davis R. Dewey, *Financial History of the United States* (10th ed.; New York, 1928), pp. 369-70; Warren F. Hickernell, *Financial and Business Forecasting*, Alexander Hamilton Institute (London, 1928), I, 311-14; *Commercial and Financial Chronicle*, IX (Sept. 25, 1869), 406; *ibid.* (Oct. 2, 1869), 437; *ibid.* (Oct. 9, 1869), 453-55 (hereafter cited as *Chronicle*).

28. Simon S. Kuznets, *National Product Since 1869* (New York, 1946), pp. 118-19. Net changes in inventories averaged $380 million in 1869-78, or 5.4% of gross national product, which was $7,033 million. For 1919-28, the figure was $1,756, or 2.2% of GNP ($81,199 million).

29. XII (Jan. 14, 1871), 37.

which hitherto had been rising in spite of falling prices, now tended to slow down.[30] Railroad earnings rose spectacularly.

Investment in building apparently went into a decline before the panic of September 1873. The indexes of both Long and Riggleman show that the peak of physical construction came in 1871. The evidence is not clear as to how soon railroad investment began to decline. One estimate gives the peak in miles built as 1871, the other, as 1872. Orders for rails began to fall off only in the spring of 1872, and "apparent consumption" of rails reached its peak in that calendar year. Orders for locomotives also show 1872 as the best year, while orders for cars boomed until the second quarter of 1873.[31] These peaks relate to physical volume only. As steel prices rose sharply in 1872, the peak in expenditures may have come later than the peak in physical expansion. In so far as the data relate to orders, physical peaks themselves may have lagged behind the dates given. Annual figures for the increase of railroad capital show a decided peak in 1873, confirming misgivings as to whether physical series provide a good guide to the peak in expenditures. Even if the value of railroad investment did not decline prior to the panic, the transport-building cycle gave every evidence of being at the peak or beyond.

The Panic of 1873

The Bureau dates the cyclical peak as October 1873, the month following the outbreak of the banking panic. If the Bureau's dating is accepted, there is no alternative but to conclude that the panic was the proximate cause of the business downturn. In principle there are many reasons for not accepting the Bureau's dates in blind faith. Not the least is the scarcity of monthly data for the 1870's. The intentionally vague definition of the business cycle employed by the Bureau, however well suited to its research methods, does not seem precise enough for present purposes. Lastly, the procedural rules employed by the Bureau give preference to later dates in cases of doubt.

Such rules, combined with lack of evidence, inevitably imply a date that others might regard as too late. But even from the standpoint of the N.B.E.R. it seems to me that September would be a

30. George F. Warren and Frank A. Pearson, *Prices* (New York, 1933), p. 197. Their index is the same for 1873 as 1872. The index of nonagricultural wages used in Chart 2 shows some rise in 1873, but it is smaller than in the preceding years.

31. John E. Partington, *Railroad Purchasing and the Business Cycle* (Washington, D. C., 1929), pp. 37-47.

better choice. The violence of the panic, which began in the latter part of September, makes it extremely unlikely that October could have been the peak month. Such monthly and quarterly series as are available seem on the whole to support an earlier date than October. A September peak is not inconsistent with the hypothesis that the panic was the immediate cause of the downturn. The evidence does not clearly rule out a date even earlier, but it seems reasonably clear that if the downturn was passed prior to the panic, the amount of the decline must have been slight. Or, to put the conclusion a little differently, the expansion probably levelled off before the panic, presumably because the limit to the expansion of the money supply had been reached.

The event that made a banking panic inevitable was the failure of Jay Cooke & Co.[32] Cooke, as the man who had financed the Civil War, enjoyed an extraordinary reputation. His downfall did far more damage than the failure of a financial pirate could have. He had taken on the risky job of financing the Northern Pacific Railroad. By May 1873, this road had spent over $15 million, had little more than 500 miles in operation through a sparsely populated region, and the two portions of its lines were still more than 1,000 miles apart. More than once Cooke had been on the verge of finding customers for his $100 million of bonds, but each time the deal fell through. Now, to keep the road going, he was advancing money obtained from depositors at short term in expectation that a European market would develop.

But the market for railroad bonds turned worse in 1873 rather than better. Tight money was perhaps the principal cause,[33] but there were several others. Twenty-five railroads defaulted on interest on their bonds between January 1 and August 31,[34] a circumstance which affected the market unfavorably.[35] The Granger movement, although still in its infancy, prejudiced capitalists against the railroads.[36] The *Chronicle* was consistently optimistic about the safety of railroad bonds and even after the panic admitted only reluctantly that railroad building had been too rapid and that "some roads have

---

32. The account of the panic that follows is based, except as otherwise indicated, on Oliver M. W. Sprague, *History of Crises Under the National Banking System*, 61st Congress, 2d Session, Senate Doc. No. 538 (Washington, D. C., 1910), pp. 1-89. See also Henrietta M. Larson, *Jay Cooke, Private Banker* (Cambridge, Mass., 1936), chap. 19.
33. *Chronicle*, XVIII (Jan. 10, 1874), 28.
34. *Ibid.*, p. 36.   35. *Ibid.*, XVII (Aug. 2, 1873), 150.
36. *Ibid.*, XVIII (Jan. 10, 1874), 28.

been built in sections of the country where they were not yet needed and could not have had any reasonable prospect of making sufficient net earnings to pay their annual interest";[37] but the *Nation* the previous year published an article claiming that "railroad securities in America are not more profitable on the whole, while decidedly less secure, than the bonds of the United States" and that in western states more roads had been built than the population could support.[38] Some investors abroad, as well as at home, evidently thought along the same lines as the *Nation*. In the summer of 1873, the *Chronicle* reported that foreign purchasers of bonds were favoring governments over railroads.[39] Despite the fact that long-term capital imports in 1873 were still high, the *Chronicle* further reported that foreigners were shunning new issues of railroad securities.[40] Although the money stringency had a good deal to do with drying up the market for bonds, investors in 1873 were turning away from newly issued railroad bonds and had good reason to do so.

Jay Cooke was not the only one engaged in the dangerous practice of advancing short-term funds for long-term use. The New York banks had loaned money to railroads that expected to raise funds for repayment by selling bonds before the notes fell due.[41] The usual midsummer ease in the money market in 1873 induced the New York banks to increase their loans further, with the intention of recalling them before money became tight in the fall.

Such unsound banking practices impinged on a situation made vulnerable by the downturn of railroad and building construction. Imports had reached their peak in 1872. Stock prices and New York clearings declined sharply in the first half of 1873. Wholesale prices resumed their downward trend after reaching a peak in the first quarter. Clearings in Philadelphia reached their maximum in the second quarter.

Cyclic weakness was less important for the panic than structural banking weakness. Under the National Banking System, there was no effective central bank to act as lender of last resort and to shield business and the stock market from panicky calling of loans in time of crisis. Banking troubles were likely to spread from New York throughout the country, inasmuch as bank reserves were concentrated

37. *Ibid.*, XVII (Nov. 15, 1873), 647.
38. XV (Aug. 15, 1872), 102-3.
39. XVII (Aug. 9, 1873), 173.
40. XVI (March 29, 1873), 407 and 408. See also *Chronicle*, XV (Dec. 21, 1872), 822.
41. *Chronicle*, XVII (Nov. 15, 1873), 647; *ibid.*, XVIII (Jan. 10, 1874), 28.

in that city. The law permitted country banks to keep three fifths of their required reserves on deposit in reserve cities. In 1873, New York banks were obligated to other banks for more than their total reserves, and 70 to 80 percent of bankers' deposits were held by seven of New York's sixty banks. Trouble in New York might lead to hasty withdrawal of bankers' deposits, undermining the position of banks both in New York and the hinterland, encouraging runs and leading quickly to contraction of loans.

Trouble was most likely to come in autumn. Moving of crops regularly caused a drain of money from New York to the interior. As the currency supply was highly inelastic, failures would be precipitated then if ever. So it was not surprising that unsound railroad financing was exposed in September. On the eighth, the New York Warehouse and Security Co., which had financed the Missouri, Kansas and Texas Railroad, was forced to suspend. On the thirteenth, the important banking house of Kenyon, Cox & Co. failed on account of indorsements of paper of the Canada Southern Railroad. These disasters wreaked havoc on the stock market but nothing more.

On Thursday, September 18, Jay Cooke & Co. failed on account of its advances to the Northern Pacific Railroad plus a heavy drain by depositors on its cash resources. This caused general distrust and a rapid calling in of loans, precipitating failure of Fisk and Hatch the next day. Stocks plummeted, and failures followed thick and fast. On September 20, two trust companies suspended. Although they later were able to resume business, immediate consequences were far reaching. One, the Fourth National, held $15 million of bankers' deposits; hence, the suspension hurt outside banks, and led to runs and the recall of funds from New York.

The panic was handled well. On September 20, the New York Clearing House Association arranged for its members to deposit approved securities with a committee of five, which then issued certificates of deposit ("clearing house certificates") up to 75 percent of the value of the securities. The certificates could be used to settle clearing house balances. Thus the policy of every bank's recalling loans, thereby ruining each other and business too, was avoided. Unfortunately, mounting calls for cash from the interior forced partial suspension of cash payments. On September 24, the clearing house banks passed a resolution that all checks issued would be stamped "Payable through the Clearing House," concentrating control of reserves in the committee's hands. Partial suspension in New York necessarily caused partial suspension throughout the country, except in California. But the committee controlling the New York reserves restored confidence by using them freely. Panic was over by September 29, eleven days after it had begun. After October 18, New York bank reserves began to increase, and by mid November the reserve ratio once again exceeded the legal minimum.

What effect did the banking panic have on business? In the first place, there was a brief paralysis of the crop movement. Secondly, on September 20, foreign exchange became blocked. However, the issue of clearing house certificates on September 24 enabled the banks to resume purchasing foreign bills. Toward the end of the week, England began to ship gold, enabling exports to move. Thirdly, the panic caused considerable hoarding, e.g. because businesses kept their cash receipts in their own vaults instead of depositing them in banks. The national banks lost 23 percent of their holdings of legal tender notes between September 12 and October 13, a symptom of the hoarding. But the New York banks used their reserves so freely that the desire to hoard stopped. In the meantime, the hoarding aggravated the effects of partial suspension (which lasted nearly three weeks) and numerous firms had difficulty meeting payrolls. These had to reduce employment because they could neither get the cash to which they were entitled nor negotiate loans. Fourthly, after the middle of October, although there was no longer any difficulty meeting payrolls, businessmen had to cut production because demand had fallen. Contributing to the decline of orders was the decline of railroad and building construction. But undoubtedly the most important immediate factor was the interruption of business during the panic. To the extent that payrolls could not be met, consumer demand was cut. More significant, businessmen during the panic presumably either cancelled orders or curtailed making new ones. The shock to confidence must have affected both consumption and investment. Once the purely monetary troubles were over, the decline of spending and ordering curtailed output, which in turn reduced spending, and so on in the familiar process. Even without a decline of long-term investment prospects to reinforce it, the panic by itself could have started a cumulative cyclical decline.

Theory of the Downturn

If theories are looked at as tools for understanding reality, very few tools have been needed to account for the downturn of 1873. I have not had to mention any of the theories of the upper turning point discussed in Chapter 2. Nevertheless, it is useful to discuss them at this point, because they can give us a more penetrating understanding. Moreover, theories can be considered as generalizations of reality as well as tools; and there is now an opportunity to test their generality with a case in which the essential processes stand out in unusual clarity. Besides, the discussion may throw some light on the history of business cycle theory, for the facts (some of which have always been widely known) are consistent with several different theories.

Monetary. According to the purely monetary theory, cyclical expansion leads to a drain of currency out of banks and into circulation as wages and incomes rise. Sooner or later the banks reach the end of their reserves and must stop expanding credit, but as the rise in wages and incomes lags behind credit, the drain of currency continues. This forces the banks to contract, initiating depression.

That is roughly what happened in 1873. The autumnal drain of cash into the interior helped set off a violent process of monetary contraction. But this is a superficial interpretation. It leaves too much out of the picture. For instance, it ignores the likelihood that greater elasticity of credit would not have saved the situation but would have permitted the multiplication of unsound financial practices, leading in the end to still greater difficulties;[42] only revival in the securities markets could have saved Jay Cooke and his ilk. The case illustrates how the monetary theory in one form or another could be so popular prior to the 1930's. The facts do not contradict it. But the monetary cycle is subsidiary to other cyclical forces.

Shortage of Capital. According to Cassel, shortage of capital causes the downturn.[43] At the beginning of the upswing, or high conjuncture, the rate of interest is low. This induces businessmen to take advantage of the opportunities provided by technical progress (e.g. railways), the opening up of new countries, and the increase of population to launch ambitious investment programs. In the upswing, production of fixed capital grows more rapidly than production of consumers' goods. For four reasons, the supply of money capital does not grow as rapidly as the output of capital goods: (1) if savings were a constant proportion of income, the relative growth of output

---

42. Schumpeter, *Business Cycles,* I, 316.

43. Gustav Cassel, *The Theory of Social Economy,* trans. Joseph McCabe (New York, 1924), Fourth bk., esp. pp. 596-628. I take Cassel as an example to represent the shortage-of-capital school primarily because he meant his theory to explain the conjunctures of the period 1870-1914. Similar remarks to those that follow in the text above could be made about Hayek's monetary overinvestment theory as summarized by Haberler, *Prosperity,* pp. 33-72.

of fixed capital would create a disparity; (2) in fact, savings are not a constant proportion of income but are relatively large at the first part of an upswing when profits are high but toward the end ("in the high conjuncture proper") fall off relatively as wages rise and profits decline, so that the interest rate rises toward the end of the upswing; (3) this is accentuated by the increased returns from fixed capital at the earlier part, which rise more rapidly than the prices of capital goods and therefore tend to raise the interest rate; and (4) in the earlier period, banks create new purchasing power at low interest rates, diverting production to capital goods, and hiding the increasing stringency of capital, but "when the banks afterward find it necessary in their own interest to cut down this excessive supply of media of payment, the real scarcity of capital is suddenly and acutely felt."[44] The high rate of interest at the end of the upswing cuts down the demand for capital goods, frequently forcing the abandonment of projects already begun. Workers in the capital goods industries lose their jobs. Usually a crisis marks the onset of depression. Crisis is defined "as a time of general inability to meet obligations which fall due."[45] It is caused by "an overestimate of the supply of capital, of the amount of savings available for taking over the real capital produced."[46]

In so far as they can be ascertained, the facts of 1865-73 fit Cassel's theory well. After a considerable period of expanding credit, money conditions became tight in 1872. Meantime, the Northern Pacific and some other roads made grandiose plans based on an overestimate of the supply of capital that would be forthcoming. When the elasticity of the credit system ceased to hide the shortage of capital, the inability of a few to meet their obligations became translated through runs into a panic and a partial breakdown of the banking system. After the crisis, foreign investors stopped buying American securities, accentuating the shortage of capital.

There is much to commend this interpretation. It turns on a fact other explanations are apt to ignore, namely, that the decline of railway investment was due to lack of investors more than lack of projects. On the other hand, one cannot help feeling that investors were chary not (or not only) because they did not have enough funds but because they recognized a change in the profits prospects of new investments. Although the shortage-of-capital theory accounts for much

44. *Social Economy,* p. 628.
45. *Ibid.,* p. 509.
46. *Ibid.,* p. 626.

more of what happened than the purely monetary theory, it still does not cover the whole ground.

Hicks.[47] The facts give the appearance of what Hicks would call a cycle of autonomous investment rather than an explosive accelerator.[48] Investment apparently declined for other reasons than collision with a full employment ceiling. One piece of negative evidence is the price of pig iron, a material important for investment goods. A collision with a full employment ceiling would reveal itself by a rise in its price. Actually, the price of pig iron declined for a full year before the peak in business.

Schumpeter and Gordon. Discussing the spurt in railroad building during 1869-71 Schumpeter said,

Two things are perfectly clear. First, that development . . . was a typical downgrade development within the meaning of our model. It was a Juglar prosperity superimposed on a Kondratieff recession,[49] a new step in what was no longer fundamentally new, but a process of carrying out what had previously been initiated . . . . This left plenty of problems for the individual case, but they were comparatively easy to solve, further eased by the growth of the environment, and of the type which is characteristic of "exploiting investment opportunity" and "pushing into new economic space." Moreover, the general features of the period support this interpretation. There was a great building boom. The well-being of all classes in the years 1869 to 1873 . . . is obviously due to the expansion of production which our schema leads us to expect in every Kondratieff recession.[50] But it is not less clear, in the second place, that that method of financing which so well illustrates our theory, was handled with such carelessness as to make it an additional cause of the situation of 1873. It not only induced but really also presupposed abnormal speculative activity and could not without it have gone to anything like the lengths it did. The

---

47. We confine the discussion in the text to the main variant of Hicks's theory. The weak cycle (or anti-damped cycle) variant is clearly inapplicable since it is relevant only if a ceiling is not encountered. The cycle in autonomous investment variant is better associated with Gordon, who has developed the idea more fully, and Schumpeter's theory, although fundamentally different, nevertheless has an important bearing on it.

48. The two alternatives are not mutually exclusive, but if there is a cycle in autonomous investment, the question of whether there was an explosive accelerator is irrelevant for analyzing the downturn. For Hicks on cycles of autonomous investment, see *Contribution,* pp. 120-22.

49. Undoubtedly a slip. It is clear from Schumpeter's model in Vol. I, his chronology on p. 396, and his statement on p. 338 that he meant Kondratieff *depression.* In my opinion, however, he would have been better off had he meant what he said (see Chap. 2).

50. Here the word "recession" is defensible—the well-being of all classes could have been the result of a Kondratieff recession that ended in 1869.

phenomena of the Secondary Wave were developed to an unusual degree thereby, and errors and cases of misconduct became possible which our model does not account for per se ... and it becomes understandable that even as regards the railroad business these things were more obviously in evidence than the underlying process and that it seemed as if construction had been brought to a stop and the success of existing lines had been jeopardized by them rather than by any "logic of evolution." But even so, nobody can deny ... that railroad construction had temporarily exhausted possibilities—a formulation which is more correct than the more common phrase of things having been overdone—and it should be easy to see that this, together with the dislocating consequences immediate and ulterior, for the economic system, of new construction was what created the situation in which the Secondary Wave broke, and with it untenable credit situations and speculative bubbles all over the field of industry and commerce.

... It is not astonishing that the impact was primarily on the new, instead of on those elements that progress had made obsolete. For, as was pointed out in our theoretical chapters, this will always happen if the new things stand on a slender and the old things on a safe financial basis. Thus, the role played in the drama by the Northern Pacific failure does not any more contradict expectation from our model than does the fact that, in general, danger signals first became visible in the railroad field.[51]

The passage quoted is a brilliant synthesis of the monetary and real forces at work. It brings out the underlying importance of entrepreneurial activity in railroads and shows how it gave rise to the excesses of the boom and the ultimate collapse. Banking panics for Schumpeter are always partly accidental, and so it was in this case; but given the institutional arrangements, his theory shows how at a time like this events make a panic understandable if not probable. That his interpretation does not make use of the shortage of capital that was manifest in 1873 is a source of strength rather than weakness, for he emphasizes a more significant fact, namely, that the railroads were ceasing to be attractive to investors. Although Schumpeter's work as a whole has been subjected to important criticisms, for this particular episode it offers a more convincing explanation than any other.

The quoted passage gives as much support to Gordon's analysis as to Schumpeter's own. Gordon's concept of a major cycle does not depend on the way the downturn begins. In fact, he says, "The decline, when it finally comes, may be ushered in by the same sequence

---

[51] By permission from *Business Cycles* by Joseph A. Schumpeter (Copyright, 1939, McGraw-Hill Book Company, Inc.), I, 335-36.

of events that we associate with minor recessions; but, as the contraction gathers momentum, the impairment of investment opportunities is increasingly recognized...."[52] Acceptance of the detail of Schumpeter's discussion of this episode does not imply rejecting Gordon, and the treatment of investment behavior in no way turns on the fundamental difference between the two, namely the question of whether there is a deficiency of long-term investment opportunities.

The Depression of the 1870's

The cyclical contraction that followed the panic of 1873 was the longest in the history of American business cycles, lasting until March 1879, a span of five years and five months. In monetary statistics, it was second in severity only to the contraction of 1929-33 among post Civil War cycles. For measuring the severity of business contractions, the records of bank transactions (clearings or debts) in effect begin only with 1875; yet the decline for 1875-78 was greater than for any other period except 1893-97 and 1929-33. It was virtually as great as 1893-97 and undoubtedly would have been greater if statistics were available from the peak of 1873.[53] One investigator used six series to measure the severity of depressions. He found that 1873-78 was second only to 1929-32, and this result was mainly due to the three monetary series used.[54]

Nevertheless, in terms of output the contraction of the seventies was singularly mild. Indexes of production for manufacturing and for transportation and communication declined markedly less than in 1893-94 and 1907-8 even though the latter contractions were much shorter; and manufacturing did not decline after 1875, actually increasing 14 percent in the last two years of the depression (see Chart 7).[55] In spite of the long depression, real income in 1879 was two

52. "Investment," p. 30.

53. Joseph B. Hubbard, "Business Declines and Recoveries," *Review of Economic Statistics,* XVIII (Feb. 1936), 18-19.

54. A. Ross Eckler, "A Measure of the Severity of Depressions, 1873-1932," *Review of Economic Statistics,* XV (May 15, 1933), 79. The period 1929-32 was the deepest depression in all six series. The contraction of the seventies was second in two monetary series (clearing and railway revenues) and third in the other (imports). It was second in one of the physical series (coal production), fifth and sixth in the other two (pig-iron production and cotton consumption; however, Eckler does not make it quite clear whether cotton consumption was a physical or a monetary series).

55. The coverage of the indexes is rather meager, so that too much confidence cannot be placed in inferences drawn from them. One need not necessarily conclude that manufacturing output as a whole increased in 1877 and 1878. Nevertheless, the figures are comparable over the whole period, 1865-1914, so that comparisons among different cycles of this period should be reasonably trustworthy.

thirds greater than in 1869. Even on a per capita basis, the increase was one third.[56] In June 1878, which was presumably as bad a time as any, Carroll Wright took a kind of census which showed only 28,500 people unemployed in Massachusetts out of a normal working force in "mechanical industries" of 318,000.[57] Although comparison with modern figures is not reliable, this looks no worse than 1930.[58]

In Britain the depression had a similar character. Prices and interest rates fell, but production fared surprisingly well. The percentage of unemployment of 1874-77 was only two thirds of the average for 1850-1914—a performance which normally would indicate prosperity. For Britain, the depression apparently originated abroad. But foreign sales in terms of volume (although not in prices and profits) were well maintained, and activity was turned to such domestic lines as shipbuilding and housing.[59]

Schumpeter's explanation of the depression of the seventies is readily disposed of. It occupied a place in his three-cycle schema comparable to that of the nineteen thirties and was explained on the same grounds—both Juglar and Kondratieff cycles were in their depression phase simultaneously.[60] The analogy rested on the belief that the depression of the seventies was severe as well as prolonged. As we have just seen, it was indeed severe in monetary terms, but not in terms of output. Schumpeter seems to have been misled by reports of three million unemployed, which made relative unemployment appear worse than in the thirties.[61] His statement was extremely cautious and guarded; yet to mention the figure at all is to give a grossly exaggerated impression. The behavior of output and unemployment was more in keeping with Kondratieff recession than depression and therefore accords with my revision of the three-cycle schema proposed in Chapter 2.

The panic of 1873, the disillusionment of investors about the railroads, the indirect effects of the decline in railroad investment, and

56. Martin, *National Income*, p. 6. It should not be necessary to stress that national income figures for this period are subject to a wide margin of error. Martin's estimates probably exaggerate the increase.

57. *Tenth Annual Report of the Bureau of Statistics of Labor*, Massachusetts Public Doc. No. 31 (Boston, Jan. 1879), pp. 6-13. Applying the ratio of unemployed in Massachusetts to the whole country, Wright estimated total unemployment in the United States at 570,000.

58. In 1930, out of a total labor force of 48.7 million, there were 4.2 million unemployed. Civil nonagricultural employment was 31.1 million; *26th Annual Report of the National Bureau of Economic Research* (New York, 1946), p. 31.

59. Rostow, *British Economy*, p. 49.   60. *Business Cycles*, I, 338.

61. *Ibid.*, I, 337.

THE CYCLES OF 1865-79

the position of the seventies in the downswing of a building cycle are fully sufficient to account for events through 1876. What need to be explained are (1) why the depression lasted so long and (2) why it was so mild in terms of output.

If the United States had been on the gold standard in 1873 at the exchange rate that then actually prevailed, cyclical contraction might have come to an end two years sooner than it did. Under gold standard conditions, a small country undergoing depression reduces imports as national income drops, but its exports are maintained. If its prices fall, both domestic and foreign buyers shift to its products and away from foreign commodities. For both reasons, depression generates a favorable balance of payments, which helps arrest cyclical contraction. The greenback appreciated a small amount between 1873 and 1876 and in the following year appreciated almost 7 percent more. The forces that under paper standard conditions caused appreciation would under gold standard conditions have been channeled into stimulating the domestic economy or arresting the fall of prices. In 1877 there is evidence of an upturn in railroad investment, building construction, manufacturing, and mining. This indicates that under gold standard conditions deflation might well have been ended by 1877, other circumstances being favorable to cyclical revival.

Since the United States was not on the gold standard, the question arises, what effect price flexibility had on the course of contraction, drawing on the theoretical discussion of Chapter 3. It is safe to assume that prices (including wages) were more flexible in the 1870's than in the 1930's. Wholesale farm prices generally are highly flexible. Inasmuch as they fell somewhat more sluggishly in the 1870's than nonfarm prices[62] (whereas they fell much more rapidly than other prices between 1929 and 1933), other wholesale prices must have been highly flexible also.

The effect of price flexibility on cyclical contraction can be brought out by contrasting two situations. First, assume that the economy momentarily rests in Keynesian underemployment equilibrium but wages and prices begin to fall. So long as they continue to fall—and there is no necessary reason why they should not fall forever—statistical series will exhibit many of the characteristics of cyclical contraction; and even if circumstances now become favorable to cyclical expansion, revival will be postponed or hindered by the general deflation. This seems to be more or less what happened in 1877 and 1878.

62. Mitchell, *Gold, Prices and Wages*, p. 54.

Second, assume that a cyclical contraction is under way. If price changes do not alter the course of aggregate spending, price flexibility increases output above what it otherwise would have been (with a given amount of spending, output is an inverse function of the price level). Of course, the fall of prices will not leave aggregate spending unchanged, but its effects work in both directions.

In the 1870's, general price flexibility probably reduced aggregate spending below what it otherwise would have been but not by enough to reverse the tendency for flexibility to mitigate the decline of output. Flexibility probably induced expectations that prices would fall further. As a matter of fact, prices had been falling, with one interruption, ever since 1865; yet until 1878 they were still above the pre Civil War normal. In addition, in the lame-duck session of early 1875, Congress passed a law providing for resumption of specie payments on January 1, 1879; and in the spring of 1877 the Secretary of the Treasury began to make effective preparations to implement the law. It must have been evident that if resumption was to be carried through, American prices would have to fall relative to foreign prices (which were also falling). The government did not in fact put effective pressure on the price level, but that would not keep the prospect of resumption from affecting short-term expectations unfavorably. Offsetting in part the factors adverse to spending was the rise in the value of currency and publicly held government debt. Because retail prices fell more slowly than wholesale prices, government obligations increased in value only a little more than 10 percent. To conclude, general price and wage flexibility probably intensified the contraction of spending, mitigated the decline of output, and prolonged the contraction phase of the cycle.[63]

Another important circumstance must be considered. The large amount of investment in railroads prior to 1873 might mean that several years would pass before the revival of railroad building. On the other hand, there was no shortage of railroads to be built. Construction of many roads had had to be abandoned during the depression before their main lines were completed, and the steady growth of population and agricultural output continually increased the inducement for the roads to expand. In view of the experience of the

---

63. The statement that price flexibility mitigated the decline of output but prolonged the contraction phase of the cycle sounds inconsistent. The explanation lies in the fact that the decline in output apparently ended around 1877, whereas the contraction (according to N.B.E.R.) continued until March 1879.

The discussion so far has been concerned with general flexibility. As noted below, selective price cuts (in the form of a railroad rate war) had an adverse effect.

1880's (the 1885 trough in railroad investment came only three or four years after the peak and was followed by a vigorous expansion), we might reasonably expect railroad activity to revive about 1876 or 1877. The evidence, although conflicting as to the exact time, indicates that it did so. The number of miles built reached its trough in 1875 and then increased substantially in the following year. The increase in railroad capital shows a trough in 1876 with a substantial revival in 1877. Orders for most types of railroad equipment revived in 1876 or 1877.[64] But all the evidence points to an early relapse of railroad investment. Why?

The continuance of deflation elsewhere in the economy provides part of the answer. Had deflation stopped, the railroads could have sparked a revival. But part of the answer must be sought within the railroad industry itself. There were three specific factors that discouraged investment in railroads: freight rate wars were acute in 1876; railroad strikes, which had to be quelled by military force, occurred in 1877; and federal, state, and local aid to railroad companies was replaced during the depression by efforts, occasionally successful, to pass legislation regulating railroads and railroad rates.

Were the adverse railroad developments endogenous or exogenous? In a broad sense, they are the endogenous results of the economic process. But in a narrower sense at least two or three are better considered exogenous. Strikes and changes in government policy are affected by other causes than the economic ones, particularly with respect to timing, and cannot appropriately be incorporated into a theory of the business cycle. Even freight rate wars, although very much a part of the Schumpeterian mechanism, are to some extent accidents dependent on the personalities involved and on details of the circumstances in which they find themselves (such as the extent to which previous history has forced the industry to recognize the advantages of collusion) that lie outside the present subject of study.

In 1879 conditions were ripe for recovery. Specie payments were successfully resumed on January 1, a step that (if we can believe the *Chronicle*) had favorable effects on business confidence. By that time, prices were well below even the pre Civil War normal. Not only was there no need to expect prices to fall farther but in fact they stopped falling. In addition, investment in railroads revived strongly in response to the new business furnished by a 50 percent increase in crop production since 1873 and the sales of railroad land grants to new settlers. During the summer it became apparent that the United States

64. Partington, *Railroad Purchasing*, p. 53.

was to enjoy unusually bountiful crops, Europe unusually poor ones, a combination which for a predominantly agricultural country on the gold standard was a powerful stimulant. Thereafter, the expansion phase of the cycle was in full sway.

Conclusions

When warfare ended in 1865, long-term investment prospects became favorable, particularly in railroads. Nevertheless, readjustment to peacetime conditions brought on a recession which lasted until the end of 1867. There was another recession in 1869-70, the causes of which are obscure. But the expansion of railroad investment went on, climaxing in a boom in 1872-73. By that time long-term investment prospects, from the point of view of the man who puts up the money, appear to have taken a turn for the worse. Nevertheless, a banking panic, originating in the excesses of the railroad boom, was the immediate cause of the cyclical downturn. The theories of Schumpeter and Cassel both fit the facts of the downturn. Of the two, I prefer Schumpeter's, although it does not account satisfactorily for the depression that followed. The depression is the longest of which there is record, lasting until early 1879. Although exceedingly severe in monetary terms, it was mild in real terms, partly as a result of price flexibility. The unfavorable long-term investment situation accounts for the depression's lasting through 1876 or 1877. About that time the outlook appears to have improved, but a number of short-run influences—the fact that the United States was off the gold standard; a high degree of price flexibility; unfavorable price expectations; rate wars, strikes, and adverse legislation in the railroad industry—delayed recovery. In 1879, the return to the gold standard put a floor under prices and increased confidence; and poor crops abroad, combined with bumper crops in the United States, gave a powerful stimulus, so that short-run as well as long-run prospects became propitious.

The hypothesis of a major cycle from 1865 to 1879 with the peak in 1873 requires a minor qualification. Although the evidence is not altogether certain, long-term investment prospects apparently changed before the business cycle peak of 1873 and trough of 1879. Strictly speaking, one should perhaps date the major cycle accordingly. But simplicity and convenience dictate dating the peaks and troughs of major cycles to coincide with peaks and troughs of business cycles. Otherwise, the hypothesis stands up.

7

THE CYCLE OF 1879-85

A BUSINESS CYCLE, counting from trough to trough, began in March 1879 and lasted until May 1885.¹ The cycle was worldwide. France, Britain, and Germany all had troughs in 1879 with the ensuing peaks coming within months of those of the United States. Only at the terminal trough of the cycle was there marked divergence, the upturn coming much sooner in the United States of America.²

The Lower Turning Point (1877-79)

The end of the depression of the seventies cannot be dated with certainty, partly because data are lacking, but mainly because the

1. Arthur F. Burns and Wesley C. Mitchell, *Measuring Business Cycles* (New York, 1946), p. 78. There is no dispute whatever in the literature about the existence of this cycle, although there is some difference of opinion about its exact dating. Cf. the investigators cited by Burns and Mitchell on p. 108.

2. There has been very little research aimed at explaining this cycle. So far as I know, the only intensive work done on it in recent years was by Arthur G. Auble in his unpublished doctoral dissertation, "The Depressions of 1873 and 1882 in the United States," Harvard University, 1949. Schumpeter, *Business Cycles*, I, 339-40 and 383-96 *passim*, and others have made some scattered comments on it, but the best published accounts are those written by contemporary observers. The *Bankers' Magazine* of New York had a number of good articles, particularly on international influences. The London *Economist* discussed the American scene at length from sources which in many cases are now difficult to find; it also contributed reports and comments of its own. In 1886 Carroll D. Wright published a study called "Industrial Depressions," *First Annual Report of the Commissioner of Labor* (Washington, D. C., 1886). Devoted almost entirely to the depression of 1882-85, it is known to modern economists as a forerunner of the mature economy thesis. But the best original source is the *Chronicle*, which had an insight into the workings of the cyclical mechanism which was quite good in view of the little that was then known about cycles. See particularly its annual review articles, to be found in the first or second issue of each year (also in *Financial Review*, published by the same company). The bimonthly *Investors' Supplement to the Chronicle* frequently had illuminating comments in its lead article.

concept of a lower turning point is ambiguous. Physical production may have turned upward as early as 1877. Real income per capita may have risen during the last two or three years of the 1870's. Monetary series, on the other hand, reached their troughs distinctly later. Bank clearings began to increase in 1878, but wholesale prices continued to decline into 1879. By the spring of the latter year, a process of cyclical expansion plainly got under way; but should the trough be dated then or earlier?

A rise in physical output tends to stimulate a further rise in physical output because it becomes profitable to replace or expand capacity; and a fall of aggregate money payments tends to shrink spending still further because it reduces income. Moreover, rising output tends to raise spending, and a decline in spending tends to lower output. If output and spending are both rising, the economy is in a period of cyclical expansion according to most economists' definitions; and if they are both falling, it is said to be in a period of cyclical contraction. But if one is rising and the other falling—as appears to have been the case in the latter 1870's—it is not in a period of either expansion or contraction. It is best to call such a period a "transition" and to avoid giving a precise date to the trough.[3]

The last chapter showed that external events strongly influenced the lower turning point. Long-term investment prospects began to revive about 1877. But the contraction of spending continued, partly from previous momentum, partly because under paper standard conditions international trade did little to break the fall, partly because the prospect of returning to the gold standard on January 1, 1879, at a higher exchange rate than then prevailed cast doubt on the future course of prices, and partly because prices were highly flexible. The contraction in spending for the time being prevented the improved investment prospects from taking effect. By the beginning of 1879 the situation had changed. The United States successfully returned to the gold standard, reviving confidence; and good crops in 1879, coupled with unusually poor crops in Europe, gave business in the United

---

3. Nothing in this is intended as criticism of the Bureau's selection of March 1879 as the trough. It selected its dates for use in statistical analyses which required it to specify exact months. In cases of doubt, it "placed the reference turn toward the close of the transition period," Burns and Mitchell *Measuring,* p. 80. As there is plenty of room for doubt in this instance, its procedure naturally yields a date early in 1879. If I had to select a particular date for the trough, I should pick the second quarter of 1878, which was the low in Frickey's (revised) series of outside clearings. If we had complete information, it might well show an upturn in both spending and physical output at about that time.

States a decisive stimulus that invigorated the tentative cyclical expansion that had already begun.

The Upswing (1879-81)

Construction of railroads was the principal factor in the upswing. The number of railroad miles built rose spectacularly from 2,665 in 1878 to 11,569 in 1882. (See Chart 4.) No accurate estimate of the amount of money invested in railroads during these years is possible, but it plainly was large enough to dominate the picture.

Ulmer prepared annual estimates of capital expenditures by United States railroads, but because their reliability is limited, he did not publish them. He did, however, publish them in the form of five-year moving averages and in addition presented a chart in which annual estimates in 1929 dollars appeared.[4] The five-year moving average in current dollars rises from a low of $113 million in 1877 to a high of $320 million in 1882. Gross national product in these years can be put in the neighborhood of $10 billion, of which gross capital formation was $2 billion or a little less.[5]

Since a moving average tends to reduce the amplitude of swings, the rise in railroad investment must have exceeded 2 percent of GNP; and since a five-year average can be presumed to have had a very marked effect in this case in reducing the peak,[6] the spurt in railroad investment from 1879 to 1881 or 1882 must have been markedly greater than 2 percent of GNP. The leverage effects of the familiar multiplier and accelerator and the investment opportunities created by railroad building add up to a factor of great importance.

Much of the railroad building consisted of completing the main lines of roads which had been stopped by the panic of 1873.[7] The Northern Pacific, for instance, completed its route. Even more important was construction of feeders and branches for parent lines.[8] In addition, repairs and improvements that had been put off during

---

4. Melville J. Ulmer, "Trends and Cycles in Capital Formation by United States Railroads, 1870-1950," N.B.E.R., Occasional Paper 43 (New York, 1954), pp. 60 and 19.

5. Kuznets estimated average annual GNP in current prices at $8.9 billion for 1874-83, $10.7 for 1879-88, of which gross capital formation was $1.7 and $2.1 respectively. Simon S. Kuznets, *National Product Since 1869* (New York, 1946), p. 119.

6. See Ulmer, "Trends and Cycles," p. 19 (chart 4).

7. *Chronicle*, XVIII (May 23, 1874), 516; *ibid.*, XXXVI (Jan. 6, 1883), 7-8; *Investors' Supplement to the Chronicle*, XXXVI (June 1883), ii-iii.

8. *Chronicle*, XXXVI (Jan. 6, 1883), 8; *Investors' Supplement to the Chronicle*, XXXVII (Aug. 25, 1883), i.

CHART 8. Bond Issues* and Railroad Bond Yields, 1865-97

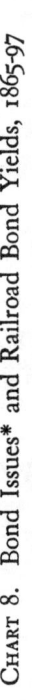

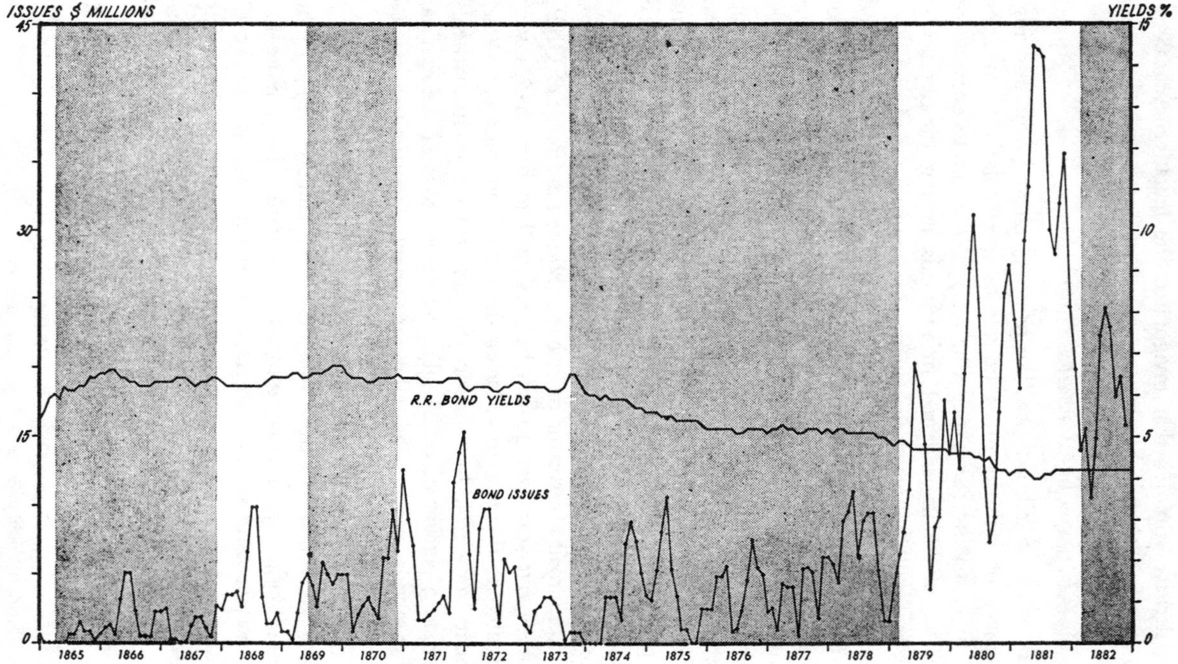

Shaded areas are business cycle contractions (N.B.E.R. dates).

SOURCES: R.R. bond yields, *Historical Statistics of the U.S.*, p. 348; bond issues,* Ayres, *Turning Points in Business Cycles*, pp. 182-90.

* New corporate bonds sold for cash on the New York Stock Exchange, converted to a three-month moving average.

THE CYCLE OF 1879-85

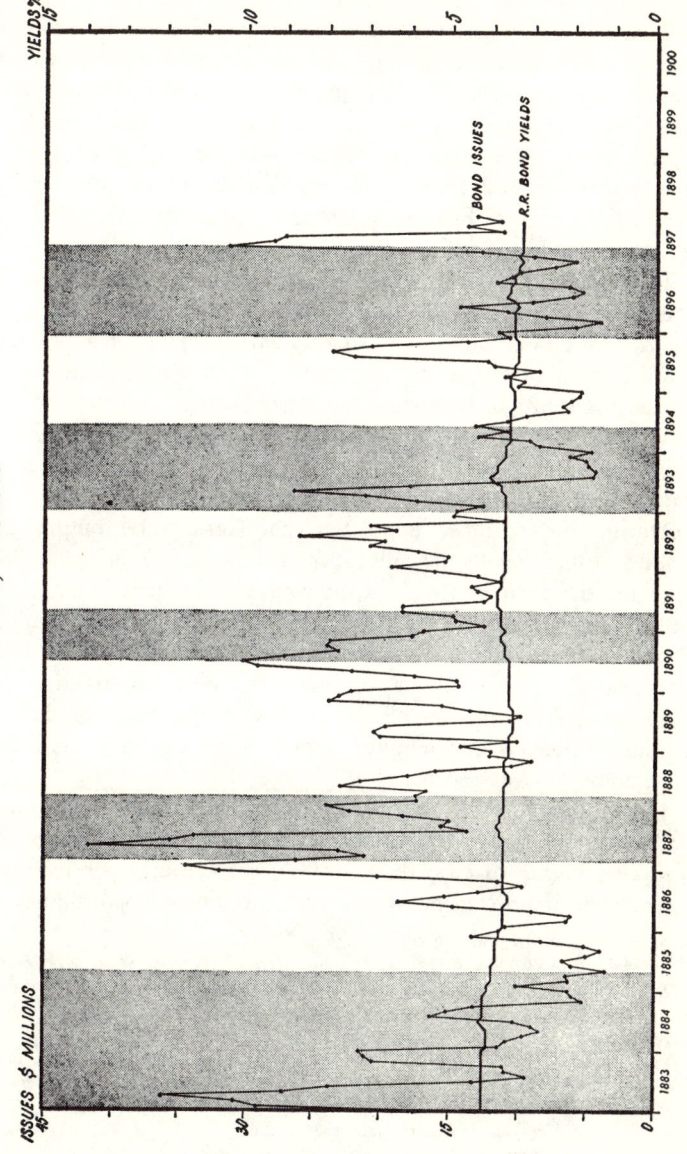

Chart 8, continued

the depression were now initiated.[9] For the most part, therefore, construction was undertaken not by new enterprises but by established lines to which it was becoming more of a routine operation than a venture into innovation.[10] "The painful process of foreclosure, settlement and reorganization" which had gone on steadily during the depression of the seventies paved the way for the upswing of the early eighties;[11] and in the ensuing downswing the new mileage was in the hands of financially stronger corporations than had been the case following 1873.[12]

Reasons for the spurt in railroad investment are not hard to find. The business cycles of the last half of the nineteenth century all belong to the same family (or Kondratieff cycle) not merely because railroad building played an important part in all of them but also because the spurts in building were interrelated.[13] Railroads, particularly those west of the Mississippi, were often built ahead of—and enormously facilitated—the growth of population and traffic that ultimately justified them and led to another spurt of railroading.[14]

During the seventies population and agricultural output grew steadily so that freight ton-miles increased two thirds in the six years following the panic of 1873. In the course of the general deflation of the seventies, freight rates had fallen. But, even so, traffic earnings in 1879 were virtually as high as in 1873, and, as a result of the decline in expenses, net earnings were higher.[15] With construction costs and interest rates considerably lower than in the boom of the early seventies,[16] projects that tempted both builders and investors became more numerous. (See Chart 8.)

But the spurt in railroad investments cannot be explained in terms of favorable objective circumstances alone. Although total net earnings were higher in 1879 than in 1873, net earnings per mile were lower. The improvement in objective investment opportunities (as-

9. *Chronicle*, XXIX (Sept. 6, 1879), 236.
10. *Ibid.*, XXXVI (Jan. 6, 1883), 8; and *Investors' Supplement to the Chronicle*, XXXVII (Aug. 25, 1883), i. This routine character of innovation was one of the chief reasons why Schumpeter (*Business Cycles*, I, 339) called this period a Kondratieff depression.
11. *Chronicle*, XXX (Jan. 10, 1880), 30. See also London *Economist*, CXLIII (May 24, 1879), 599; *ibid.*, CLI (March 12, 1881), Supplement, 28; and *Bankers' Magazine*, XXXIV (Feb. 1880), 654.
12. *Bankers' Magazine*, XXXVII (Jan. 1883), 486.
13. This is based on Schumpeter, *Business Cycles, passim*.
14. Cf. *Bankers' Magazine*, XXXIV (March 1880), 712.
15. U. S. Bureau of the Census, *Historical Statistics of the United States, 1789-1945* (Washington, D. C., 1949), p. 201. See also *Chronicle*, XXX (Jan. 10, 1880), 36.
16. *Chronicle*, XXXVI (Jan. 6, 1883), 8.

sisted by a stimulus from abroad) initiated the spurt in railroad building, but it developed only with the help of a plentiful supply of capital and a not wholly rational wave of optimism.

As is usually the case at the beginning of cyclical expansion, the money market was easy. (See Chart 3.) Moreover, as was not usually the case in the nineteenth century, the upswing developed no more than brief hints of stringency.[17] Not only was domestically mined gold retained but there were large gold imports in 1880 and 1881, partly—perhaps largely—because the foreign trade balance was favorable. (See Chart 9.) More remarkable than easy money was the ample domestic supply of long-term capital. Whereas English capital financed a great part of the railroad building boom that pre-

CHART 9. Merchandise Exports and Imports, 1865-97 (fiscal years).

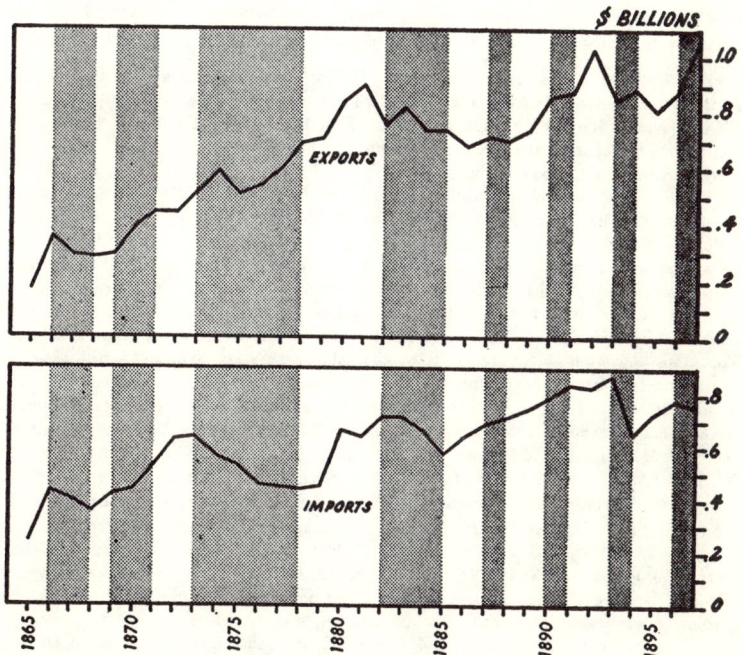

Shaded areas are business cycle contractions (N.B.E.R. dates).
SOURCE: *Historical Statistics of the U.S.*, p. 244.

---

17. See the articles on the money market in the various issues of the *Bankers' Magazine*, and the *Chronicle*, particularly XXXII (Jan. 8, 1881), 29-30; XXXIV (Jan. 7, 1882), 8-10; XXXVI (Jan. 6, 1883), 8-9; and XXXVIII (Jan. 5, 1884), 9. For an extended discussion of this point see Auble, "Depression," pp. 159-75.

ceded the panic of 1873, American railroads now floated their security issues more largely in the United States.[18]

Interest rates were lower than in the earlier period, when bonds were often floated at prices which yielded 10 percent or more. The change reflected the secular growth of capital in the United States, the general fall in interest rates during the era of falling prices between 1873 and 1896, and the surplus of the federal government (see Chart 10) that developed during the upswing and was used to retire the national debt, freeing funds for railroad building.[19]

The *Chicago Tribune,* commenting sadly on the overoptimism of 1879-81, said:

Why is it that in such a time as that, funds are contributed by all classes of people for almost any enterprise whose promoters promise great returns? It is because they see business active all around them, people in enterprises already established winning large profits, and everything apparently inviting them to be rich. They are seized with the craze of money

---

18. "We have almost ceased to borrow for corporate undertakings in London and Paris" (*Commercial Bulletin* [Sept. 16, 1880], as quoted by *Bankers' Magazine,* XXXV [Nov. 1880], 323). On the other hand, the London *Economist,* CLIV (Feb. 18, 1882), 7, reported that in the first half of 1881 London subscribed £20 million to new American railroad issues.

Contemporary sources are conflicting in their statements about international capital movements. The December 1880 issue of the *Bankers' Magazine* said on p. 436: "Whether more American stocks and securities have been marketed abroad than have been purchased abroad, during the year past, is a doubtful question"; and on p. 484: "The gloomy views which are prevalent in some quarters as to the monetary future, are probably due in part to a want of appreciation of the large amounts of foreign capital which are flowing into the United States to an extent never known before." The same journal in February 1881, p. 587, March 1881, p. 678, and April 1881, p. 753, argued vigorously that during 1880 the amount of railroad shares held abroad diminished. For other statements on international capital movements see *Chronicle,* XXXII (Jan. 8, 1881), 29; London *Economist,* CLIV (Feb. 18, 1882), Supplement, 6; *Bankers' Magazine,* XXXII (April 1879), 745; *ibid.,* XXXIII (Nov. 1879), 329; *ibid.,* XXXIV (Aug. 1880), 84; *ibid.,* XXXVIII (Oct. 1883), 247. The very conflict of opinion, however, shows a marked difference between 1879-83 and 1869-73.

19. George S. Boutwell, "The Political Situation," *North American Review,* CXXXVI (Feb. 1883), 158; George M. Weston, "Advantages of Paying the National Debt," *Bankers' Magazine,* XXXVII (Nov. 1882), 328-29; *Investors' Supplement to the Chronicle,* XXXIV (Feb. 1882), ii. It should be remembered, however, that the federal surplus between 1869 and 1873, although smaller, was substantial.

A government surplus is usually regarded as deflationary, but, if investment opportunities are numerous, funds need not be hoarded; and if bank credit and long-term capital are in joint demand, the net result of paying off government debt may be inflationary. If the government continues to retire debt after investment opportunities cease to be numerous, it will indeed become deflationary; and, by hastening the exploitation of investment opportunities, it may hasten the cyclical downturn. Hence, it is possible for a government surplus both to accentuate the upswing and to contribute to the downturn.

THE CYCLE OF 1879-85

CHART 10. Federal Receipts and Expenditures, 1865-97 (fiscal years).

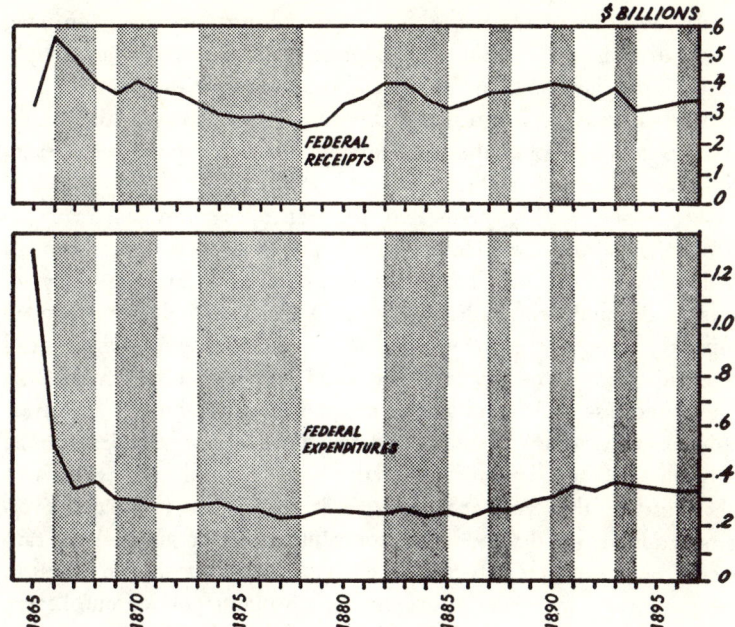

Shaded areas are business cycle contractions (N.B.E.R. dates).
SOURCE: *Historical Statistics of the U.S.*, pp. 296-97 and 299-300.

making, and become incapable of reasoning on any project that is presented for their consideration. It is easy for unscrupulous men to humbug them at such a time. Even the promoters of enterprises often half-believe the lies they tell, and partake of the prevailing mania. . . . It is appalling to consider how many of the corporate enterprises of the country have secured their capital by taking advantage of these investment—or, rather, speculative —epidemics.[20]

The word "boom" was first used in its political sense in 1878. Naturally, its first application to business cycles was for the expansion of 1879-81, and with some justification.[21] Contemporary observers were impressed by the growth of speculation. Already in November

---

20. Quoted by *Bankers' Magazine*, XXXIX (March 1885), 688. For similar statements see *Investors' Supplement to the Chronicle*, XXXVIII (June 1884), 2; and anonymous, "Hydraulic Pressure in Wall Street," *North American Review*, CXXXV (July 1882), 54, 60, and 64.

21. "Two years covered the whole of the 'boom' commencing in the summer of 1879, and ending in the summer of 1881" (*Bankers' Magazine*, XL [Nov. 1885], 339).

1879 the London *Times* said, "The spirit of railway speculation [in the United States] is probably as rampant now as it ever has been."[22] Later the *Bankers' Magazine* thought the country had been "on a big speculative drunk."[23] But the doings referred to were largely peripheral. Financial recklessness of the type that led to the panic of 1873 appears to have been much less common,[24] and, however one might wish to define "boom," the word is more applicable to the early seventies than to the early eighties.

Prosperity quickly permeated the entire economy. Already in September 1879 the steel mills were reported to have orders enough to keep them working at capacity on into 1880.[25] Stimulated by increased demand from railroads, the iron and steel industry expanded capacity,[26] and there is evidence in manufacturing of what I call the "superaccelerator"—investment based on the assumption that the rate of increase of demand will be maintained in the future.[27] Outside clearings (quarterly) doubled, and the wholesale price index rose 29 percent. As the *Chronicle* summed it up: "We built 28,554 miles of new road in the years 1880, 1881, 1882.... This stimulated overproduction in all the industries contributing to, or allied with, railroad property, which in turn affected every other branch of business in the same way."[28] Moreover, as one commentator pointed out, "every railroad which is constructed, and especially in the West and South, creates fresh opportunities for investments in agriculture, mining,

---

22. Quoted by the London *Economist*, CXLVII (March 13, 1880), Supplement, 52. See also *Chronicle*, XXX (Jan. 10, 1880), 30, and *Investors' Supplement to the Chronicle*, XXXIII (Dec. 31, 1881), i.

23. XXXVII (Jan. 1883), 486. The *Bankers' Magazine* had too many articles on the subject of speculation to cite here. These dealt primarily with the growth of speculation as a result of development of organized exchanges. An obviously exaggerated article on this subject is Henry D. Lloyd, "Making Bread Dear," *North American Review*, CXXXVII (Aug. 1883), 124-26. See also *Chronicle*, XXXIV (Jan. 7, 1882), 8.

24. "The depression is not likely to be so severe and last so long as the one that began in 1873. The country has not sunk so much money in bad investments as it had just previous to that event" (*Bankers' Magazine*, XXXVIII [Oct. 1883], 244).

25. *Chronicle*, XXIX (Sept. 6, 1879), 236; cf. London *Economist*, CXLVI (Jan. 31, 1880), 118.

26. *Bankers' Magazine*, XXXVIII (Oct. 1883), 242. Pig-iron production doubled between 1878 and 1882. This involved building a considerable amount of new capacity despite the fact that numerous obsolete blast furnaces were idle even at the peak of prosperity.

27. *Ibid.*, XXXVII (Feb. 1883), 568. Of course, both accelerator and superaccelerator later contributed to the downturn.

28. *Investors' Supplement to the Chronicle*, XXXVIII (June 1884), 2; cf. *Bankers' Magazine*, XXXVIII (Oct. 1883), 241.

mills and foundries."[29] The annual circular of Dun, Barlow and Company for 1879 said, "The number of unemployed is less than at any time within the past seven years."[30] This, of course, was merely an impression that could have been erroneous, as it implies that early in the upswing there were less unemployed than at the cyclical peak of 1873. At any rate, employment seems to have been reasonably full in the early eighties in spite of accelerated immigration, for the *Bankers' Magazine* in 1882 remarked, "In this country . . . labor can always find employment."[31] The memory of the unemployment of the seventies would not have faded so fast if unemployment had not been pretty well obliterated for several years.

Although overshadowed by the railroads, construction of buildings was also an important factor in the upswing. (See Chart 4.) Stimulated by the population increase, the general development of the country by the railroads, and the low level of construction during the seventies, the value of construction permits rose two and a half times between 1879 and 1883. Although the index cannot be trusted very far, it gives a rough idea of what was going on.[32]

During the upswing, the economy appeared to be peculiarly responsive to the international equilibrating mechanism of the gold standard. (See Chart 9.) The spurt of railroad building did not develop strongly until the favorable foreign markets of 1878 and 1879 gave the upswing its start. Imports of raw materials rose in consequence of the increased business activity,[33] and manufactured goods were diverted from exports to the home market.[34] Thus a disturbance of equilibrium that resulted in increased exports stimulated consumption and investment, which in turn increased imports and retarded the expansion of exports. The favorable balance of trade increased gold supplies, providing a basis for the expansion of money needed to support increased activity; and, it may reasonably be inferred, higher real income

29. Weston, "Advantages," p. 332.
30. Quoted by *Bankers' Magazine*, XXXIII (Feb. 1880), 641. Cf. also the statement that "labor rejoices in fair wages and full employment" in an article signed by twenty-two men, including J. Pierpont Morgan, J. J. Astor, and Cyrus W. Field, "The Political Situation from a Financial Standpoint," *North American Review*, CXXXI (Nov. 1880), 471.
31. XXXVII (Sept.), 162.
32. Newman's index as given by *Historical Statistics of the United States*, p. 173. Long's value index tells much the same story as Newman's.
33. *Bankers' Magazine*, XXXIV (July 1880), 7-9. This magazine displayed some excellent insights into the equilibrating process, and, although it suffered from absence of a theoretical apparatus, it provides striking confirmation of modern ideas about how the gold standard worked.
34. *Ibid.*, XXXIV (Oct. 1880), 242.

was made possible by rising employment as the unemployed found jobs and as prosperity stimulated immigration.[35] Increased prices in the United States also contributed to the equilibrating process.

In the middle of 1880 the cyclical expansion received a brief check. Prices of a number of articles went so high that their markets became flooded with foreign goods, resulting in collapse.[36] There is some evidence, however, that this pause in the upswing was partly a reaction to excessive accumulations of inventories. Aside from this episode, the foreign trade position continued to be favorable until merchandise imports and exports came into approximate equality toward the end of 1881[37]—just before the expansion died—and did not become favorable again until 1883, that is to say, until (and in part because) the downturn had been passed. No doubt other forces were more important for cyclical developments, and a measure of coincidence is involved. But there is evidence here of the equilibrating mechanism of the gold standard at work, hindering the American economy from getting out of line with that of other countries.

The Upper Turning Point (1881-83)

Most major depressions begin spectacularly. The famous crash on Wall Street ushered in the depression of the 1930's. Bank panics in 1873, 1893 and 1907 occurred at, or close on the heels of, the downturns of those years. The depression of 1920-21 began with a collapse of prices; that of 1937-38, with a collapse of production.[38] In contrast,

---

35. The figures on immigration exhibit a pronounced cyclical movement (see Harry Jerome, *Migration and Business Cycles* [New York, 1926], p. 35). See also *Bankers' Magazine*, XXXIV (Oct. 1880), 274-75. Modern writers on the theory of international trade have often overlooked the fact that in the heyday of the gold standard, immigration was part of the equilibrating mechanism.

36. The best discussion of this episode is in the *Chronicle*, XXXIV (Jan. 7, 1882), 8; see also *ibid.*, XXXII (Jan. 8, 1881), 28. Cf. *Bankers' Magazine*, XXXV (July 1880), 6 and 77; *ibid.*, XXXV (Aug. 1880), 127; *ibid.*, XXXV (Oct. 1880), 280. Cf. also London *Economist*, CLI (March 12, 1881), Supplement, 22.

37. Exports declined heavily in the fourth quarter of 1881. The *Economist*, CLIV (Feb. 18, 1882), Supplement, 1 and 10, the *Bankers' Magazine*, XXXVI (Feb. 1882), 571, *ibid.*, XXXVI (March 1882), 726, and Lloyd, "Bread," pp. 124-26, emphasized a decline in exports of wheat and other farm products which they attributed to speculators' driving up prices. More important, perhaps, was the decline in crop production (see Chart 6); cf. also *Bankers' Magazine*, XXXVII (Sept. 1882), 202; *ibid.*, XXXVII (Dec. 1882), 405; *ibid.*, XXXVII (Jan. 1883), 486.

The *Bankers' Magazine* attributed the rise of imports in the first part of 1882 to rising wages and prices, XXXVII (July 1882), 1-5.

38. I do not mean, however, to indorse Keynes's much disputed statement that "the substitution of a downward for an upward tendency often takes place suddenly and violently" (John M. Keynes, *The General Theory of Employment, Interest and Money*

the downturn of the early eighties was slow and quiet. The bubble of overoptimism was pricked in the summer of 1881, and the force of the expansion began to die down in the latter part of the year.[39] The following year was generally regarded as unsatisfactory, particularly with respect to profits;[40] yet output and wholesale prices (except for the fourth quarter) continued to rise, and outside clearings remained high. During 1883 business grew steadily worse;[41] nevertheless, some important statistical series such as outside clearings and the index of manufacturing indicate that 1883 was a better year than 1882. Not until 1884 did the contraction become pronounced. It is helpful to single out a particular date to mark the cyclical peak, and the date chosen by the Bureau—March 1882—seems to be about right.[42] But

---

[London and New York, 1936], p. 314). My statement is confined to major depressions; and in several of the cases cited in the text, notably 1929, the upper turning point itself was by no means sudden and violent.

39. "Indeed, the slackening of speed began in some respects in the last half of 1881; and from the first of July in that year, when the country was temporarily paralyzed by the appalling death of its chief magistrate, there was a change in the spirit of advance, and almost exaltation, which had taken possession of our business world since 1878" (*Chronicle*, XXXVI [Jan. 6, 1883], 7. There is a minor error here. President Garfield, although shot on July 2, did not die until September 19). See also *ibid.*, XXXIV (Jan. 7, 1882), 10-11; the *Railroad Gazette*, XIII (Dec. 30, 1881), 742; the statistics of freight ton-miles in *Historical Statistics of the United States,* p. 334, and of outside clearings. A somewhat rosier view of 1881 can be found in the London *Economist,* CLIV (Feb. 18, 1882), Supplement, 10-11.

40. "A careful retrospect of 1882 presents only the view of a diminishing pressure in the force which had pushed everything forward, and by no means a retrograde movement; the gross amount of business was, in some departments at a maximum—the largest ever transacted in a single year—but it was in the net proceeds, in the cash profits realized, that the results were sometimes less satisfactory than in prior years" (*Chronicle*, XXXVI [Jan. 6, 1883], 7). "That there should be such an increase of late in the number of failures, in view of the general prosperity of the country is a very unpleasant fact. The spectacle is presented that, while the trade of the country is not in the most healthy or desirable condition, the country itself was never before more prosperous than at the present moment" (*Bankers' Magazine,* XXXVII [Feb. 1883], 568).

41. "Although this is hardly a time of abnormal business depression, a great part of the industrial energies of the country are unemployed" (Henry George, "Overproduction," *North American Review,* CXXXVII [Dec. 1883], 584). See also *ibid.*, pp. 588-89, and *Chronicle,* XXXVII (Dec. 22, 1883), 680.

42. Burns and Mitchell, *Measuring*. Other investigators have put the turning point a bit later. This is odd in view of the N.B.E.R. rule to take the later date in case of doubt. Partington put the change from prosperity to recession in September 1882; Ayres put the downturn in November; Kitchin, in December; and Persons put the end of prosperity in June of the following year (John E. Partington, *Railroad Purchasing and the Business Cycle* [Washington, D. C., 1929], p. 235; Leonard P. Ayres, *Turning Points in Business Cycles* [New York, 1939], p. 29; Joseph Kitchin, "Cycles and Trends in Economic Factors," *Review of Economic Statistics,* V [Jan. 1923], 14; and Warren M. Persons, *Forecasting Business Cycles* [New York, 1931], p. 198).

it is also helpful to think of the entire period from the middle of 1881 until the end of 1883 as a gradual transition from prosperity to depression.

At the middle of 1881 the basic situation of the railroads was weaker than the overoptimism that normally accompanies a major upswing would indicate. A hard winter had increased expenses and reduced traffic. The spring brought poor crop prospects, implying poor traffic prospects. The booming stock market was "inflated" in the sense that non-dividend-paying shares sold at substantial prices. The fatal shooting of President Garfield in July, which was regarded as an event unfavorable to business interests, became the occasion for recognizing these weaknesses. People began to feel vaguely distrustful and insecure. The stock market went into a year-long decline, never in this cycle to regain the peak of mid 1881. It became more difficult to float new securities. The verve had gone out of the expansion.[43]

As time went on, railroad prospects continued to deteriorate. The railroad building and consolidation of the preceding years led to rate wars, and it was charged that railroad officials sold out securities in their own companies and deliberately prolonged the wars in order to get their securities back at lower prices. During the period of transition from prosperity to depression, rate wars and mismanagement (if not fraudulent management) recurrently undermined public confidence in railroad stocks and bonds.[44]

These events were slow to exert their influence. The railroads built even more miles in 1882 than in 1881.[45] But this added to the belief, which was already gaining ground at the beginning of the year, that railroads were multiplying too rapidly to be profitable.[46]

In spite of the favorable harvest of 1882 and the revival of opti-

43. *North American Review,* CXXXV (July 1882), 54-55; *Bankers' Magazine,* XXXVI (Aug. 1881), 87-88, 157, and 159; London *Economist,* CLIV (Feb. 18, 1882), Supplement, 10. It is difficult to believe that the assassination of Garfield had as much effect as the last two references claimed.

44. London *Economist,* CLIV (Feb. 18, 1882), Supplement, 8 and 10-11; *ibid.,* CLVIII (Feb. 23, 1884), Supplement, 7; *Bankers' Magazine,* XXXVI (Jan. 1882), 567; *ibid.,* XXXVI (March 1882), 690; *ibid.,* XXXVII (Jan. 1883), 482 and 558; *ibid.,* XXXVIII (Sept. 1883), 238; *ibid.,* XXXVIII (Oct. 1883), 316; *North American Review,* CXXXV (July 1882), 54-55 and 59.

45. Various evidence could be assembled in an effort to date the peak of railroad investment (cf. the discussion in Auble, "Depressions") but I do not think it profitable to do so. The number of miles built, which reached its peak in 1882, is obviously an unreliable guide.

46. London *Economist,* CLIV (Feb. 18, 1882), Supplement, 7 and 10; *Bankers' Magazine,* XXXVII (Dec. 1882), 405-6 and 479; *ibid.,* XXXVIII (Oct. 1883), 242.

mism it engendered,[47] the difficulty in raising capital for railroad building became pronounced by the end of 1882. According to the *Railroad Gazette*, "We would have built even more than we have in 1882, if capital had been as easy to get for such purposes during and after as before the railroad war and the bad harvests."[48] Moreover, "it is said that it is now [the end of 1882] almost impossible to get capitalists or their representatives to listen to a proposition to take part in any new railroad enterprise. There is a good deal of work in hand, however, some of which makes slow progress because of the difficulty of getting money, but for most of which means seem to have been provided already."[49] As in 1873, there was no lack of railroad routes to be built—the peak in number of miles added was not reached until 1887—but, unlike 1873, there was scarcely any evidence of a lack of capital seeking investment.[50] Apparently capitalists were unwilling to put money into railroads. Their unwillingness evidently stemmed from belief that further building would not prove profitable.[51] Their

47. *Bankers' Magazine*, XXXVII (July 1882), 77. There was a real connection between good harvests and good business, not only because good crops meant larger traffic for the railroads but also (and more important) larger exports of crops meant more spending by farmers on American products. This relationship was well known in the latter part of the nineteenth century. Hence, good crop prospects regularly increased confidence.

48. XIV (Dec. 29, 1882), 804.

49. *Ibid.* See also *ibid.*, XIII (Dec. 30, 1881), 743. Cf. *Bankers' Magazine*, XXXVI (May 1882), 886; *ibid.*, XXXVII (Jan. 1883), 486; *ibid.*, XXXVIII (Oct. 1883), 315-17; and London *Economist*, CLXII (Feb. 23, 1884), 2-3 and 5.

50. A hint that railroad building declined because of shortage of capital is contained in an article in the *Investors' Supplement to the Chronicle*, XXXVI (June 1883), ii-iii: "It will be asked, then, why was not the improvement in [railroad stock] prices maintained when abundant harvests [in 1882] became an assured fact? Because it was found that the derangement of various industries resulting from the decline in railroad building, poor crops of 1881, &c., together with the more important fact that the market had been loading up for three years with new railroad securities, were more serious matters than at first supposed, and their lasting effect had been underestimated." But the article went on to say: "Then there has been some apprehension as to the effect of the opening of so many new lines of road. ... There was also in the past few months a return movement of stocks this way from Europe, mainly of the speculative sort, which were sent back after the holders had lost the hope of making money by a great rise in their prices." This sounds more as if the boom came to an end because it had spent its inner force than because it was throttled by lack of capital.

51. Carroll Wright's conclusions may be cited in support of this statement. "This full supply of economic tools to meet the wants of nearly all branches of commerce and industry is the most important factor in the present industrial depression" ("Industrial Depressions," p. 257). He particularly singled out the railroads: "In the United States the mileage of new railroads constructed has been out of all proportion to the increase of products to be carried." Wright's opinion should perhaps be discounted, inasmuch as he wrote at the bottom of the depression and seems not to have

money did not find outlets in other forms of permanent investments but either remained idle or went into the money market.[52] And as railroad building was great enough to dominate the upswing, its decline is enough to account for the major downturn, although federal debt retirement and worsening of exports were contributory causes.[53] Compared to that in the early seventies, railroad financing was on a strong basis; hence, there was at the time of the turning point no financial debacle like the panic of 1873.

The Downswing (1883-85)

The downswing of the early eighties was severe enough for most investigators to rate it a major depression.[54] Statistics and contemporary comment alike bear out the view that, although not so bad as the 1870's, 1890's, or 1930's, the depression of the early eighties was no mere recession. But, like the depression of the seventies, it was severe primarily in financial series like outside clearings and wholesale prices rather than in indexes of production. As Carroll Wright said, "The volume of business and of production has not been affected disastrously by the depression, but ... prices have been greatly reduced,

---

realized that the capital equipment of the country would not have been so superabundant if there had been full employment. Nevertheless, he was one of the best qualified of contemporary observers, and his conclusions should be regarded as a primary source of considerable importance.

52. *Bankers' Magazine*, XXXVIII (Oct. 1883), 316. Cf. London *Economist*, CLXII (Feb. 23, 1884), 2-3.

53. If one accepts the N.B.E.R. date of March 1882 for the cyclical peak and takes the evidence of number of miles built as showing that railroad investment did not decline sooner than the latter part of 1882 (both assumptions could be questioned), the question arises how the cyclical downturn could precede its cause. But this is not difficult. The cyclical downturn can be attributed initially to international trade developments, and it can then be argued that the results would have been no more serious than in 1880 (see above) but for the decline in railroad investment.

54. Thus Persons (*Forecasting*, p. 7) called it a "major depression," Axe implied that it was a severe depression (Emerson W. Axe, "Generally Low Prices and Cheap Money Suggest a Bull Market This Year," *Annalist*, XXXVII [Jan. 16, 1931], 92), and Schumpeter (*Business Cycles*, I, 396) called it a "Juglar recession and depression." Hubbard and Eckler both put it in the same category with 1907-8, Hubbard calling it a "decline of considerable severity," Eckler a "decline of the third order of magnitude" (Joseph B. Hubbard, "Business Declines and Recoveries," *Review of Economic Statistics*, XVIII [Feb. 1936], 18, and A. Ross Eckler, "A Measure of the Severity of Depressions, 1873-1932," *Review of Economic Statistics*, XV [May 1933], 79). Burns and Mitchell are jointly an exception, excluding it from their list of severe depressions; but they concede that it is the most severe of those they exclude in the period between 1873 and 1933 (*Measuring*, pp. 455, 458, and 462).

THE CYCLE OF 1879-85   129

wages frequently reduced, and margins of profits carried to the minimum range."[55]

The downswing gathered momentum slowly in 1883. The decline in railroad construction not only eliminated the jobs of many workers directly employed in railroad building[56] but also spread depression to other industries.[57] As one would expect, the iron and steel industry was particularly affected.

In January, 1880, steel rails were worth $71 per ton; in December, 1883, large contracts for steel rails were placed at $33 to $35 per ton. American pig iron was worth at the earlier date $35 per ton, and about January 1, 1884, it sold at $20 per ton. . . . Blast furnaces were blown out; rail mills were shut down; wages were reduced; hands were discharged. Other branches of mining and manufacturing suffered increasingly as the year wore on, and in the later months there was quite a general movement towards curtailing production and reducing all possible expenses, including the wages of operatives.[58]

At first producers tried to maintain output. They either accumulated inventories they did not want or induced dealers to take them by offering longer dated bills. But the stocks hanging over the market put pressure on prices, and more and more firms failed as their bills fell due. Production declined, and, in spite of abundant money, banks became reluctant to make new loans.[59] Belief that

---

55. "Industrial Depressions," p. 254. In the same volume (pp. 65-66) Wright estimated unemployment in 1885 at 7½% compared to normal unemployment of 2-2½%, but his methods of estimation were not such as to inspire confidence in the results (see also T. V. Powderly, "The Army of the Discontented," *North American Review*, CXL [April 1885], 369). For a vivid but probably exaggerated description of the unemployed see William Godwin Moody, "Working-men's Grievances," *North American Review*, CXXXVIII (May 1884), 505.

56. Wright ("Industrial Depressions," pp. 242-43) cited with approval the estimate of Edward Atkinson that half a million fewer workers were employed in railroad building in 1883 than in 1882 and added that the estimate had never been contradicted. There is no reason for confidence in the order of magnitude indicated (the less so since a decline in miles built of less than one half was supposed to reduce the number of workers employed by two thirds), but if the cyclical mechanism had not been working in the way indicated, somebody would have denied Atkinson's estimate and Wright would have heard about it.

57. *Chronicle*, XXXVIII (Jan. 5, 1884), 8.

58. *Ibid*. Cf. *Bankers' Magazine*, XXXVII (Dec. 1882), 405, and London *Economist*, CLVIII (Feb. 24, 1883), Supplement, 32. Pig-iron production, however, was only a trifle lower than in 1882 (*Historical Statistics of the United States*, p. 149). This was due partly to inventory accumulation, partly to lower prices which reduced imports (London *Economist*, CLVII [Feb. 24, 1883], 27).

59. *Bankers' Magazine*, XXXVI (June 1882), 971; *ibid*., XXXVII (Feb. 1883), 568; *ibid*., XXXVIII (Aug. 1883), 92-93; *ibid*., XXXVIII (Sept. 1883), 161-62; *ibid*., XXXVIII (Oct. 1883), 315-16; London *Economist*, CLXII (Feb. 23, 1884), Supplement, 30 and 50.

prosperity was just around the corner gave way to general pessimism before 1883 was over.[60]

Although the railroads appeared to be at the bottom of the trouble, their own business in physical terms was better than ever. Nevertheless, railroad stocks declined as the public, its faith in railroad managers diminished, tried to unload securities that had no prospect of yielding an income.[61] Although railroad profits in the aggregate probably held up pretty well, in many particular instances they were disappointing. Profit prospects declined more than actual profits because of the general business depression, poor crops, and increasing competition among railroads.[62] The stage was set for a further decline of railroad building in 1884.

In that year the pace of the downswing accelerated. Frickey's index of manufactures shows a decline for the first time during this cycle,[63] and outside clearings, the cyclical peak of which occurred in the third quarter of 1883, declined drastically in the second half of 1884. As expected, railroad profits declined, and, though the percentage decline in aggregate earnings was not large, the number of railroad miles built suffered a further decline in 1885.

The year 1884 was also marred by a bank panic in New York. On May 8 a brokerage firm named Grant and Ward failed, dragging down with it the Marine National Bank, which had overcertified a Grant and Ward check for $750,000. Five days later the Second National Bank had to close its doors because the president had stolen three million dollars. A run caused the Metropolitan Bank to close the next day, and panic ensued: stock prices plummeted as attempts were made to raise cash and recall call loans. Interest at one point rose to 4 percent for twenty-four hours, country banks started to recall their funds, and there were many more failures or suspensions.

The coincidence of the Marine and Second National Bank failures started panic only because it occurred at a time of increasing business depression; but the government's silver policy, which undermined

60. *Bankers' Magazine*, XXXVIII (Oct. 1883), 241.
61. *Chronicle*, XXXVIII (Jan. 5, 1884), 9-10.
62. *Investors' Supplement to the Chronicle*, XXXVIII (April 1884), 1-3.
63. Cf. *Chronicle*, XL (Jan. 3, 1885), 9: "In no department was the decline in activity more conspicuous than in the flagging manufactures, the decreased mining, and the comparatively small amount of railroad building. Not only was there no inducement to engage in new work, but in manufactures and mining the low prices of products necessitated the cutting down of work and wages in every way possible, and many furnaces, mills and mines were closed. The production of pig iron was cut down . . . but still the demand fell off more rapidly than the production, and prices did not strengthen."

confidence, was a contributory cause. Under an act of 1878 the Secretary of the Treasury had to buy and coin between two and four million dollars' worth of silver every month. In practice he always bought the minimum, but, as silver sold at a discount, this meant coining upward of $24 million of silver a year. The depression in 1883 made money redundant. The banks therefore held onto their gold and made payments to the Treasury in silver. This led to fears that the gold standard could not be maintained, especially when the subtreasurer in New York City hinted that the Treasury might have to settle its clearing house balances in silver. Foreigners started selling American securities, and gold flowed out, depleting Treasury reserves still further. Beginning in the fall of 1884, the Treasury found various ways of complying with the act without endangering the currency, and there were no serious repercussions from the silver policy until the 1890's.[64]

The panic did not last long. Steps were taken immediately to issue clearing house certificates. The defalcation of the Second National was made good, and both it and the Metropolitan reopened at once. Capital flowed in from Europe to take advantage of high interest rates and low stock prices. Confidence returned quickly. During the panic the New York banks contracted their loans noticeably, but this was largely made up by an inflow of funds from country banks. The downswing seemed to accelerate during and after the panic, but this does not prove that the panic intensified the downswing. Any significant influence of the panic on business must have operated through increasing pessimism.[65] The fact that the panic did not dangerously affect the financial position of business is further indication of the comparatively sound condition of business at the onset of the depression.

The Lower Turning Point (1885)

As 1884 wore on into 1885, few signs were visible to indicate the coming end of the downswing.[66] Interest rates were low (see Chart

64. William J. Lauck, *The Causes of the Panic of 1893* (Boston and New York, 1907), pp. 19-23.
65. Oliver M. W. Sprague, *History of Crises Under the National Banking System*, 61st Congress, 2d Session, Senate Doc. No. 538 (Washington, D. C., 1910), pp. 108-23. See also *Chronicle*, XL (Jan. 3, 1885), 8.
66. The *Chronicle*, however, thought differently: "The fact that the downward course [of security prices] has been steadily in progress for nearly four years . . . that 'liquidation' in almost every trade and business has been thorough and complete, that we have been through a financial crisis of large dimensions, that this came after

3), but this was significant more as showing that one of the conditions for an expansion was present (namely, a money supply capable of expansion) than as a factor for stopping contraction. Crops in 1884 were good (see Chart 6), but not good enough to expand either the value of exports or the profits of railroads. The *Chronicle* from time to time pointed out railroad securities that appeared undervalued on the market, but it did not urge investments in new building, which alone would have had real influence on business.

Nevertheless, contraction gradually came to an end and gave way to weak revival in the course of 1885.[67] The Bureau dates the trough in May, which agrees reasonably well with statistical data, contemporary comment, and the findings of other investigators. The most obvious and probably the most important factor limiting contraction was construction of buildings. (See Chart 4.) Throughout the downswing this industry not only did not decline but actually continued to expand. Nor is this surprising. The mechanism of the building cycle, which reached its trough about 1878-80, apparently makes for upswings in building nearly a decade in length. Rents adjust slowly to supply-demand conditions, and the amount of building in any one year can have only a small effect on the total number of buildings in existence.[68] If much of the stimulus for building came from the opening of new territories by the railroads, the influence of the mileage added from 1880 to 1883 would be felt for some years more. Other factors were the large amount of immigration in the early eighties and the cyclical decline of interest rates.

But railroad building itself, which was to experience a great rise in 1886 and especially 1887, was at its lowest ebb at the time of the cyclical upturn. Thus the upturn occurred not because of the behavior of

---

a shrinkage of great magnitude, and must therefore have uncovered the weak spots in the situation, that the general mercantile community is unusually strong, and that the banks carry a surplus never before known in our history, would seem to argue that if we are not on the eve of a change for the better, we have at least seen the worst of the present era of depression" (*Investors' Supplement to the Chronicle,* XL [Feb. 1885], 1). Much of the *Chronicle's* argument, however, seems to be that, because matters have been so bad, they can't get any worse. Whatever we may think of such reasoning, if the business community in general believed it, it would constitute a psychological factor that would help bring contraction to an end.

67. London *Economist,* CLXX (Feb. 20, 1886), Supplement, 51.

68. The historical evidence does not give a clear picture about the normal length of the building cycle, inasmuch as wars have so often exaggerated the troughs and lengthened the postwar upswing. But for building to continue to expand throughout the depression of the early eighties is what we should expect to find even if we suspect the building cycle upswing would normally be less than a decade.

railroad construction but in spite of it. The upswing did not become pronounced until railroad building revived, but the lower turning point itself cannot be explained by any change in long-run investment prospects. Nor can it be explained by external events. The contraction process simply came to an end by itself, limited by what is nowadays called "autonomous" investment, by impossibility of induced disinvestment exceeding depreciation, and presumably by the tendency for consumption to fall less than income.[69]

As the prospects for business in general improved, so did the prospects for railroad investment. The first half of 1885 was marred by railroad wars, such as the attempt of the New York Central to crush the competing West Shore road. This particular battle was settled in August, whereupon the trunk lines formed a strong pool to maintain—and soon to raise—rates. Harmony among railroads then spread throughout the country, considerably improving prospects. The stock market rose, making possible large speculative profits out of worthless stocks. Meanwhile, those few roads in default on bonds were successfully reorganized, and traffic continued to increase with the growth of the country. Thus the stage was set for revival of railroad investment in 1886. But it seems more than coincidence that railroad building turned up after the cyclical upturn. The improvement in general business was one of the causes of railroad revival.[70]

The upswing continued to be sluggish during the first part of 1886.[71] But with good crop prospects and expanded investment in railroad and building construction, the revival became vigorous in the last half of the year.[72]

69. Although knowledge of recent business cycles makes it almost certain that inventories play an important role, lack of data makes it difficult to assess their part in the upturn of 1885. One scrap of evidence, however, may be given, for what it is worth: "The discouragement of 1884 in all the branches of industry was carried over into 1885. There was generally a large stock of manufactured goods to be worked off at low prices, and this to a considerable extent was accomplished, so that at the end of 1885 the surplus stocks were believed to be much less than at the beginning of the year" (*Chronicle*, XLII [Jan. 9, 1886], 37-38). This seems to indicate that the end of contraction enabled businessmen to dispose of excess inventories rather than that contraction came to an end because businessmen had worked them off.

70. The factors entering into the revival of railroad investments are discussed by the *Chronicle*, XLII (Jan. 9, 1886), 37-39, and *ibid.*, XLIV (Jan. 8, 1887), 38, and in the *Investors' Supplement to the Chronicle*, XLI (Aug. 1885), 1-2; *ibid.*, XLI (Dec. 1885), 1-2; *ibid.*, XLII (June 1886), 1; *ibid.*, XLIII (Aug. 1886), 2. See also London *Economist*, CLXX (Feb. 20, 1886), Supplement, 6 and 28.

71. *Bankers' Magazine*, XL (May 1886), 802.

72. *Chronicle*, XLIV (Jan. 8, 1887), 38.

Conclusions

Gordon's threefold classification of cycles—major, minor, and hybrid—was described and discussed in Chapter 2. The contraction of 1882-85 does not fit neatly into any of his categories. He himself preferred to regard it as a major contraction on grounds of the decline in investment opportunities in railroads, but he noted that it had "some of the earmarks of a hybrid."[73] To judge by performance, investment opportunities in the important field of building construction not only remained favorable throughout the cycle but actually improved.

The cycle conforms well to Schumpeter's theory. The burst of railroad investment, which provided the motive power of prosperity, began, as it should, after the upturn of business in general. Schumpeter's schema calls for a relapse (or Kitchin cycle) during the prosperity phase; this can be identified with the interruption of expansion in 1880. The period from the middle of 1881 to the end of 1883 is a good example of Schumpeterian recession. The railroad boom died out partly because available opportunities were pretty well used up and partly because of increasing disequilibriums growing out of innovation and the competing-down process (i.e., increasing competition among railroads made it more difficult to calculate costs and revenues). The behavior of outside clearings gives some (although not wholly convincing) evidence of the Kitchin prosperity we might expect in 1883. The year 1884 and much of 1885 Schumpeter rightly called Juglar depression—a movement away from equilibrium as a result of the cumulative mechanism. As one would expect from Schumpeter's theory, the momentum of depression died out of its own accord. The burst of railroad building in 1886-87 can be considered as belonging to Kitchin prosperity as well as Juglar recovery.[74] It may be thought awkward to regard the spurt of railroad investments of the early eighties as belonging to Juglar prosperity and that of the middle eighties to Kitchin prosperity, but the difficulty can be overcome by considering the changing nature of railroad innovation. In the

---

73. Robert A. Gordon, "Investment Behavior and Business Cycles," *Review of Economics and Statistics,* XXXVII (Feb. 1955), 31n.

74. The chart which Schumpeter gave on p. 213 (*Business Cycles,* I) suggests that the Kitchin prosperity should come before the end of Juglar depression, but this is not a necessary part of Schumpeter's three-cycle schema. Only at positions of equilibriums are the phases of the three kinds of cycles rigidly determined. Alternatively, one could regard the date which Schumpeter himself gave for the end of Juglar depression (near the end of 1885) as too early, and by shifting it forward we could get Kitchin prosperity into Juglar depression in a manner that would be consistent with the facts and favorable to the theory.

middle eighties railroad investment was a routine part of railroad operations. The main lines had been completed in 1882 or before; what remained was to build feeder or complementary lines. A change of this sort in the character of innovation had been going on throughout the railroad Kondratieff, the early innovators paving the way for the later ones as Schumpeter's schema would lead us to expect; but one can appropriately mark a change in the eighties and interpret events in accordance with Schumpeter's schema rather than in opposition to it.

It is not surprising that the facts of this period seem to bear Schumpeter out, for his theory was deliberately designed to fit history, particularly the history of the railroad era. But the facts also fit another theory, that of Hicks.[75] His explanation of the lower turning point fits 1885 very well indeed. Autonomous investment is plainly visible in the form of buildings as well as some railroad mileage. A certain amount of evidence, direct and indirect, can be found for the proposition that excess capacity developed in the downswing, and we can reasonably infer that this was instrumental in bringing the downswing to an end. In this case the excess capacity (in the railroads at least) was worked off more through the growth of population and crop production than physical deterioration, but this is scarcely an important qualification to our judgment of Hicks's theory. As far as the upturn is concerned, Hicks's theory is more illuminating than Schumpeter's.

Hicks's theory supplies two main explanations of the downturn.[76] In the first, the upswing ends because of a ceiling to output set by full employment and limits (if any) to expansion of the money supply. The downturn follows as a result of the acceleration principle. In the case of 1882, neither of these checks was apparent. The labor supply was increasing rapidly, and no real stringency was felt in money markets. The railroad boom seemed to die out from lack of momentum rather than external check.

Hicks's other explanation of the downturn (the one on which he lays less stress) applies when the accelerator is explosive only in the sense that it would generate cycles of ever increasing amplitude if nothing interfered. The first cycle, on this assumption, need not reach full employment, and since every downswing is apt to be interfered with by the limit to induced disinvestment, every expansion may be considered as the start of a "first" cycle. Hence, the interaction of the multiplier and the accelerator may produce the downturn without

---

75. *Contribution.* See Chap. 2 above.
76. Hicks has five explanations of the downturn. See Chap. 2 above.

the operation of the ceiling even though the accelerator is (slightly) explosive.

This explanation needs only a little adaptation to be applied to 1882. In that year no ceiling was reached in spite of full employment. This is a possibility which apparently was not precisely envisaged by Hicks but which fits very nicely into his theory. The downturn may have resulted because the accelerator was too small to produce exponential growth. The fact that freight ton-miles did not increase at all from the first quarter of 1882 through the second quarter of 1883 affords evidence that the acceleration principle caused the decline in railroad building.[77]

But Schumpeter's theory—involving a burst of innovation which dies out because opportunities are used up and because disequilibriums develop while the competing-down process brings on recession—is more illuminating and convincing than any attempt to regard the railroad boom and collapse as part of a process of interaction between multiplier and accelerator.[78] Inasmuch as Hicks's theory is more useful than Schumpeter's at the lower turning point, the cycle as a whole supports a synthesis of the two theories.

77. It is difficult to understand why freight ton-miles did not continue to rise in view of the rise in the indexes of manufacturing, crops, and transportation and communication. Moreover, gross earnings of railroads rose in 1882, a fact which is hard to reconcile with the behavior of freight ton-miles and the probable behavior of freight rates.

78. Cf. W. W. Rostow, "Some Notes on Mr. Hicks and History," *American Economic Review*, XLI (June 1951), esp. 321-22.

8

THE CYCLE OF 1885-88

THE RECESSION OF 1887-88 has received little attention in the literature. It usually gets treated as a blemish on a larger movement or major cycle, beginning in 1885 and extending past the middle nineties. This is natural enough. A recession has none of the drama and none of the historical impact on larger affairs of a depression like the nineties. Moreover, the material available for study, although by no means scanty, is so limited that it looks like a less promising field for investigation than it actually is.

American experience differed sharply from that of other countries. Although contraction began in France, Britain, and Germany within months of the 1882 peak in the United States, the subsequent upturn came earliest in America.[1] In Britain and Germany the contraction lasted until the summer of 1886. In France the trough did not occur until August 1887, by which time the expansion that began in the spring of 1885 in the United States had run its course and given way to a new contraction. All three European countries experienced their next peak at about the same time as the American peak of 1890. Thus the contraction 1887-88 was uniquely American—an extra cycle.

Upswing

The trough was in May 1885. The preceding cyclical contraction apparently came to an end by itself, stopped by autonomous investment (primarily construction of buildings), by the fact that induced disinvestment cannot exceed depreciation, by the tendency for consumption to fall less than income, and by easy money conditions. The im-

---

[1]. All dates of turning points in this paragraph are from Arthur F. Burns and Wesley C. Mitchell, *Measuring Business Cycles* (New York, 1946), pp. 78-79.

provement in general business helped set the stage for a spurt in railroad building, which was at low ebb in 1885. During the first half of that year, rate wars discouraged investment in railroads, but in the second half railroad managers were able to get together in agreements to raise rates. Their ability to agree no doubt stemmed in part from improvement in their business. The growth of the country was gradually expanding railroad traffic, the rates of interest at which capital could be obtained were in a long period of decline, and those roads that defaulted on bonds in the preceding depression were being reorganized. Railroad stock prices went up during the latter part of 1885, reflecting the improved prospects. The business cycle upswing, sluggish during the first half of 1886, became vigorous in the second half as railroad miles built increased from less than 3,000 in 1885 to more than 8,000 in 1886. (See Chart 4.) Expansion was helped by the crop situation.[2] (See Chart 6.) True, over-all crop production shows only a small rise in 1886 compared to that in 1885. Moreover, the importance of good crops for business conditions must not be overrated. Although a country that was an important supplier of food for Europe might expect a major stimulus from good crops through international trade, total merchandise exports amounted to only about 6 or 7 percent of gross national product. Only extraordinarily good crops in the United States and extraordinarily poor ones elsewhere would increase exports by as much as 1 percent of GNP. The increase of exports that the United States actually experienced in fiscal 1887 (cf. Chart 9) was not large compared to gross national product. Nevertheless, the crop situation helped. Good crops meant business for the railroads, giving them both means and need to buy railway equipment and encouraging them to build more road; and this in turn meant business for iron and steel. Moreover, since poor crops could have a serious effect, assurance that crops were not poor helped confidence.

The character of railroad building in 1886 and 1887 differed from that in earlier cycles. Previous spurts of construction involved a good deal of activity by new and often shaky companies engaged in starting or completing their main lines. In the early 1880's this kind of work had largely been finished. The construction of 1886-87 was done by

---

2. "The last half of the year [1886] showed a far better record [than the first half]. The turning point is always passed when it is known that good crops are assured, and in 1886 this became tolerably certain at an early date, and the wheat crop was reported about 100,000,000 bushels larger than in 1885," *Chronicle*, XLIV (Jan. 8, 1887), 38. See also *Bankers' Magazine*, XLI (Sept. 1886), 237-40.

comparatively strong companies building feeder or complementary lines.³

Railroad construction and the general development of the country still had a reciprocal relationship. "Of course, in a measure, the opening up of new territory has followed simply from the extension of the railroad mileage, making districts accessible that were previously very hard to reach—the railroad being in this sense the pioneer of progress; but it is also true that the occupation of new land and the building of new mileage go hand in hand, and are interdependent, neither being able to advance very far without the aid of the other."[4]

The spurt in railroad construction began after business conditions had been slowly improving for some time. In the analysis of the N.B.E.R., the quarterly series of miles of railroad track laid on main lines is lower in Stage II of the reference cycle than in Stage I, Stage II being the first stage of expansion, in this case the last half of 1885, while Stage I is the trough, in this case the second quarter of 1885. Improved business made it easier to maintain rates; this meant better earning prospects and higher stock prices.[5] And capital was abundant, making interest rates low.[6]

3. *Chronicle*, XLIV (Jan. 8, 1887), 39-40.

4. The rest of the passage is worth quoting for its description of the whole era of railroad building: "There could be no very great or continuous opening up of new territory without the necessary facilities in the way of railroads. On the other hand, most new mileage on the borders of our Western territory is prosecuted with the idea and expectation that it is to pave the way for an accession of new settlers and an extension of the area of land devoted to their uses. The success of the enterprise depends upon the realization of that idea. Should the expectation be disappointed, and the railroad fail of getting that support from the extension of local industries and local activity upon which it so confidently counted, railroad building of course would have to stop right there . . . until the growth of our industries had again overtaken the growth of transportation facilities. We have had one or two such periods—that is, when new avenues of transportation had been multiplied so fast that for the time being it seemed as if all future wants had been most liberally discounted, and the venture would therefore prove permanently unprofitable—but in each case there was a quick recovery, and the country soon grew up to give employment to all the existing facilities, and to require more besides." *Investors' Supplement to the Chronicle*, XLIII (Oct. 1886), 1-3. It is interesting to note how this passage confirms one aspect of Schumpeter's theory of the Kondratieff cycle, or, more accurately, how Schumpeter built the process described by the passage into his theory. However, he would say not that there was overbuilding but rather that as much had been accomplished as was feasible at the time (*Business Cycles*, I, 161-74).

5. *Investors' Supplement to the Chronicle*, XLIII (Aug. 28, 1886), 2. Revenue per freight ton-mile did not in fact increase in 1886 (it even declined a bit), but this is neither decisive nor relevant. Revenue per freight ton-mile has decided limitations as an index of freight rates, especially if there is a shift in the composition of freight traffic toward bulky, low revenue goods like coal. In any event, the point discussed in the text is a psychological one.

6. See *Bankers' Magazine*, XLI (March 1887), 648.

The increase in railroad investment was not confined to constructing new lines. "The demand ... has been enormous for the replacement and renewal of old plant and rolling stock and motive power, which have not been equal to the demands made by freight traffic on old roads. ..."[7] Similarly, part of the increased demand for steel rails was for replacement; steel rails were replacing iron, and the weight of rails was being increased.

In the latter part of 1886, increased railroad activity gave a lift to the rest of the economy, which created more business for the railroads, setting the stage for still greater construction in 1887. Earnings and dividends improved; in consequence, railroad stocks continued to rise.[8]

Increased railroad investment stimulated the iron and steel industry directly through increased purchases of rails and equipment. Until about the end of the year, the industry responded by utilizing capacity more fully and increasing output, sales and unfilled orders, rather than by advancing prices or accumulating inventories for speculative purposes.[9] Fear of foreign competition motivated this behavior.[10] By the end of the year the *Bankers' Magazine* was reporting of the iron industry, "There is scarcely ... any branch of this industry that is not only not fully employed to its utmost capacity, but also that is not contracted ahead for three to six months for its entire production."[11]

Building construction increased in 1886, but not from the revival of the rest of the economy. Indexes of building construction show a rise from 1880 which was not interrupted by the depression of the mid eighties.[12] (See Chart 4.) In so far as housing is concerned, the *Bankers' Magazine* credited low interest rates, a smaller decline in immigration than during the depression of the seventies, and absence of other opportunities for use of capital; yet near the end of 1886, it felt there was a housing deficiency in both quality and quantity, asserting that tenement dwellers could be housed cheaper and better

---

7. *Ibid.*, XLI (Oct. 1886), 320.

8. *Ibid.*, pp. 316 ff.; London *Economist*, CLXXIV (Feb. 19, 1887), 7.

9. London *Economist*, CLXXIV (Feb. 19, 1887), Supplement, 32 (which quotes *Bulletin* of the American Iron and Steel Association); *Bankers' Magazine*, XLI (Oct. 1886), 320.

10. London *Economist*, CLXXIV (Feb. 19, 1887), Supplement, 30.

11. XLI (Dec. 1886), 476. See also *ibid.*, XLI (Oct. 1886), 320; and London *Economist*, CLXXIV (Feb. 19, 1887), Supplement, 32.

12. U.S. Bureau of the Census, *Historical Statistics of the United States, 1789-1945* (Washington, D. C., 1949), p. 173. The picture for 1884 is not, however, entirely unambiguous. Compare with Clarence D. Long, *Building Cycles and the Theory of Investment* (Princeton, N. J., 1940), p. 226, where a decline for the year is indicated.

in modern apartments and rows of small houses.[13] The increase in building in 1886 over 1885 was not impressive compared to that of 1885 over 1884; in fact, Long's index of number of permits issued for nonresidential building for 1886 shows no rise whatever.

The character of revival in business generally was similar to that in iron and steel.[14] Agriculture was slow to benefit from the general recovery; in fact, the estimate of gross farm income indicates a decline in 1886.[15] (See Chart 6.) Statistics on the visible supplies of wheat, oats, and corn indicate considerable accumulation of stocks toward the end of the expansion phase of the cycle, but this may be spurious, representing merely a change of ownership from farmers to others.[16]

As the cyclical expansion proceeded, the banks expanded loans and investments; and although the monetary gold stock increased (despite a more than seasonal decline in 1886), reserve ratios declined. Interest rates on commercial paper and call loans went up. (See Chart 3.) On December 14, 1886, a temporary but severe stringency developed, apparently the result of manipulators trying to depress the stock market.[17] Nevertheless, the tightening of the money market in 1886 was no more than normal for an expansion. Even during the seasonal increase in demands on New York banks in the fall for crop moving purposes, the members of the clearing house in that city continued to have excess reserves.

Output in 1886 undoubtedly exceeded any previous year. (Cf. Chart 7.) Because population was rising rapidly, this did not necessarily mean full employment. One may hazard the guess that full

13. XLI (Nov. 1886), 346-48.

14. "It is the general report from most branches of business that the amount of trade this fall has been far in excess of last year, and larger than an average. It has been done on a smaller margin of profit, however. Although prices have generally improved on manufactured goods, the raw material has advanced as much or more, and left the manufacturers' profit very small; as consumption has not sufficiently overtaken production to materially reduce the competition among dealers. . . . But the business done, has been upon a safer basis than for years, both as to its class and as regards long credits. When they have sold a bill of goods, it has been to some one who wanted them for immediate use, who resold them, and who had the money to pay for them when the bills became due, instead of the goods piled up on their shelves. Stocks are therefore small in second hands, while the actual demand has been large enough to keep them moderate in first hands." *Ibid.*, p. 396.

15. Frederick Strauss and Louis H. Bean, *Gross Farm Income and Indices of Farm Production and Prices in the United States, 1869-1937*, Dept. of Agriculture, Tech. Bull. 703 (Washington, D. C., 1940), pp. 22 and 24.

16. *Bankers' Magazine*, XLI (Nov. 1886), 397. For further discussion of accumulation of grain stocks, see *ibid.*, XLI (Oct. 1886), 317.

17. *Chronicle*, XLIV (Jan. 3, 1887), 40.

employment was not reached till the end of the year. Even thereafter, except for bottlenecks, lack of labor could not have done more than slow down the rate of increase, since the labor force was increasing rapidly. The scattered and meager evidence about inventory investment seems to indicate that it did not play an important role during 1886.

Expansion in the United States tended to generate expansion elsewhere rather than the other way round; the behavior of exports was so irregular and the increase in imports so large that for the United States international trade was a leakage inhibiting the expansion. (See Chart 9.) The London *Economist* reported of 1886, "for whatever improvement may have taken place we are very largely indebted to India and the United States."[18]

Downturn

According to the Bureau, the expansion reached its peak in March 1887. This date seems a month or two early. But inasmuch as analysis and interpretation in this instance are not affected by a shift of this order, discussion of the dating problem is relegated to an appendix.

Burns and Mitchell ranked the contraction of 1887-88 as the mildest occurring between 1879 and 1933.[19] Although the data used are subject to serious limitations, there are no grounds for disputing their conclusion that 1887-88 was about as mild as any contraction worthy of the name. The only difference of opinion to be found in the literature is whether it should be recognized as a cyclical contraction at all.[20]

18. CLXXIV (Feb. 19, 1887), Supplement, 4. Cf. Wesley C. Mitchell, *Business Cycles* (Berkeley, Calif., 1913), p. 46.

19. *Measuring*, p. 403.

20. Kitchin omitted it from his chronology (Joseph Kitchin, "Cycles and Trends in Economic Factors," *Review of Economic Statistics*, V [Jan. 1923], 10-16). Partington omitted it from his table, although his text recognized that a recession occurred (John E. Partington, *Railroad Purchasing and the Business Cycle* [Washington, 1929], pp. 235 and 257-58). A number of important series—railroad freight ton-miles, railroad earnings, total imports, total loans and discounts of national banks, and individual deposits of national banks—were so little affected by the contraction that the Bureau has not marked off any specific cycle peak in the vicinity of this period. Contemporary journals do not indicate that a decline in business of any consequence took place. Moore has shown that there is a tendency for the amplitude of contractions to be correlated with their diffusion. The highest percentage of series contracting during the downswing of 1887-88 occurred in February of the later year and was 65.0. Although this seems quite enough to establish that there really was a business cycle contraction, it is the second lowest maximum for cyclical contractions occurring between 1882 and 1938 (Geoffrey H. Moore, "Statistical Indicators of Cyclical Revivals

It is no less significant to study for that. The most practical question about business cycles is why some contractions are gentle and others catastrophic, why some never make much headway while others gather momentum like a truck rolling downhill. Although economists know a good deal about this problem, much more knowledge is needed. Once started, a vicious spiral is difficult to stop. Unless the United States is to pursue a policy of perpetual inflation, the government must be able to judge, at the time a contraction is just getting under way, whether vigorous action must be taken at once or whether it is safe to rely on built-in flexibility and central bank policy together with the inherent tendency (if any) for contractions to die out of themselves. In seeking the answer, the contractions that die out quickly are just as significant objects of study as those that are more dramatic and disastrous.

The 1887-88 contraction is especially interesting because clues as to the cause of the downturn are abundant. Railroad construction reached its all-time peak of nearly 13,000 miles added in 1887, creating bottlenecks in the iron and steel industry, with a drastic decline the next year to less than 7,000. (See Chart 4.) Building construction also fell off in 1888, though not as drastically. Interest rates, seasonally adjusted, were high in the vicinity of the peak, indicating that tight money may have been a factor. (See Chart 3.) A decline in federal expenditures, unfavorable crop conditions, a small drop in exports, and a rise in failures all require looking into. Since investigation of recent cycles has shown that those of small amplitude can usually be called inventory cycles, it is necessary to investigate the scanty evidence on the behavior of stocks.

Railroad building, for many years the dominant form of investment, presents an ambiguous picture. One would like a quarterly series on gross railroad investment. There are a number of series bearing on the question, none of which tells nearly enough.

---

and Recessions," N.B.E.R., Occasional Paper 31 [New York, 1950], pp. 47-58). The connection between diffusion and amplitude was previously pointed out by Burns and Mitchell, *Measuring*, p. 106. Although Hubbard found other contractions even milder, he considered 1887-88 to be a decline of small magnitude (Joseph B. Hubbard, "Business Volumes During Periods of Decline and Recovery," *Review of Economic Statistics*, XII [Nov. 1930], 183). Hubbard used clearings to measure severity. To Eckler, it was of the sixth order of severity—one of only two cases mild enough to fall into this classification (A. Ross Eckler, "A Measure of the Severity of Depressions, 1873-1932," *Review of Economic Statistics*, XV [May 1933], 78-79). Eckler used six series to measure severity. Serious doubts could be raised about the adequacy of any one of these methods of measuring the severity of the contraction of 1887-88, but they all point to the same undoubted conclusion—it was one of the mildest on record.

Obviously the statistics on railroad mileage must have been an unreliable indicator of gross investment. Since most of the mileage was built by companies already in existence, there could be no close connection between investment in construction of new lines and investment in equipment and terminal facilities. Additions to track simultaneously increased a road's need for other forms of investment and lowered its ability to make other investment at that particular time. Moreover, the work of renewing old track and equipment, increasing the weight of rails, replacing wooden bridges with iron ones, and so on, might have reached its peak at the same time as construction of new lines but might well have been deferred till after the spurt in additions to mileage was over. Moreover, there was wide variation in the costs of building a mile of road, because of geography and other factors. Railroad investment probably did not nearly double in 1887 and then fall off more steeply than it rose, although this is what the annual figures of mileage added suggest.

Ulmer has recently published estimates of railroad investment which throw some light on the question.[21] For every third year on the average, he derived an estimate from reports of state railroad commissioners, which gave him a sample representing 20 to 70 percent of the total. For the intervening years he interpolated on the basis of miles of track operated.[22] His results prove that miles built are a misleading indicator of investment. Gross capital expenditures in constant dollars reached successively higher peaks in the early seventies, the early eighties and the early nineties, whereas number of miles added reached its all-time high in 1887. Unfortunately, his figures tell us little more about year to year changes than we can get from a series on miles of railroad added; they cannot throw more light on the question whether there was an intermediate peak in 1887, much less on how great was the decline. But his figures suggest that railroad investment in constant dollars was less in 1887 than in the peak years of the early eighties and early nineties.

The N.B.E.R. has a quarterly series (#2, 84a) called Miles of Railroad Track Laid on Main Lines. It unfortunately ends with the third quarter of 1887. It has a marked seasonal pattern, with the first (winter) quarter decidedly lower than the other three. The figures for 1886 and 1887 are given in Table 2. Since the total for the year 1887 was nearly 13,000, or about 7,000 more than

---

21. Melville J. Ulmer, "Trends and Cycles in Capital Formation by United States Railroads, 1870-1950," N.B.E.R., Occasional Paper 43 (New York, 1954).
22. *Ibid.*, pp. 52-53.

TABLE 2. Miles of Railroad Track Laid on Main Lines, 1886 and 1887

	1886		1887	
	Unadjusted	Adjusted*	Unadjusted	Adjusted*
1st quarter..............	406	944	739	1,719
2nd quarter.............	1,174	1,210	1,243	1,281
3rd quarter.............	2,453	1,804	3,919	2,882
4th quarter.............	3,241	2,593	.....	.....
Totals.............	7,274	6,551	(5,901)	(5,882)

*For seasonal variation.

the total for the first three quarters, the peak must have come in the fourth quarter of that year even after adjustment for seasonal variation.[23] Nevertheless, there was a decline in the first half of 1887 from the peak in the fourth quarter of 1886, even after allowing for the normal seasonal pattern. These figures indicate some decline in one form of railroad investment in the neighborhood of the cyclical peak; this may have influenced the timing of the downturn. But since they indicate a decided spurt in the second half of 1887, there may be here an important reason why the contraction phase of the business cycle made so little headway. The explanation is not complete, since railroad building presumably suffered a more than seasonal drop in the first quarter of 1888 (the trough of the business cycle) and thereafter.

Addition to railroad mileage was by no means the whole of railroad investment. One might expect a bulge in consumption of rails in 1887, with the decline in the following year smaller than the decline in additions to mileage, since a considerable part of rail consumption must have been for replacement; and this is what in fact one finds. Apparent consumption fell off by about one third in 1888.[24] These are annual figures. The quarterly series on orders, together with a monthly series on the wholesale price, tell an interesting story—a drastic decline of nearly 75 percent in orders in the third quarter of

23. The unadjusted total of miles of railroad track laid on main lines for 1886, as shown in Table 2, is 7,274, about 10% less than the 8,000 miles added according to the commonly used series. By reducing the nearly 13,000 miles built in 1887 by the same proportion, one gets a little more than 11,500 as a rough estimate of track laid on main lines. Since 5,901 were built in the first three quarters, this leaves more than 5,500 for the fourth quarter, compared to 3,919 in the third quarter (unadjusted). Since the seasonal peak comes in the third quarter, there is little doubt that the peak in track laid on main lines can be assumed to be in the fourth.

24. Partington, *Railroad Purchasing*, p. 79.

1887 accompanied by a considerable fall in price. Orders revived in the fourth quarter, but the price continued to fall. I do not know what the lags were between orders and deliveries or between deliveries and use, but it seems clear that the rails needed for the construction activity of the last half of 1887 must have been ordered well in advance; on a calendar year basis, the bulge in orders came in 1886 rather than 1887.[25] If so, this qualifies the conclusion reached above, that increased railroad construction in the last half of 1887 helped brake the cyclical contraction; the decline in orders for rails had an adverse effect on the iron and steel industry from virtually the beginning of the contraction. Presumably the decline in orders foreshadowed the decline in additions to road mileage, and additions to road mileage were about to decline because investment opportunities in that direction were getting used up.[26] Since there was no over-all shortage of investment opportunities, the development in steel rails can be considered a maladjustment in the structure of production.

Such statistics as are available on railway rolling stock indicate that purchases were steady, as far as yearly totals are concerned,

25. This statement is based on calendar years because the figures on apparent consumption are on a calendar year basis; and I wanted to bring out the point that the bulge in orders came a year before the bulge in production and consumption. This way of putting matters should not obscure the fact that the bulge in orders could be better described as coming in the year ending June 30, 1887. The figures on orders come from Partington, *Railroad Purchasing*, p. 221.

26. As early as May 1887 the *Bankers' Magazine* was saying, "Doubtless the rapid growth of our country calls for railway extension to a quite unparalleled degree as compared with other nations, yet even here there is a limit to profitable railway building. It is not profitable to go far beyond immediate wants in extending existing lines, or building new ones. It is not profitable to build a railway that will not be needed for five or ten years to come. . . .Yet this has been done again and again, and is likely to be repeated during the present season of prosperity. It is as certain as anything can be that many of these new railways will not be needed for many years, and that in the intervening period their projectors or the holders of their bonds will foreclose and sell these properties, incurring heavy losses without obvious gain to anybody. As soon as this period of railway building ceases—and it certainly will stop as soon as people have expended their money and exhausted their confidence—the reaction will set in" (pp. 802-3). Cf. the following passage from the *Investors' Supplement to the Chronicle*, XLV (Sept. 1887), 2: "The Chicago & Northwestern and one or two other large companies have recently resolved, it is reported, that when present extensions are completed they will undertake no further new work till the result of their latest ventures is determined. This resolution, if adhered to, might reduce materially the total of new mileage for 1888. . . ."

What constitutes an investment opportunity in my usage (not Gordon's) is a subjective matter, dependent on the thinking of investors of the time. I doubt if I would have regarded many of the extensions of 1887 as investment opportunities, but that is irrelevant. In the minds of those making the decisions, opportunities in railroad building were more abundant in 1887 than in 1888.

THE CYCLE OF 1885-88

neither reinforcing nor offsetting the decline in additions to mileage. Cars and locomotives owned by railways at the end of the year show fairly steady rises during these years.[27] Annual totals of quarterly series on orders of cars and locomotives tell the same story; in fact, 1888 shows an increase over 1887.[28] But the quarterly figures themselves are another matter: most of the ordering of 1887 was done in the first and fourth quarters, with the second and third quarters a good deal lower. Partington said the decline "was probably in large part a reaction from the swell of orders in the latter part of 1886 and the first quarter of the new year."[29] He also noted that railway journals of the time ascribed it to uncertainty about the effects of the Interstate Commerce Act. In addition, the railroads may have been putting so much of their financial resources into construction of new mileage that they had to be cautious about ordering equipment for the time being. After making due allowance for the presumption that production of rolling stock was more regular than orders, one can still ascribe the beginning of the contraction phase of the business cycle in some small part to the decline in orders for railway equipment, and the end of contraction to the resumption of orders.

The preceding discussion does not yield firm conclusions about aggregate investment by the railroads.[30] Aggregate investment apparently held up at least through the end of 1887, with important shifts

27. Thor Hultgren, *American Transportation in Prosperity and Depression* (New York, 1948), pp. 149-50.
28. Partington, *Railroad Purchasing*, p. 221.
29. *Ibid.*, p. 78. Partington's figures exaggerate the decline because they are not adjusted for seasonal variation.
30. *Historical Statistics of the United States*, p. 201, gives a series for investment in railroad and equipment. By taking first differences, one can get estimates of the investment made each year. Such estimates are exceedingly untrustworthy. The series given in *Historical Statistics* comes from *Poor's*, which compiled it from reports by the railroads. Even if *Poor's* had done its work well, the series would have serious deficiencies. The figure for each railroad is based on the close of its own fiscal year; since the fiscal years ended on different dates (December 31, September 30, and June 30 are typical), an aggregate of these figures does not relate to any one point of time. If the one railroad whose books I have had occasion to investigate closely is representative of railroad accounting practices of the nineteenth century, the basic records would be incapable of yielding reliable estimates of the amount of investment, as that term is understood today. I have some reason to question how good a job *Poor's* did in aggregating the figures. Under the circumstances, the series is not good enough to stand the strain of first differencing. For what it is worth, first differencing gives investment of more than half a billion dollars in 1887 and 1888, declining to a quarter of a billion in 1889. If this could be believed, it would imply no fall in railroad investment until after the business cycle contraction of 1887-88 was over.

in the components of the aggregate. Sometime in 1888, presumably early in the year, there may have been a decline.

The bulge in railroad building naturally enough led to bottleneck phenomena in the iron and steel industry, particularly in steel rails.[31] It appears that steel rails could have been sold at profitable prices in even larger quantity in the first half of 1887, if more could have been produced. The industry met the situation by working overtime and raising prices. Did this contribute to causing the recession? I believe on the contrary that the bottlenecks were stabilizing. Greater output of steel rails in the first half of 1887 would have led to an even greater reduction in the second half.

The period from about 1878-80 to 1890-92 represents the upswing of a building cycle (if there is such a thing). (See Chart 4.) Annual figures on permits record a temporary reduction in 1888, both in number and value; and Long's monthly index shows a decided peak in March of 1887, with the trough in February 1888. Even after allowing for a lag between the issuance of a permit and the act of investment, the timing is almost perfect for explaining the cyclical phenomena of 1887-88. The chief problem is to explain why building construction declined during a period when—to judge by the active building of subsequent years—investment opportunities in this field were still numerous. Contemporary opinion cannot give much help. The statistics showing the lull in building were not compiled till long afterwards; in the absence of statistics, a contemporary observer of an industry as scattered as building might know and explain the development in one locality but not in a number of cities. And Riggleman's indexes for seven regions show that the decline was not confined to one part of the country; although the timing differed, it affected all

31. "Manufacturers of all kinds of goods are still running full time and regular force as a rule; but they are working less overtime, or have ceased altogether, whereas in many branches, especially in iron, overtime and extra force was the rule earlier in the season. 'Behind orders' was the general complaint for the first nine months of the year in many lines of this great industry. But now we are told that most of them 'have caught up with their orders,' and few have enough to keep them running beyond January, 1888. . . . the steel rail men are caught up with their orders from new roads, and have been letting down the price in order to induce old roads, which have been holding off for the railroad building to subside, and lower prices, before increasing or renewing their old plant or rolling stock. . . . Steel rails have thus come down $6 per ton from the top, and a good many kinds of manufactured iron and steel have sympathized. . . , yet there was advance enough during the past year to admit of this receding of prices without loss or stopping production. . . ." *Bankers' Magazine*, XLII (Nov. 1887), 407-8.

THE CYCLE OF 1885-88   149

regions.³² This suggests looking for a general cause. One can be found in stringent money conditions.³³ (See Chart 3.)

Contrary to the usual seasonal pattern, money was tightest in the spring, especially June. For the building industry, this is a worse time of year for stringency to occur than the crop moving season, when winter is approaching. If commercial paper rates are used as an index of stringency, money was tighter in 1887 than at any other time in the decade except during the panic of 1884. Although money eased somewhat during the last half of the year, commercial paper rates remained high. Quite aside from the credit rationing that probably occurred, interest is an important part of the cost calculations involved in putting up buildings. The tightening of money in 1887 was no local phenomenon confined to the New York money market; on the contrary, the condition in New York resulted from pressure from the rest of the country. It seems plausible to attribute the decline of construction in 1887 to the shortage of credit.

Money became tight because output and business activity grew more rapidly than the monetary base. As a very rough guess, total output grew 10 percent during the cyclical upswing. Meanwhile, between June 30, 1885, and June 30, 1887, gold and currency in circulation (including that held by banks) grew about 2 percent, or $25 million.³⁴

32. Series 2,37 through 2,43 in the N.B.E.R. files.

33. ". . . the demand [on the New York City banks] for loans was heavy, and the only complaint from customers was the common one of late years, that the banks loaned so largely on securities that they could not give sufficient accommodations on mercantile paper. The maximum surplus reserve was reached on January 29, when it was $22,298,450, and the minimum on June 25, when it was $3,345,900 . . . . The tendency of operations was to draw funds away from the Atlantic cities to the Interior and keep them there, as the railroad building in the far West and South, the speculation in town lots, and the wheat corners in Chicago and San Francisco, all called for a large amount of money. On the other hand, the demand in New York and Boston, to carry new railroad bonds in the hands of bankers and syndicates, was very large, while the call for money on stock speculation was moderate. Rates were easy in this market till March, when they began to harden, this tendency increasing in April. . . . There was no further stringency in money till after the middle of June, when the markets were greatly unsettled by the collapse of the coffee bubble here and the wheat bubble in Chicago, and the consequent demand for money. On the 24th of June there was a sharp calling in of loans. . . . During the last half of the year there was never any great stringency in money, but there was great trouble in August and September in borrowing on any railroad collaterals except those that were first-class, and the fear of tight money influenced the stock market. The Treasury came to the relief of the situation, first by purchasing on proposals over $25,000,000 of bonds and then in October by offering to place its surplus with depositary banks on Government bond security. . . ." *Chronicle,* XLVI (Jan. 7, 1888), 10.

34. *Historical Statistics of the United States,* p. 274.

Because the banks had had large excess reserves in 1885, they were able to increase their total deposits 20 percent during these two years,[35] but by the middle of 1887 the rate of expansion had to slow down.

The failure of the money base to grow more rapidly was partly due to gold exports in the fiscal year 1886. The merchandise balance deteriorated by $121 million (far more than the $40 million change in gold flows), primarily because imports experienced the rise usual during cyclical upswings.[36] (Cf. Chart 9.) During 1887 the gold flow was reversed, even though the merchandise balance became a little worse, on account of capital movements—both an export of securities and an import of short-term funds attracted by high interest rates.[37] This is the normal result of a business cycle upswing originating in the United States and operating in conjunction with the international mechanism of adjustment to the gold standard. It tends to confirm the hypothesis that both the gold flows of classical theory and the income effects of modern theory are part of the adjustment process.

Although three different policies of the Treasury Department each had a strong impact on the money market, their net effect appears to have been small. The Treasury was struggling to keep the chronic government surplus from depriving the money market of needed funds. Between June 30, 1885, and the same date in 1887, money held in the Treasury increased $38 million.[38] The surplus was much larger than this, most of it being used to retire bonds. Since national bank notes had to be secured by government bonds, this form of money decreased $32 million. Meanwhile, the government was pursuing an inflationary silver policy, so that silver money outside the Treasury increased $62 million.[39]

Although the federal surplus was large, exceeding $100 million in the fiscal year 1887, its impact on the income stream was not. (See Chart 10.) In the short run, changes in the surplus are more significant than the absolute amount. The rise in the surplus between the fiscal years 1885 and 1887 was only $40 million, or less than half of one percent of national income. The increase in the surplus was only a trifle greater than the rise in collections of import duties, which was, of

35. *Ibid.*, p. 262.
36. *Ibid.*, p. 244.
37. *Chronicle*, XLVI (Jan. 7, 1888), 11.
38. Not including precious metal held in trust against gold and silver certificates in circulation—*Annual Report of the Secretary of the Treasury* (Washington, D. C., 1928), p. 552.
39. *Historical Statistics of the United States*, p. 275.

course, in turn the result of the upswing itself. The surplus, therefore, represented mainly a leakage which operated only because and to the extent that business activity increased.

Besides, one must avoid double counting. Inelasticity of the money supply served to check the cyclical expansion in the vicinity of the peak, and the surplus was a factor offsetting the inflationary silver policy of the government. Although the surplus operated both on the money supply and on the income stream, the two effects are not additive.

The same is true of the income effects of the deteriorating balance of international trade. The large and steady rise in imports represented a leakage. The smaller decline in exports, which did not begin till the cyclical expansion was far advanced, presumably came about because markets were improving faster in the United States than abroad. Both were leakages. Moreover, they kept the gold supply from growing. The two effects, however, are not additive.

Federal expenditures must be analyzed in a somewhat different way. In terms of the N.B.E.R. method of analysis, they declined from Stage V (the cyclical peak) to Stage VIII (the last stage before the trough). The decline was not great, being less than one half of 1 percent of national income. Although multiplier effects must be allowed for, they take time to work themselves out; and both the pattern of federal expenditures and the length of the recession were such that multiplier effects must have been small. On the other hand, a considerable part of the income effects must have been felt after the money stringency was at its height and therefore to some extent can be considered an additional factor. Timed at the start of one of the mildest contractions on record, they might have made the difference between a recession and a pause to activity too slight to come under the N.B.E.R.'s definition of a business cycle.

The index of crop production for 1887 declined.[40] (See Chart 6.) On psychological grounds, poor crops in the United States must be considered unfavorable. Bigger crops meant more business for the railroads and more exports, so that business expectations tended to vary directly with crop expectations. Whatever influence the psychological factor had took effect early in the downswing. Moreover, the poor crops led to disinvestment in inventories. The N.B.E.R.'s

---

40. Strauss and Bean, *Farm Income*, p. 130. A notable exception was cotton, output of which reached a new high.

analysis of the visible supplies of wheat, oats, corn, and cotton shows the decline clearly.[41]

The behavior of stocks of nonfarm commodities is more ambiguous. The *Economist* in early 1888 generalized, "The new year has opened with materially reduced stocks of staples" in the United States. Most of the support for the statement lay in figures of farm commodities, but it reported that crude petroleum stocks were down to 25 million barrels from 33 million and that stocks of anthracite coal had been reduced as a result of a miners' strike.[42] Pig iron in the hands of manufacturers, on the other hand, increased from 225,629 gross tons at the end of 1886—an extremely low percent of annual output—to 301,913 at the end of 1887.[43] This accumulation may not have been unintentional even though it resulted from diminished demand. The *Bankers' Magazine* reported in November 1888, "Already many of the iron manufacturers are changing to the manufacture of staple goods that can be piled up in stock and held for a market to the best advantage. . . ."[44]

Liabilities of business failures in the third quarter of 1887 were the highest for any quarter during the decade except for the quarter in which the panic of 1884 occurred.[45] In addition, there had been important bank failures in June. Failures are a symptom of recession; their magnitude is one of the tests to apply in deciding whether or not a recession occurred. They also have a causal force, intensifying a recession by locking up funds, interrupting the spending stream, and damaging confidence. In part the failures must have been the result (as well as the cause) of money stringency and of the other forces that slackened business activity. In part they resulted, particularly the more spectacular ones, from the exuberance and speculative activity that sustained cyclical upswing is apt to generate.[46] Such boom-like phenomena were not widespread and did not go very deep.

41. Series 5,01; 5,84; 5,21; 5,03—all in the N.B.E.R. files. According to the London *Economist*, CLXXVIII (Jan. 28, 1888), 112, rye, lard, sugar, and coffee stocks were also down, but tobacco was up.
42. CLXXVIII (Jan. 28, 1888), 112.
43. American Iron and Steel Association, *Statistics of the American and Foreign Iron Trades for 1896* (Philadelphia, 1897), p. 61.
44. XLIII, 407.
45. *Historical Statistics of the United States*, p. 349.
46. "The month of June will be known from the rest of the months of 1887 as the month of panics and failures. Not general panic, however, such as results from an unsound and overdone condition of legitimate business, but speculative panics confined to the markets in which speculation has been carried to an unsafe point"—*Bankers' Magazine*, XLII (July 1887), 74. Cf. *ibid.*, XLI (May 1887), 801-4.

THE CYCLE OF 1885-88

The money stringency eased during the last half of 1887. There was considerable apprehension lest the federal surplus cause serious difficulties, but the Secretary of the Treasury managed to get rid of the extra money in time to avert trouble. Presumably, anticipation of further stringency exerted some small temporary restraining influence.

Easing of the stringency was the normal result of slackening business activity, which reduced the need for money. Presumably the recession also helped by keeping the balance of trade from deteriorating more rapidly (it continued to deteriorate). As already noted, gold flowed in as a result of capital imports, and gold continued to be produced by American mines in excess of the amounts used in the arts. Perhaps in consequence of easier money, building revived early in 1888.

The maladjustment centering in steel rails but affecting the entire iron and steel industry tended to work itself out. A drastic decline in orders for steel rails as railroad building neared its climax brought a marked reduction in their price from the very high level to which it had been pushed. The reduction in price in turn stimulated orders for rails for replacement. Meanwhile the railroads were increasing orders for equipment. Aggregate railroad investment very likely held up well. In addition, demand for iron and steel products for miscellaneous purposes continued to grow.

The downswing gathered so little momentum and the upswing got under way so gradually that it is difficult to date the trough with any precision. The N.B.E.R. puts it in the first quarter of 1888, or, on a monthly basis, April. There cannot be much quarrel with these decisions.[47]

As noted in the preceding paragraph, bad weather accentuated the

---

47. Frickey's series of outside clearings for seven selected cities shows the first quarter as lowest. The N.B.E.R.'s series for outside clearings in a growing number of cities shows the fourth quarter of 1887 and the first quarter of 1888 as virtually the same (*Historical Statistics of the United States*, p. 337). Pig-iron production declined more than 20% from a peak in October 1887 to a trough in March 1888 (*ibid.*, p. 333). Just about 50% of Moore's statistical indicators were expanding in the month chosen for the trough, which is as it should be ("Statistical Indicators," p. 14). The *Bankers' Magazine*'s monthly commentaries on the business situation did not observe improvement in business until June; unusually bad weather throughout the winter and most of the spring was blamed, as well as the coal strike which occurred during the winter, XLII (Feb. 1888), 576-83; *ibid.*, XLII (March 1888), 649; *ibid.*, XLII (April 1888), 736-42; *ibid.*, XLII (May 1888), 821-29; *ibid.*, XLII (June 1888), 915-21; *ibid.*, XLIII (July 1888), 6-7. Cf. *Economist*, CLXXIX (April 28, 1888), 535, and *ibid.*, CLXXIX (May 5, 1888), 567. This is not necessarily a reason for selecting May as the trough, since a contemporary observer could not be expected to see anything but continued "depression" until the improvement became marked.

decline in business activity during the winter months by interfering with transportation. But there was an offsetting external factor: federal expenditures rebounded at about the time of the cyclical trough. Probably no significance need be attached to the anthracite coal strike. Although it had an obvious impact on pig-iron production in the vicinity of the mines, this cannot be taken as a net loss of output to the industry since demand was declining.

Conclusions

Historical business cycles can be considered the result of the following factors: (1) external or exogenous shocks; (2) aggregate investment opportunities; (3) maladjustments in the structure of production, which are the result both of shocks and of using up investment opportunities of particular kinds; (4) constraints, such as full employment, limits to expansion of the money supply, international trade (which operates as a constraint when one country expands more rapidly than the rest of the world), or the tendency of tax receipts to vary with national income; (5) the reinforcing mechanisms, which tend to convert an increase (or decrease) in aggregate activity into a further increase (or decrease), in extreme cases resulting in booms (or vicious spirals); (6) bunching mechanisms, such as the one described in Schumpeter's theory which leads to bursts of innovating activity; (7) destabilizing mechanisms, which accentuate an expansion at the expense of making the next contraction worse.

In terms of these categories, the recession of 1887 resulted from external shocks in the form of reduced federal expenditures, poor crops and a hard winter; a maladjustment in the structure of production resulting from relative exhaustion of investment opportunities in a particular direction, namely, additions to railroad trackage, and affecting primarily steel rails; constraints, particularly that imposed by the money supply on building, but also international trade, government finance and full employment; and the mechanism that caused a bunching of investment in railroad trackage and thereby produced the maladjustment in the structure of production. There is some element of a destabilizing mechanism, in that the optimism generated by the upswing led to speculative activity with disastrous results in certain quarters, but this was peripheral. Although in the later stages of the upswing investment opportunities probably were used up faster than new ones were created, aggregate opportunities were not seriously deficient.

THE CYCLE OF 1885-88

Although the bunching mechanism can be described in Schumpeterian terms, it was not what Schumpeter's theory would suggest first. No key innovator appeared on the scene in 1885 or 1886, breaking new paths, to be followed in 1886 and 1887 by a host of imitators. By the mid 1880's, railroad building was thoroughly understood by a considerable number of railroad men. They were led to do the same thing at the same time not by a new man in a new company but by something quite different.

The most important immediate cause of bunching lay in the realm of finance. In 1886 and 1887 it became much easier for railroads to raise money, and they responded by laying more track. Financing became easier as a result of previous business cycle developments (which ultimately might be explained on Schumpeterian grounds), together with the growth of the country, which in terms of population and agriculture went on in spite of the depression. At the same time, these developments increased the willingness of railroad men to carry out such undertakings.

Bunching cannot be explained on grounds of financing alone. It was also the result of the logic of railroad development, which dictated at this stage, when the main lines had largely been completed, that feeders be built first, with other kinds of investment (improving old roadway, adding equipment, building terminals, etc.) to follow. And perhaps there was a competitive element as well. The survival of many railroads as independent firms depended on the outcome of a competitive struggle. Additional investment was not always something that could be deferred; with competitors ever taking away business on through routes or at least driving down rates, a firm's only chance might lie in building more road.

The behavior of railroad investment of these years can fit into any of the usual theories of investment, which aside from the Schumpeterian can be labeled induced (or acceleration principle) investment, exploitation of investment opportunities, and response to interest rates. The rapid rate of adding to the mileage operated can properly be considered a little of each.

Nevertheless, what went on corresponds pretty well to what one would expect from Schumpeter's model. In Schumpeter's chronology, the period from late 1885 to the end of 1888 was the recovery phase of a Juglar cycle. In his model, the depression phase carries the economy below Walrasian equilibrium; in recovery the economy returns to equilibrium as the result of firms and workers seeking their best position. Aside from the complications caused by multiplicity of cycles, there is no innovation during recovery, but this does not mean absence of investment associated with saving (and consequent lowering of the interest rate), the growth of population, and pushing into new economic space created by the previous prosperity. Railroad investment during 1886 and 1887 can be described in such terms.

As summarized above, four different kinds of factors combined to bring about the recession. One might try to assess their relative importance, but this would be futile, since it took the combination of them all to bring about even a mild and gentle decline. The question is, why did they all happen at once? There is only one reasonable answer—coincidence. If there was any mechanism that caused crops to be poor at the same time that federal expenditures dropped off or caused the constraint of an inelastic money supply to develop just when a maladjustment in the structure of production was imminent, it is hard to see what it might be.

From the point of view of finding an intellectually satisfying theory of the business cycle, this result is disappointing. One does not like to fall back on coincidence. Yet it is not only a quite reasonable result but also what might be expected in the future. A growing economy develops maladjustments in the structure of production all the time, some of them more serious than others. It is also subject to numerous external shocks. A prosperous economy cannot entirely avoid the effects of constraints. Occasionally there will be a coincidence of enough unfavorable factors to reverse an expansion process. Such a verdict could be passed on 1953 as well as 1887.

Why did the recession end? The sum of the forces initiating it was barely enough to get it started. Consequently, the decline in activity was slow and gentle. Under unfavorable circumstances, a contraction that starts slowly may gather momentum and develop into a vicious spiral. But circumstances in 1887 were not unfavorable: investment opportunities were still plentiful, and so far as I can tell inventories were rather low. The milder the contraction the more easily it is brought to an end. Moreover, the forces responsible for the recession were either single shocks, the effects of which spend themselves, or were the sort that get corrected quickly (maladjustment in the structure of production and the constraints, particularly the constraint that the money supply imposed on building). In the vicinity of the trough there occurred two outside shocks, a rise in government expenditures and bad weather. (I omit the fall in exports, since they had increased temporarily in the last half of 1887; presumably multiplier effects from the rise more or less offset the subsequent decline.) Neither of these shocks was large in magnitude, and they were opposite in direction. This is the most interesting feature of the trough—it cannot plausibly be explained on the basis of external events. Without ever degenerating into a depression, the contraction came to an end by itself.

Thus the episode is testimony to a kind of stability in the American economy. Of course, in some ways the economy was highly unstable. The most important forms of investment opportunities (in railroads and in buildings) were liable to temporary exhaustion, and the banking system was vulnerable to panics. But when such dangers could be avoided, the recession of 1887-88 gives evidence of stability in the sense that a small downward movement tended to be self-reversing rather than cumulative.

The significance of this finding can best be discussed in terms of Colin Clark's econometric study of the United States.[48] He used a six-equation model which included the multiplier, the acceleration principle, a ceiling, a floor, and exogenous shocks. The values of his parameters, particularly for the inventory-accelerator equation, were such as to generate a high degree of instability. The downswings of 1923-24 and 1926-27 came to a quick end not because they were self-reversing but because of external factors. Clark's findings may be taken as an example of a general view of the business cycle which is significant for two reasons. First, the question of how unstable is the economy we live in is of practical importance to government officials charged with the duty of preventing depression. Second, the question of whether there are effective self-reversing mechanisms is important for business cycle theory.

The test must lie in mild downswings like that of 1887-88. If the hypothesis of extreme instability is correct, it should be possible to find that every minor downswing came to an end in part because external factors on balance were favorable. It may confidently be predicted that this will be the case for every recession of the future, because the government will deliberately engineer favorable shocks for this purpose. It is also true (or at least it can plausibly be argued that it was true) for all recessions since World War I. To disprove the hypothesis of extreme instability, one must find at least one

[48]. "A System of Equations Explaining the United States Trade Cycle, 1921 to 1941," *Econometrica*, XVII (April 1949), 93-124.

case (preferably more) in which external factors were not on balance favorable to a significant degree. Such a case was 1887-88.

Of course, 1887-88 is not decisive. Knowledge of what happened then is necessarily limited. One cannot be absolutely certain, for instance, that there was a decline in aggregate demand; and if aggregate demand did not decline, proponents of the instability hypothesis are entitled to argue that there was no cyclical downswing in the relevant sense. The light that events of 1887-88 shed on the world of 1959 is questionable in view of the great changes of the last seven decades. Some of the changes are plainly in the direction of greater stability, namely, the increase of built-in flexibility. Others are plainly in the direction of less stability, for instance, the growth of consumer credit and the greater postponability of consumption expenditures as levels of living rise. Where to strike the balance no one can be absolutely certain. But those who are optimistic about the net effect on stability of structural changes in the American economy can derive a measure of comfort from the events of the latter 1880's.

9

THE CYCLE OF 1888-91

THERE WAS a business cycle in the United States of America which, counting from trough to trough, extended from April 1888 to May 1891, with the peak in July 1890.[1] The downswing was singularly mild, qualifying as no more than a recession. Elsewhere in the industrial world the contraction was so long and deep that (except for the U. S.) 1890 is generally counted as the peak of a major cycle.[2] As the upturns of 1888 and 1891 were uniquely American, the cycle as a whole bears little resemblance to experience elsewhere.

Upswing

The start of the upswing was delayed by an unusually bad winter. During the rest of 1888, recovery proceeded steadily. The three best statistical series for cyclical movements within the year are bank clearings outside New York, railroad freight ton-miles, and pig-iron production. (See Chart 11.) Outside clearings revived sharply in the second and third quarters. This probably overstates the speed of revival, since exclusion of New York clearings by no means eliminates the effects of speculation from the figures; and both New York clearings and contemporary comment indicate that speculative activity revived during the same two quarters.[3] Freight ton-miles, which had reflected the recession only by briefly ceasing to grow, resumed a steady upward march. Pig-iron production also increased throughout the year, but in spite of its upward trend it did not exceed the high of

---

1. Arthur F. Burns and Wesley C. Mitchell, *Measuring Business Cycles* (New York, 1946), p. 78.
2. Gustav Cassel, *The Theory of Social Economy*, trans. Joseph McCabe (New York, 1924), p. 508.
3. London *Economist*, CLXXIX (May 5, 1888), 567.

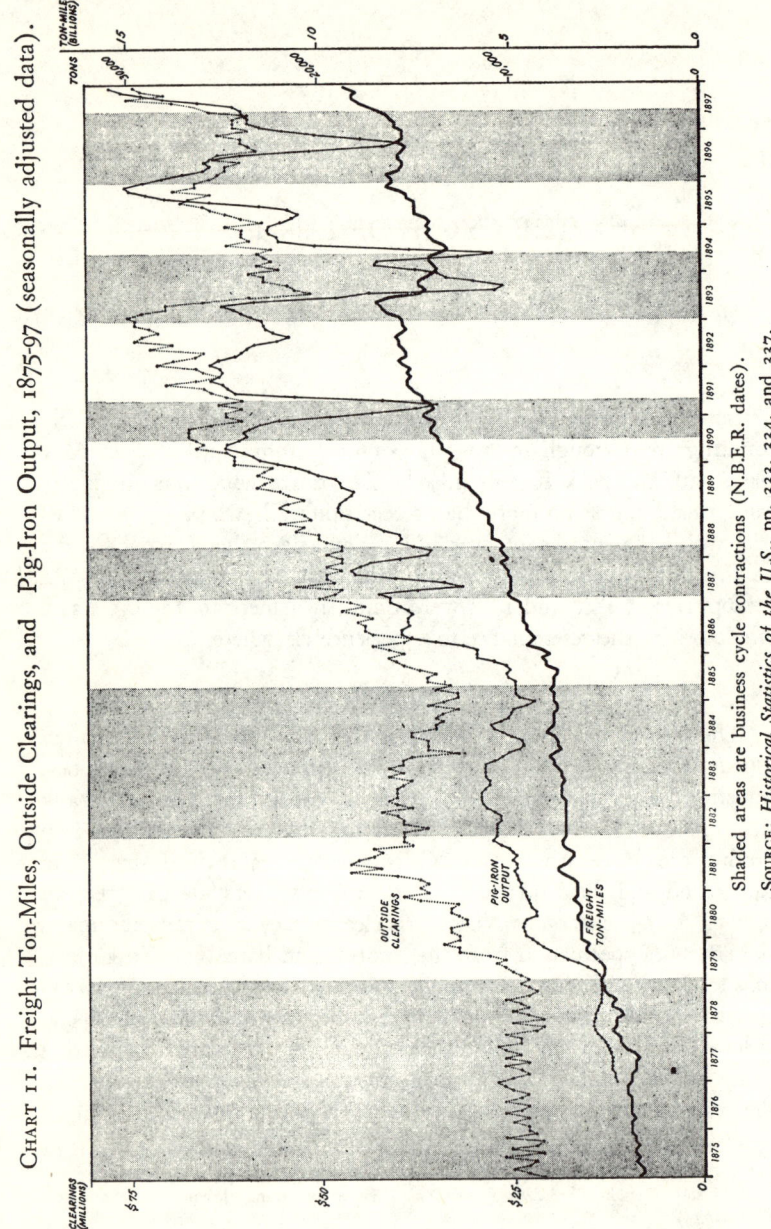

CHART 11. Freight Ton-Miles, Outside Clearings, and Pig-Iron Output, 1875-97 (seasonally adjusted data).

Shaded areas are business cycle contractions (N.B.E.R. dates).

SOURCE: *Historical Statistics of the U.S.*, pp. 333, 334, and 337.

1887 until the year's end. About 1888 as a whole, the *Bankers' Magazine* said, "Few industries have been idle, and the number of unemployed has been below the average. . . ."[4] Nevertheless, full employment in the sense of as many job vacancies as qualified jobseekers was probably not reached in 1888. Not only had there been a recession but in addition the work force was increasing 3 percent per year.

Three developments were mainly responsible for the revival during the last three quarters of 1888. First, building construction, after declining throughout the cyclical contraction, turned up, presumably in response to easier credit conditions. (See Chart 3.) Second, declining prices for iron and steel increased sales and output for this important industry, partly at the expense of imports. Third, crops were developing favorably for the United States—good crops at home, not so good crops abroad. (See Chart 6.) This had an immediate, favorable effect on expectations.

Aggregate railroad investment probably declined. The rise in maintenance and replacement expenditures and the increased demand for equipment were not enough to offset a drastic fall in building more railroad mileage. (Cf. Chart 4.) It is too bad that one cannot be more certain about the facts, because the case points to a remarkable kind of economic stability. An outlet for investment funds that accounted for more than 15 percent of gross capital formation during the eighties[5] went into a decline at a critical point in the business cycle. Nothing more should have been necessary to prolong the downswing, perhaps even to bring on a major depression. Yet in fact revival gathered momentum. One may surmise that the decline in railroad investment could not have been very great.[6]

Moreover, there was probably a small offset in the form of reduced corporate savings. Although railroad business increased in 1888, competition drove profits down. Dividends, as is usually the case, were not reduced nearly so much, with the result that undistributed profits went down perhaps $25 million.[7] But this was small in comparison with GNP, which was running in the vicinity of 10 or 12 billion dollars.

4. XLIII (Jan. 1889), 486.
5. Melville J. Ulmer, "Trends and Cycles in Capital Formation by United States Railroads, 1870-1950," N.B.E.R., Occasional Paper 43 (New York, 1954), p. 11.
6. *Ibid.*, p. 19. Ulmer's estimating method was such that no confidence can be placed in year to year changes.
7. U. S. Bureau of the Census, *Historical Statistics of the United States, 1789-1945* (Washington, D. C., 1949), pp. 200-1. Cf. *Investors' Supplement to the Chronicle*, XLVIII (Jan. 26, 1889), 1-2.

Despite the cyclical revival, there was no crowing over profits in 1888.[8] The money market, unlike the previous year, did not develop stringency.[9] According to the *Chronicle*, railroad securities continued to be exported in large quantities until the St. Paul passed its dividend in September.[10] Capital imports for the period 1885-90 have been estimated at more than a billion dollars.[11]

Exports did not revive until the fourth quarter of 1888, but thereafter continued to increase irregularly until near the end of the following year. (See Chart 9.) Imports also revived in the fourth quarter but not so rapidly. The merchandise balance gave the United States a distinct stimulus during the rest of the upswing. But there was no stimulus from the side of the federal government. (See Chart 10.) Budget expenditures increased very little prior to the middle of 1890, whereas receipts responded to the revival by rising steadily.

During 1889 the upswing continued unabated. Between the fourth quarters of 1888 and 1889, outside clearings rose 8 percent, railroad freight ton-miles 13 percent, and pig-iron production 14 percent. (See Chart 11.) The rise in building construction was especially marked. Crops were even better than in 1888, but their total value was markedly lower.[12] (See Chart 6.) Employment indexes of Jerome and Frickey both begin with 1889 and exhibit an increase during the year, although in the case of Jerome's the rise is negligible.

Although contemporary accounts differed as to the degree of prosperity achieved, they agreed that there were no symptoms of a boom. According to a more optimistic view, "In the business of the country at large, in agriculture, manufacturing, and general trade, there was great activity, and usually plenty of work, good wages, and fair profits to the capitalist. [But] there were several clouds which spread more or less gloom in certain quarters. Among these may be named the depression in wool and woolen manufactures, the decrease in anthracite coal production, the severe pressure of mortgages on the farmers in some parts of the West, together with the unprecedentedly

---

8. According to the *Bankers' Magazine*, "the . . . year has been one of the largest sales and smallest profits on record," XLIII (Jan. 1889), 487. In similar vein the *Chronicle* reported, "During 1888, while prices and profits have been by no means satisfactory, the volume of business has been steadily enlarging . . . ," XLVIII (Jan. 5, 1889), 6.

9. *Chronicle*, XLVIII (Jan. 5, 1889), 13.

10. *Ibid.*, p. 11.

11. C. J. Bullock, J. H. Williams, and R. S. Tucker, "The Balance of Trade of the United States," *Review of Economic Statistics*, I (July 1919), 226-27.

12. Cf. *Bankers' Magazine*, XLIV (Nov. 1889), 326-29, where it is reported that farmers were burning corn instead of coal.

THE CYCLE OF 1888-91

low prices of corn and oats. . . ."[13] In a pessimistic account, the year was neither "generally prosperous nor disastrous; and the business of this country has been neither good nor bad; but half and half."[14] The year "has probably been more disappointing and unsatisfactory, from a business point of view, than any of the past five; partly because more had been expected of it; and partly because the substantial and permanent improvement in the iron trade during 1888 . . . has not extended beyond some of its allied interests, while it has utterly failed to pull its closest ally—the coal trade—out of the worst Slough of Despond into which it has fallen since 1876-77. . . . The woolen manufacturing interests have had a still worse year than the coal trade. . . ."[15]

Aggregate earnings of the railroads improved, thanks to the Inter-State Railway Association, organized to prevent rate cutting.[16] Revenue per freight ton-mile declined only a little in 1889. Railroad investment presumably held up well, expenditures on maintenance of way and structures rising while the number of miles built continued to decline. Such building as occurred was confined to short lines and branches, with only two roads laying as many as forty miles in the first half of the year.[17]

"Iron was active beyond all expectations, and the demand increased in the later months of the year, pushing up prices of pig iron fully $2 per ton as compared with the closing prices of 1888. This general demand, for industrial purposes of all sorts, was the less anticipated, since it was well known that railroad construction was falling off. . . ."[18] As already noted, the price rise was in the face of a large increase in output, resulting from expansion of the industry, especially in the South.[19]

It is difficult to say what was happening to inventories. According to a traditional line of thought, good crops such as were experienced in 1888 and 1889 lead to inventory accumulation, stimulating the economy. The figures on visible stocks in the files of the N.B.E.R. indicate that this was not true for corn and cotton.[20] For the first half of the

---

13. *Chronicle*, L (Jan. 4, 1890), 10. Elsewhere on the same page, the *Chronicle* conceded that "profits were often small. . . ."
14. *Bankers' Magazine*, XLIV (Jan. 1890), 501.
15. *Ibid.*
16. *Chronicle*, L (Jan. 4, 1890), 12 and 14.
17. *Ibid.*, p. 12; *Bankers' Magazine*, XLIV (Aug. 1889), 98.
18. *Chronicle*, L (Jan. 4, 1890), 12.
19. *Bankers' Magazine*, XLIII (May 1889), 820.
20. Series 5,21 and 5,03. For cotton, this is contradicted by figures in *Bankers' Magazine*, XLIV (Jan. 1890), 506.

cyclical upswing, the same could be said of wheat and oats (the crop of wheat in 1888 was poor), but in the second half the visible supply of wheat rose a little, that of oats a great deal.[21] As far as they go, these figures fail to confirm the expectation. Evidence on the behavior of other kinds of stocks is scattered and inconclusive. The wool industry seems to have experienced a little inventory cycle of its own, accumulating stocks in 1888 and decumulating in 1889, partly under the pressure of hardening credit.[22] Stocks of cotton goods were said to be small, stocks of coal excessive.[23] The visible supply of petroleum declined 41,000 barrels.[24] Pig-iron stocks also fell off.

Late in the year, when the seasonal demand for money was at its height, stringency developed. Whereas the United States had net imports of $25 million of gold in the fiscal year 1888, $50 million was exported in the next fiscal year, even though the merchandise balance moved in a favorable direction. The most likely cause was a fluctuation in capital imports. The golden part of the money supply declined between June 30, 1888, and the same date in 1889; consequently, the money supply expanded very little. Deposits and loans, on the other hand, grew substantially. For the first time in a number of years, the autumnal demand for money lowered the reserves of the New York City banks below the legal minimum. Commercial paper rates rose noticeably, although not quite as much as in 1887, and call loan rates in extreme cases hit 30 and 40 percent.[25] (Cf. Chart 3.) The *Bankers' Magazine* commented that probably never before had such money and bank conditions existed with so little effect on business. Formerly, tight money had been regarded as an unfavorable symptom, likely to cause alarm, calling of call loans, and bear markets, but now the government policy of buying bonds as long as necessary had led the banks to exhaust their reserves without fear.[26] The force of the comment is vitiated somewhat because it was written early in the fall, before reserves fell below the legal minimum.

Credit conditions became easier in the first half of 1890. In part this was a normal seasonal development. In addition the gold supply increased a little. With the merchandise balance of trade continuing good, the United States exported very little gold during the fiscal year 1890. The country therefore was able to retain most of the excess of gold production over the amounts used in the arts. Meanwhile,

---

21. Series 5,01 and 5,84.
22. *Bankers' Magazine*, XLIV (Jan. 1890), 502.
23. *Ibid.*
24. *Ibid.*, p. 507.
25. *Chronicle*, L (Jan. 4, 1890), 13.
26. XLIV (Oct. 1889), 245.

the government's silver purchase policy was increasing one part of the currency supply while its policy of repaying debt (which served as backing for national bank notes) was decreasing another. The net result of these various forces was to increase currency outside the Treasury by 3.5 percent between the middle of 1889 and the middle of 1890. Presumably this was just about adequate for the rate at which the economy was growing, but not enough to prevent recurrence of stringency in the fall, let alone to provide a margin of safety. Consequently, although money conditions in the first half of 1890 were easier, they were not as easy as one would normally expect at this time of year.

In spite of this, the cyclical expansion continued throughout the first six months of 1890. Investment by the railroads probably increased, the downward trend in number of miles added being temporarily reversed. (See Chart 4.) Railroad building continued to be of the spur and feeder variety. Although the statistics on construction of buildings are conflicting, they indicate that investment in this direction was high and possibly increasing.[27] Helped out by railroad and building activity, pig-iron production kept rising until May, although some weakening of prices and accumulation of stocks indicated that output might be growing more rapidly than demand. (See Chart 11.)

Beginning with 1890 and continuing throughout the decade, exogenous events played an important role. The immediate impact of the first external shock was ambiguous. The legislative discussions that led to passage of the Sherman Silver Purchase Act in July and the McKinley Tariff Act in October induced expectations of rising prices. Although the evidence of speculative accumulation of inventories is scattered and untrustworthy, in this instance it is certainly reasonable to believe it; and the marked rise in imports during the second and third quarters, followed by a decline in the fourth, offers some corroboration. (See Chart 9.) To the extent that inventory accumulation represented increased imports, however, it had a deflationary impact, since it must have been financed with credit that otherwise would have been available for use within the country. To the extent that money was spent abroad, it contributed to the impending money stringency. The expectations set up by the silver bill

---

27. Blank's estimates of house building, one in current and the other in constant dollars, both show 1890 lower than 1889, but this is not inconsistent with a rise during the first half of 1890. David M. Blank, *The Volume of Residential Construction, 1869-1950*, N.B.E.R. (New York, 1954), p. 69.

worked in the opposite direction. In so far as they stimulated investment in stocks of home-produced goods, they increased spending. It is difficult to ascribe much net influence to these two pieces of legislation prior to the cyclical downturn, although the "buoyancy" that the *Chronicle* later attributed to the second quarter may very easily be ascribed to this source.[28]

The short-lived buoyancy was not a speculative boom. Throughout the first half of 1890, the *Bankers' Magazine* continued to take a gloomy view of the business situation, even saying the one hopeful aspect was that matters could not very well get any worse.[29] This was gross exaggeration, but it points up a characteristic of this upswing which is in contrast with those in the early eighteen seventies, the early eighteen eighties, and the late nineteen twenties—an absence of exuberance, recklessness, and (if outward symptoms can be trusted) high profits. The same can be said for the following upswing of 1891-92. In terms of the Schumpeterian schema, the secondary wave was almost nonexistent, as one might expect at the end of a Kondratieff cycle.

Upper Turning Point

The N.B.E.R. dates the cyclical peak in the third quarter of 1890, a decision with which there can be no quarrel.[30] The month chosen by the N.B.E.R. for the peak is July. It is rarely possible to select a precise month with much confidence. There must always be an arbitrary element in the choice. Moreover, for present purposes, the exact month is of little consequence.[31]

---

28. LII (Jan. 3, 1891), 9.   29. XLIV (Feb. 1890), 580.

30. This is the peak quarter in outside clearings and in Frickey's index of employment. Although liabilities of business failures and Jerome's index of factory employment had their peaks in the fourth quarter, the peak in pig-iron production came in the second. As will appear shortly, a narration of the events of the last half year makes the third quarter appear to be the peak. The amount of freight ton-miles in this instance gives no help since it went on rising throughout the cyclical downswing. Other statistics could be cited, but they would contribute little to the picture.

31. It does, however, help to have in mind a more exact picture of the turning point than the quarterly date gives. I am inclined to feel that no month earlier than July could reasonably be defended, whereas August or September are likely candidates. Persons, Hubbard, Ayres, and Partington all chose dates even later than September. It may be mentioned that the N.B.E.R. series on outside clearings and the B.L.S. series on wholesale prices have their peaks in September, and Jerome's index of factory employment (which for this period is based on Massachusetts data only) did not reach its peak until the following January. Thus the third quarter may be called the peak in the complete sense: each of the three months composing it was probably higher than any of the months immediately preceding or following.

THE CYCLE OF 1888-91

The downturn occurred mainly because exogenous events caused prolonged monetary disturbance. Contrary to the usual seasonal pattern, stringency in the New York money market developed early in the summer, the direct result of a drain of gold abroad. Much of British foreign investment had been going to Argentina. A period of growing economic difficulties there were climaxed by a revolution. British financial houses were caught with a large amount of Argentine securities which they could neither sell, except at ruinous prices, nor obtain advances upon. In order to raise funds to keep their businesses going, they sold their good securities, American as well as British. The resulting gold drain, coming at a time when bank reserves were none too plentiful, led to tight money which persisted and intensified during the rest of the year.[32]

One intensifying factor was passage of the Sherman Act in July, providing for increased monetization of silver. Its domestic consequences will be discussed below. Internationally, it gave foreigners another reason for selling American securities.[33] Its importance was not as great in 1890 as later when the threat to the gold standard became clearer, but its passage initiated a period of more than six years of distrust of American money and a reversal of the normal flow of foreign capital into the United States. Perhaps a billion dollars of American securities were sold abroad in the late eighties, an average of $200 million a year, with a substantial reverse flow between 1890 and the end of 1896.[34] Not much confidence can be placed in the figures, but if they are anywhere nearly right, they indicate a shift of prime importance. A net change in capital imports on the order of a quarter of a billion dollars a year in an economy with a national income of perhaps twelve billion could not fail to have a marked effect on its investment, money supply, rate of progress, job opportunities and immigration. The reversal of the capital movement cannot be blamed solely on the Sherman Act, nor can the depression of the nineties be blamed solely on capital movements. But they go a long way toward explaining the recession of 1890-91.

At first the money stringency probably had little effect on business other than to slow down expansion. Loans, discounts, and the money supply continued to grow. During the rest of the year there were

---

32. London *Economist,* CXC (Feb. 21, 1891), 1; *Chronicle,* LII (Jan. 3, 1891), 10-12; *Bankers' Magazine,* XLV (Aug. 1890), 86-87; and William J. Lauck, *The Causes of the Panic of 1893* (Boston and New York, 1907), pp. 63-78.
33. *Chronicle,* LII (Jan. 3, 1891), 10.
34. Bullock *et al.,* "Balance," pp. 226-27.

recurrent periods of stringency, climaxing in November. A gold drain of $16 million in nine weeks led the New York banks, faced with the usual fall drain of money to the interior, to contract call loans in August. Interest shot to what would be fantastic rates for any other type of loan. The Treasury came to the rescue by offering to redeem $20 million of bonds before maturity,[35] thus performing a function which normally belongs to a central bank. It came to the rescue again in September when some speculators "cornered" the Treasury, going long on government bonds and short on the stock market at a time when importers were borrowing to acquire stocks in anticipation that the higher duties of the McKinley tariff would go into effect in October.[36] Thus they at once drove down stock prices, creating fears of a panic, and drove up prices of government bonds, so that when the Treasury felt compelled to relieve the situation by buying governments, it profited on both ends of the operation. There was further stringency in October. Then on November 11, the firm of Decker, Howell & Co. failed, involving a prominent bank and nearly creating a banking panic. Prompt issuance of clearing house certificates, which banks short of reserves could use to meet adverse balances at the clearing house, averted the danger. Four days after the failure of Decker, Howell & Co. came the collapse of Baring Bros. in London, a delayed reaction to the Argentine problem. Because it was followed by near panic there, more selling of American securities, and increased stringency here, the crisis of 1890 is usually associated with the name of Baring. Although runs on banks were avoided, there is some evidence of hoarding.[37] The pressure to contract fell almost entirely on the New York banks—the interior drain of cash was met so effectively by the Treasury that the cash reserves of the banks as a whole fell very little between July and December, but the country banks increased their reserves at the expense of the reserve city banks.[38] Thereafter, the London crisis eased, the seasonal need for money subsided, business activity contracted, and the money situation grew easier.

Meantime, the monetary disturbance had set in motion a downswing. The reversal of capital imports has already been noted. In addition, the money problems restricted railroad building by making

35. *Bankers' Magazine*, XLV (Sept. 1890), 177.
36. *Ibid.*, XLV (Oct. 1890), 248-49. Subsequently the effective date of the new tariff was postponed.
37. *Ibid.*, XLV (Jan. 1891), 489.
38. Oliver M. W. Sprague, *History of Crises Under the National Banking System*, 61st Congress, 2d Session, Senate Doc. No. 538 (Washington, D. C., 1910), p. 147.

it difficult to sell bonds[39] and put on pressure to liquidate inventories.[40] Very likely it also was responsible for initiating the decline in building construction recorded by Long's index of permits.[41]

Such is the principal explanation for the downturn of 1890, but a number of other factors need to be discussed. The value of exports, seasonally adjusted, fell off irregularly from $80.9 million in October 1889 to $62.4 million in August 1890. Converted to an annual rate, the decline appears quite large, even after allowance is made for the distortion involved in comparing the very highest month with the very lowest. It helps explain why expansion came to an end as soon as it did and why the gold supply was not greater when the Argentine crisis developed. But exports rose in the last four months of 1890, exceeding the corresponding period of the preceding year. This countercyclical behavior forbids giving exports a prominent place in the explanation of the downturn.

Crops were poor in 1890. Ordinarily, this would be an unfavorable influence, perhaps one of decisive importance. But in this case world prices were high, with the result that farm income actually rose. (Chart 6.) American farmers apparently disinvested in inventories.[42] Adverse effects were confined mainly to worsening prospects for some of the railroads.

In Schumpeter's account, the two and a half years from the beginning of 1889 to the middle of 1891 represent the prosperity phase of a Juglar (ten-year) cycle, i.e., a burst of innovating activity. This implies that the contraction of 1890-91 belongs to a Kitchin cycle, if it fits into his schema at all.[43] In his later thought Schumpeter leaned to the view that Kitchins were not caused by innovation. Fields of innovation mentioned by Schumpeter include alloys; organization of Carnegie Steel, Illinois Steel, Colorado Fuel and Steel, Edison

39. *Chronicle*, LII (Jan. 3, 1891), 11.
40. *Bankers' Magazine*, XLV (Dec. 1890), 412, and *ibid.*, XLV (Jan. 1891), 492.
41. Series 2,04 in the files of the N.B.E.R., or Clarence D. Long, Jr., *Building Cycles and the Theory of Investment* (Princeton, N. J., 1940), p. 228.
42. *Chronicle*, LIV (Jan. 9, 1892), 48.
43. "The sixth Juglar (1889 to 1897) illustrates our proposition about the irregularity of panics or crises. The course of things in the last quarter of 1890 and the first half of 1891 interrupted and distorted what, nevertheless, we consider as the prosperity phase of that Juglar," *Business Cycles*, I, 396-97. This passage makes it appear that the contraction of 1890-91 is an irregularity, which Schumpeter would explain in terms similar to those used above. His three-cycle schema, however, would lead us to expect a Kitchin recession and depression at precisely this time. Cf. the illustrative chart, *ibid.*, I, 213. Probably Schumpeter thought that the Kitchin was more pronounced than usual as a result of the monetary disturbance.

Electric Light, Edison General Electric, American Tobacco, and International Harvester; fertilizers; glass (tank furnaces); Portland Cement; electric trolleys.[44]

A shortage of investment opportunities had little part to play in the downturn of 1890. Although both railroad investment and construction of buildings later went into an extended decline, 1892 indicates that in favorable circumstances they could still absorb a large volume of investment funds. By 1890 they were more closely dependent both on general business prosperity and on ease of raising funds than formerly on account of the near saturation that had already occurred; and in that sense a weakening of investment opportunities, by making the economy more vulnerable to disturbances, contributed to the downturn of 1890. Contemporary accounts mention the growth of municipal bonds, as well as "industrials," as outlets for investment funds.

Evidence on the behavior of inventories is scattered but, such as it is, does not indicate an inventory cycle like Metzler's theory. The main exception is pig iron. Although the peak in price had been reached in January and the peak in output in May (see Chart 11), stocks were low at the beginning of summer, and there was some evidence that a shortage of pig iron was a bottleneck.[45] By the end of the year, stocks of pig iron had built up to unprecedented heights, even though output had declined. Although the picture is complicated by the money stringency, which reduced demand, output apparently had caught up with needs; this permitted stocks to accumulate to desired levels and beyond. Something similar may have happened to the shoe industry.[46] Aside from these industries, either stocks were low at the end of 1890 compared to a year previous in consequence of monetary conditions,[47] or they had been built up in anticipation of the McKinley tariff[48] and of free silver.

The McKinley Tariff Act, providing increased protection, had mixed effects. Along with the silver bill, it led to expectations of higher prices and created for the moment the appearance of new in-

---

44. *Ibid.*, I, 383-96.

45. "Some branches of the iron trade have been very active the past month, with larger orders in the market than could be placed, because mills would not contract far ahead, in view of the limited supply of pig iron. The pipe mills especially have been driven beyond their capacity. . ." —*Bankers' Magazine*, XLV (Aug. 1890), 90.

46. *Bankers' Magazine*, XLV (Nov. 1890), 326.

47. *Ibid.*, XLV (Jan. 1891), 492; *ibid.*, XLV (Dec. 1890), 412-13; *ibid.*, XLV (Oct. 1890), 250-52; *Chronicle*, LII (Jan. 3, 1891), 11.

48. *Economist*, CXC (Feb. 21, 1891), Supplement, 1-2; *Bankers' Magazine*, XLV (Oct. 1890), 251.

vestment opportunities in the protected industries.[49] But the election of 1890 made it uncertain how long protection would last.[50] Meanwhile, the act induced stocking of imported commodities, contributing to the money stringency without increasing domestic business.[51]

The effects of the Sherman Silver Purchase Act on domestic anticipations add less to the explanation of the 1890 downturn than to the picture of how the business community reacted to legislation it disliked. The subject is of general interest, since external events are part of the field of business cycle analysis; and one of the most difficult problems concerns how much the political and social developments that businessmen deplore affect their business decisions. Is it plausible to blame the stagnation of the nineteen thirties on the New Deal? Should public policy in the nineteen fifties give first priority to increasing confidence?

The belief in the spring of 1890 that a free silver bill would become law gave rise to inflationary expectations. This would not in itself be remarkable, since the bill was designed to be inflationary. What seems strange is the reaction to the free silver threat later in the decade, which appears to have been entirely adverse. The behavior in 1890 is hard to reconcile with one aspect of the usual interpretation of 1896.

But the free silver bill did not become law after all. In its place Congress passed the Sherman Act, providing that the Treasury should purchase 4,500,000 ounces of silver a month, issuing Treasury currency to a corresponding extent. This compromise eventually proved worse than either a full gold standard or free silver, but this was not anticipated. Instead, it was felt that the Sherman Act would provide some stimulus to business by making money more plentiful without leading to inflation and ultimate collapse.[52]

In sum, the net effect of silver legislation in 1890 was close to zero. On the one hand, it contributed something to a reversal of the international capital flow which would have taken place anyhow. On the other hand, it gave rise to favorable domestic expectations.

Downswing and Upturn

By early 1891 the attitude toward silver had already undergone a subtle change. The Sherman Act had failed to prevent a shortage

49. *Bankers' Magazine*, XLV (Nov. 1890), 323-24.
50. London *Economist*, CXC (Feb. 21, 1891), Supplement, 1-2.
51. It seems to me that the *Economist* exaggerated the unfavorable effects of the tariff on the business situation in the United States, largely because it was well aware of its unfavorable effects on business in the United Kingdom.
52. *Chronicle*, LI (July 12, 1890), 34-35; *Bankers' Magazine*, XLIV (May 1890), 824-25 and 828; *ibid.*, XLV (Aug. 1890), 96.

of money in November, and perhaps this in an irrational way had something to do with the change in sentiment. By January, stringency had been replaced by surfeit, yet neither the stock market nor commodity prices had gone up. "The chief reason for this," according to a contemporary account, "is the distrust created in the minds, both of investors and those engaged in mercantile or industrial calling, in regard to the basis of future values, as dependent on the financial legislation now pending in Congress. Everybody is still delaying new commitments, either for investment or for the development of new, or the extension of old enterprises, until the silver question is settled, for the present session of Congress at least."[53]

Any account that blames unfavorable business developments on unfavorable political developments is subject to a discount which sometimes may properly be set as high as 100 percent. The temptation to blame the malfunctionings of a system one likes on interferences one dislikes is irresistible; and when the interferences are indeed at fault, the fault is sure to be exaggerated. Besides, it is always easier to explain events on grounds of obvious external factors than on the inner workings of the economy; this was particularly true in 1891 when understanding of the business cycle was at a primitive stage. The silver agitation in Congress could not be taken to explain declining activity in the winter of 1891 even if the expectations of the writer of the passage from which the above quotation is taken had not been clearly disappointed, as he later admitted.[54] The quotation has been given here partly to record when the change in attitude toward silver took place, partly as a clear example of why one must be cautious in assessing better founded allegations of the same sort that were made a few years later. Decline in the winter of 1891 can be accounted for by the normal workings of the contraction mechanism following the events of 1890. The problem is to explain not why contraction occurred but why it was so short and mild.

The N.B.E.R. dates the trough in May. The contraction lasted only ten months, making it one of the shortest on record, comparable to that in 1887-88 and shorter than that in 1948-49. Closer examination makes it look shorter still. Decline was barely perceptible until the autumn of 1890; nor was there much decline in the month or so prior to May 1891. The contraction appears more pronounced than that of 1887-88, partly though not entirely because it began and ended

---

53. *Bankers' Magazine,* XLV (Feb. 1891), 574.
54. *Ibid.,* XLV (April 1891), 750.

THE CYCLE OF 1888-91

more spectacularly. From the highest month to the lowest, outside clearings declined 11 percent. (See Chart 11.)

Since analysis of the upturn hinges on the precise date of the trough, it is necessary to go into details. Liabilities of business failures, naturally enough, were at their peak in the last quarter of 1890, the time of the so-called crisis. The trough of orders of rails came in the same quarter; for railroad equipment, in the first quarter of 1891. Frickey's index of employment declined only in the first quarter of 1891, and very slightly at that; Jerome's index behaved similarly. Long's index of building permits reached bottom in January, of outside clearings and number of incorporations, in March, of pig-iron production, in April (see Chart 11). Thus enough important series were going up by May to make it implausible to believe the cyclical trough should be dated later.

Until August, however, revival was not obvious. "The first seven months [of 1891] formed a period of depression, low prices and meagre profits. The last five months were marked by a decided hopefulness in tone, extraordinary buoyancy at times in Stock Exchange securities, and a moderate improvement in business towards the close of the year in all parts of the country except the South."[55] Although the *Bankers' Magazine* noted signs of revival as early as March, it observed later that "The general business situation has not improved during the midsummer month, but has been more stagnant than usual. . . ."[56] Thus the transition from contraction to expansion was gradual, as is often the case, extending over a period of perhaps as much as five months.

The upturn is generally attributed to a coincidence, similar to that in 1879, of bumper crops in the United States and crop failure in the rest of the world. Wesley C. Mitchell was emphatic, declaring that this was the only case between 1890 and 1911 in which a propitious event caused the upturn; in other cases, propitious events merely aided a revival that had already started by itself.

Although this view requires qualification, there can be no doubt that the crop situation was of first importance. It explains why American experience sharply diverged from European, prosperity returning here while business grew worse abroad. In the fiscal year 1892, American exports increased about $150 million over 1891, at least 1 percent of GNP, in spite of foreign depression. (See Chart 9.) When the effects of the multiplier, induced investment (for instance,

---

55. *Chronicle*, LIV (Jan. 9, 1892), 56.
56. XLVI (Aug. 1891), 96.

in railroad equipment),[57] improved anticipations, and reversal of gold exports are all allowed for, here was an external event with a great deal of leverage. Moreover, the impact on export statistics in value terms first became marked in August, precisely the month when business revival first became clearly noticeable.

But this is not to agree fully with Mitchell's statement that the propitious event "cut short what promised to be an extended period of liquidation . . . and suddenly set the tide of business rising."[58] If the trough occurred no later than May and was preceded by a month or two of virtual stability, the end of "liquidation" cannot be attributed to the direct effects of crops on exports. True, inasmuch as winter crops abroad failed, there was some impact on our exports in early spring, but this would hardly be guessed from looking at the statistics.[59] If the end of contraction in early spring and the ensuing period of stability are to be explained by crops, the explanation must proceed via expectations.

It is therefore necessary to review anticipations during the critical months. The *Bankers' Magazine* first reported on the crop prospects at the beginning of April.[60] In its next issue, it said,

The month of April has seen an almost complete revolution in public sentiment in regard to the future of business and values in this country. Since the panic of last fall, fear, doubt and foreboding of evil to come, have hung over the business and markets of this country. . . . But during the past month all this has given way to higher prices and unusual activity in our produce, and especially our breadstuffs markets, has finally extended to the market for railway shares, is now beginning to revive the iron and other allied trades, and will soon communicate to all manufacturing industries, all because the agricultural prospects of this country have suddenly and unexpectedly become brighter than in ten years.[61]

But in the same issue it also said,

There has been more uneasiness, however, in business circles, toward the close of the month, over the prospects of the money market next fall, when the great crops in prospect will be moved earlier and in larger volume than usual, and on a higher range of prices to meet the deficit in the crops of Europe, which will require more money than for many

---

57. *Bankers' Magazine*, XLV (May 1891), 844.
58. Wesley C. Mitchell, *Business Cycles* (Berkeley, Calif., 1913), p. 453.
59. As fine an economist as Sprague attributed the gold outflow of the first half of 1891 to a decline of exports resulting from liquidation in Europe (*History of Crises*, p. 154).
60. XLV (1891), 756-57.
61. XLV (May 1891), 837.

years; and at a time when the Treasury of the United States for the first time in years will be unable to come to the relief of the money market, should it need it. . . . On the other hand, however, the very cause of such a stringency, should it occur, will, in time, bring its own relief, in imports of gold from Europe, to pay for their heavy exports of our wheat and flour. . . ."[62]

The next month's report was similar,[63] with the additional observation that "London has begun buying our railway shares again, for the first time since the panic. This occurred near the end of the month, because of Europe's big crop deficit and our large surplus, which insures increased earnings for American railways the coming year."[64]

Although it did not recant previous comments, the next month it threw doubt on how significant the revolution in sentiment really was: "The first month of the summer [June] has been one of suspense rather than important development . . . to business in general. . . . few have cared or dared anticipate the future. . . ."[65] Moreover, "The iron trade has shown very little change in price or activity in demand, as the railroad interests are slow about placing orders for new rails or equipment. . . ."[66] At the beginning of August it reported, "The absence of speculation and the general fear of tight money have made both banks and business houses trim their sails for a squally autumn. The enormous exports of gold since the first of January have also tended in the same direction. . . ."[67] Despite enormous crops and the favorable outlook for the railroads, "there is not yet enough confidence in the future of these great properties to enable them to sell their equally enormous crop of new bonds, to say nothing of their stocks. . . . The roads themselves generally seem to be in an unsatisfactory condition financially, even with the enormous crops . . . , as they are still suffering from last year's short ones, and their depleted equipment for handling these crops is not yet being renewed."[68] This was causing stagnation in the iron trade.

In sum, the crop situation had a decided effect on expectations as early as April, soon enough to have been a factor in ending the contraction of business activity. The purely negative contribution of ending the pessimism that characterizes cyclical downswings, particu-

62. P. 840.
63. XLV (June 1891), 933.
64. *Ibid.*, p. 935.
65. XLVI (July 1891), 17.
66. *Ibid.*, p. 24.
67. XLVI (1891), 98. Cf. p. 96: "Higher time rates have brought new enterprises to a halt."
68. *Ibid.*, pp. 99-100. Of course, this exaggerates the importance of crops for railroad earnings.

larly one that follows an international crisis, should not be discounted. Until August the favorable anticipations led more to a policy of watchful waiting for the anticipations to materialize than to positive action. Moreover, there was an offset because the crop conditions also led to fears, however foolish, of renewed monetary disturbances.

Hence, without denying that favorable anticipations played a positive role, one can doubt that the role was of great importance. Unlike the contraction of 1887-88, the downswing did not simply come to an end by itself, and the incident does not demonstrate that the American economy was stable. Yet its responsiveness to such a small influence (plus easy money conditions) is itself an indication of stability. The crop situation could not have taken effect so promptly—nor could it have had so great an effect later—had not conditions generally, and investment opportunities particularly, been favorable for the time being.

Now to define the sense in which Mitchell's statement, cited above, is correct. Given the decline in business activity abroad,[69] the silver policy of the United States, the gold exports, and the reluctance of foreigners to invest here, the United States in the absence of a propitious event would have been dragged down by Europe, would have encountered so much sooner the difficulties in maintaining the gold standard that were to plague Cleveland's second administration, and might easily have wound up in a banking panic before 1893. In this sense, the crop coincidence temporarily saved the United States and caused the upturn. But to say that a combination of unpropitious external events will plunge an economy into depression in the absence of a countering propitious one is not to say that that economy, if undisturbed, would have experienced extensive liquidation by virtue of its internal operation.

Conclusion

Both turning points resulted primarily from events abroad, with complications from domestic legislation, rather than from the internal workings of the American cyclical mechanism. What would have happened in the absence of outside disturbances is problematical. The expansion might have continued for a year or so longer and then come to an end because of those fundamental factors—using up of investment opportunities and Schumpeter's competing-down process—that in fact entered into the crisis of 1893.

69. Of course, business might have recovered abroad if the crop situation had not been unfavorable to Europe.

THE CYCLE OF 1888-91

But the decision to treat international disturbances as external events in this study, however advisable as a way to delimit the subject, involves taking an unduly narrow view. No doubt the international downturn of 1890 could be analyzed as the inevitable result of the international upswing. Although from the standpoint of the United States the recession of 1890-91 was nothing but an irregularity with very little claim to the name "cycle," in a broader view the United States shared in 1890 (although not in 1891) a movement of a fundamental sort.

The downturn of 1890, to revert to the more narrow view, is interesting as one of the few cases that almost certainly could have been avoided by more elasticity in the money supply. In the absence of a central bank, a more rapid increase in the gold supply would have been helpful. This raises the problem of the international gold standard and its mechanism of adjustment. The modern theory, based on the work of Ohlin[70] and Keynes, relies on income effects rather than the classical gold flows. The modern theory has a basic fault: the process it describes is not likely to be fully equilibrating. There is no reason to believe that the income effects from an initial disequilibrium in the balance of payments will be precisely enough to restore equilibrium. Accordingly, the modern theory alone is inadequate to explain why the gold standard worked successfully over a period of decades.

The modern theory supplanted the classical because economists came to doubt that the money supply had much influence on the level of activity. The downturn of 1890 shows gold performing an equilibrating function, keeping the United States in line with the rest of the world. Not in the classical way, to be sure; but the instance supports the hypothesis that gold could on occasion play a supplementary role.

The way that gold took effect in 1887 as well as in 1890 requires further discussion. Statistics are not available to establish that the total money supply actually contracted in either of those years, although some contraction very likely took place in the fall of 1890. Whether or not an expansion of the money supply is a necessary condition for cyclical expansion has not been settled. Some still maintain that stability of aggregate demand (i.e., a money supply increasing no more rapidly than is needed to offset the secular decline in velocity) is the proper goal for governmental policy. The position that the money

---

70. Bertil Ohlin, *Interregional and International Trade* (Cambridge, Mass., 1935), Part V.

supply itself should be held constant is not altogether without adherénts. Certainly if a cyclical upswing is financed by an increase in money, cessation of monetary expansion will produce maladjustments which could easily cause business to turn down. An industry like construction builds up capacity and a work force whose activities are financed by new credit; once the supply of new credit gets shut off or seriously reduced, the industry must contract. To be sure, with the money supply constant it is possible for some other industry to expand simultaneously, but this is not likely to take place rapidly enough. Even a marked slowing down in the rate of increase in the money supply can produce maladjustments.[71] The argument does not and cannot use the secular decline in velocity, inasmuch as in the short run velocity tends to rise during cyclical expansion. Nor does it necessarily require that investment be sensitive to small changes in the interest rate, since credit rationing is all that is needed. The argument, however, is akin to the shortage-of-capital theories. The difference is that the shortage-of-capital theories are aggregative, trouble arising because the total supply of loanable capital is inadequate. The present argument is in terms of the supply of capital to a particular market through a particular channel which gets cut off.

71. Saying this does not imply going as far as Warburton, who seems to think that a drop of the rate of increase of money to something like 3% a year is sufficient to cause a downturn. Clark Warburton, "Hansen and Fellner on Full Employment Policies," *American Economic Review*, XXXVIII (March 1948), 128-34. See also his "Quantity and Frequency of Use of Money in the United States, 1919-45," *Journal of Political Economy*, LIV (Oct. 1946), 436-50.

10

THE CYCLE OF 1891-94

THE BUSINESS CYCLE that reached a peak in January 1893 and a trough in June 1894 was peculiar to the United States of America. For the rest of the industrial world, the Baring crisis of 1890 marked the beginning of a protracted decline, which continued until the middle nineties. In the United States, depression was postponed until 1893. When it came, it was characterized by violent banking troubles from which other countries were free.

Upswing

Although the cyclical trough came in the second quarter, recovery during the rest of 1891 was less obvious to contemporary observers, except in crops and exports, than it is in modern statistics. Nearly twice as much pig iron was produced in December as in March. The rise in building permits was nearly as great. Railroad freight ton-miles and outside clearings showed modest gains. (See Chart 11.)

Contemporary accounts registered cautious optimism over the future rather than elation over the present. They described the improvement as moderate, making due qualifications for the South, where the large cotton crop had brought low prices and depression; they noted the reduced construction of track mileage by the railroads and the unwillingness of foreigners to invest in the United States. This attitude persisted through much of 1892. Although gains in output were recognized, what mainly attracted attention was low profits. Even at the end of the year, when the view grew rosier as the debacle grew nearer, the rosy view was expressed only with qualification. There was no exuberance.

Gross capital expenditures by railroads probably reached a new high at about this time.[1] Journalists of the day would hardly have agreed. Railroad mileage built, although somewhat higher in 1892 than in 1891, was at a level that a decade earlier would have been associated with depression. Nor did railroads seem to contemporary observers to be buying equipment at anything like the rate needed for the large crops; and the price of pig iron continued to sag. With foreigners unreceptive to American securities and the American public bemused by "industrials" or trusts, the railroads had no easy time floating securities.

Nevertheless, it would be difficult to explain the high output of 1892 on the hypothesis that railroad investment reached its peak in 1887 when 13,000 miles were built and then fell off proportionately to the decline in additions to track, for then one would have to discover some other form of investment to fill the gap, and such obvious candidates as foreign trade and building construction are scarcely enough, apart from induced investment,[2] to stimulate the rate of growth between 1887 and 1892, let alone fill any gaps.[3] Orders for railroad equipment in fact were high. Cash from new security issues on the New York Stock Exchange rose in 1892. Building new mileage and adding equipment are not the most likely forms of investment at this stage of the game; all sorts of improvements—reducing grades, replacing wooden bridges, building new stations—are more appropriate.[4] One need not doubt that railroad investment was high in 1892.

But railroads did not provide the driving force for expansion, as they had done after the Civil War. Opportunities for profitable investment constituted an underlying favorable factor, but their exploitation required a favorable economic climate. They created a situation in which some autonomous force could have powerful effect but did not themselves constitute such a force. That role was

1. Melville J. Ulmer, "Trends and Cycles in Capital Formation by United States Railroads, 1870-1950," N.B.E.R., Occasional Paper 43 (New York, 1954), pp. 19 and 60. Net capital expenditures appear a little lower than the peak in the early eighties. In both the gross and the net figures, annual data place the peak in 1893, but this need not be taken seriously in view of Ulmer's method of estimation.

2. Induced investment must be excluded because the difficulty is to find any kind of investment, induced or autonomous, to fill the gap.

3. Between two cyclical peaks, such as 1887 and 1892, GNP in current dollars could hardly have increased at less than 3% a year compounded annually (the secular rate of growth of real output appears to have been higher than this), or something like one and a half or two billion for the five-year period. On a fiscal year basis, exports rose only $300 million in the same period. (See Chart 9.)

4. *Bankers' Magazine*, XLVII (Nov. 1892), 329-30.

played by the crop coincidence, which led to a rise of exports by $150 million in the fiscal year 1892, providing through the multiplier and induced investment the needed stimulus and through the gold flow the needed monetary base.

Although bountiful harvests created such a shortage of railroad equipment in the winter of 1891-92 that it was referred to as a "blockade,"[5] although dividends and earnings improved in 1892, and although all this contributed temporarily to a high rate of investment, the longer-run prospects of the railroads were not good. Much of their bonded indebtedness had been incurred at a time when bond yields were more than 6 percent instead of less than 4 percent; and despite opportunities for refunding at lower rates, older roads that had not been through bankruptcy could not entirely rid themselves of the burden. This might not have mattered if the competitive struggle had not been continually lowering freight rates. The competitive struggle temporarily had a salutary effect, since it meant that each railroad found it imperative to invest in improvements, but the ultimate results were bound to be very different.[6] Political hostility toward railroads was growing and had a perceptible effect on railroad building. Railroad investment of an autonomous character had been financed by a combination of local capital, motivated by desire for local development, with outside capital of a risk-taking (if not reckless) nature. With virtual completion of the railroad network, the former source dried up; and with repeated experience of bankruptcy, the latter was more and more disillusioned. Even in 1892 railroad profits turned out to be a disappointment; and although statistics are not available for verification, one can see in contemporary sources how this episode might have contributed to Mitchell's hypothesis that profits decrease toward the end of expansion.[7]

The iron and steel industry exhibits a similiar picture. Pig-iron output was stimulated to a new high for the fiscal year 1892. (Cf. Chart 11.) But the pace was not maintained: from the peak in February 1892, output fell off one sixth by September; then it started

---

5. E.g., *Bankers' Magazine,* XLVI (April 1892), 764.

6. Since some of the investment in equipment was in response to physical shortages, it may be interpreted in terms of the acceleration principle, but investment in improvements was of a very different sort even though it may in a sense be regarded as induced rather than autonomous.

7. "Increased gross and reduced net earnings, is the disappointing story told of the late enormous traffic of our great railway systems, by their last monthly statements just published"—*Bankers' Magazine,* XLVII (Dec. 1892), 409. Cf. Wesley C. Mitchell, *Business Cycles* (Berkeley, Calif., 1913), pp. 494-503.

a revival which, strangely, continued beyond the cyclical peak, though without regaining the level of February 1892. Very likely some kind of inventory cycle lurks behind this behavior. More significant is the behavior of the price of pig iron, which continued with very little interruption the decline that had set in prior to the cyclical peak in 1890. Complaints about profits were mixed with complaints that older plants could compete with the newer. This implies that investment was probably taking place, though one cannot tell how fast or how it compared with the years of rapid increase in output between 1885 and 1890. For this purpose the low of 1885, a cyclical trough, should not be compared with the high of 1890. To gauge the growth in capacity (and thereby get a rough idea of the investment needed), the best comparison is between the peak month of 1890 and the peak month in the neighborhood of the cyclical peak of 1882. This comparison shows more than a doubling of output compared to a rise of about 3 percent between the peaks of 1890 and 1892. Between 1885 and 1890 obsolescent firms could enjoy a tolerable existence because demand was rising rapidly, but after the latter year their position became increasingly more difficult.[8]

Discussion of other industries such as coal and dry goods might be attempted, but it would have to be based on still less adequate information and would not yield substantially different results.[9]

Except for failures, which were exceedingly low, the upswing of 1891-92 conforms with unusual clarity to Schumpeter's concept of recession. This, of course, involves no paradox, since Juglar recession in the three-cycle schema encompasses the revival, prosperity, and recession phases of the Kitchin. Schumpeter dated Juglar recession

8. Cf. Mitchell's comment that because the liquidation of 1891 was interrupted, it had not cleaned out all the weak firms, so that at the beginning of 1893 their banking creditors were not as sound as they seemed (*ibid.*, p. 54).

9. A quotation may serve to summarize the situation: "no one would hesitate to say that 1892 has proved far more prosperous than either 1891 or 1890. . . . But . . . if we were to gather accurately the consensus of the whole business community, the result obtained would not support the idea that this has been a conspicuously prosperous year. Consumption of almost every article of merchandise has been large and the cotton goods industry has probably thrived beyond any other; the grocery trade in nearly all its branches has likewise enjoyed a good share of activity with fairly remunerative prices ruling. On the other hand, large and important departments of business and sections of the country have shared to a very small degree in the better conditions as to profitableness, while there has been almost everywhere an absence of buoyancy and an entire unwillingness to invest in undertakings at all venturesome. Stated in brief, we have apparently been in the midst of prosperous conditions, and yet as a people without achieving prosperity"—*Chronicle*, LVI (Jan. 7, 1893), 4-5. The *Economist*, CXCVIII (Jan. 14, 1893), 8, gave a similar summary of the American scene.

from the middle of 1891 to the middle of 1893.[10] If one takes account of the N.B.E.R.'s date for the peak of the business cycle, January 1893, one can call most of the first half of 1893 Kitchin (as well as Juglar) recession. Thus one can attribute expansion in the N.B.E.R. sense to the Kitchin, the absence of profits to the Juglar. The default of failures to conform to expectation can be laid at the door of an external event, the crop coincidence. The Kondratieff cycle too has a role to play. That the characteristics of recession stand out in unusual clarity can be explained on grounds that the Kondratieff of steam and steel was nearing its end and was imposing readjustments, the need for which had been accumulating over the entire epoch. The Kondratieff can be used in this way only if it is thought of as a two-phase cycle, consisting of prosperity and recession.[11]

The Upper Turning Point

The N.B.E.R.'s choice of January 1893 as the peak of the business cycle appears correct. It could not be wrong by more than a month.[12]

Once more the behavior of exports played a prominent part. In the fiscal year 1893 the value of merchandise exports declined a trifle

10. *Business Cycles,* I, 397. It would be more accurate to make April 1893 the last month of recession.

11. In Schumpeter's own exposition, the Kondratieff has four phases, so that the Juglar under discussion lies wholly within a Kondratieff revival—an awkward circumstance.

12. The peaks of the more important statistical series available exhibit a good deal of scatter. The highest month of pig-iron production came in February 1892, but there was a secondary peak in May of the following year. For orders of railroad equipment and for orders of rails, the peaks came in the first quarters of 1892 and 1893 respectively. The high for number of incorporations came in August 1892, for building permits and for both individual deposits and investments of national banks in September, for business failures (inverted) in the third quarter, for loans and discounts of national banks in December, for imports in January 1893, for outside clearings and wholesale prices and currency outside the Treasury in February, for employment in Massachusetts in April, for railroad gross earnings in May, for railroad freight ton-miles in June. By that time a larger proportion of series with acceptable conformity to business cycles was declining than at any time during the recession of 1887-88, although less than half of them were declining in the first two months of the year (Geoffrey H. Moore, "Statistical Indicators of Cyclical Revivals and Recessions," N.B.E.R., Occasional Paper 31 [New York, 1950], p. 14). Statistics therefore give little guidance to the exact date of the turning point. The usually pessimistic *Bankers' Magazine* reported there was improvement in January, paralysis in March (XLVII [Feb. 1893], 566; XLVII [April 1893], 782). Of February it said somewhat ambiguously, "The last month of the severest winter on record, for recent years, has not been characterized by any radical improvement in the business situation, when it has been about all the country could do to keep warm, from East to West, if not from North to South. The paralyzing breath of such extreme cold weather has affected every branch of trade, if not all industries," XLVII (March 1893), 644.

more than it had risen the previous year—almost $300 million, fully 2 percent of GNP. (See Chart 9.) This resulted from continued business contraction abroad and return to more normal crops. Even though expectations were not affected,[13] an economy growing at a rate of 4 percent a year could hardly have absorbed such a shock under the best of circumstances.[14] But quite apart from the silver situation, other circumstances were more favorable for collapse than for expansion.

It took time for declining exports to turn the tide. The monthly rate fell $10 million immediately after the bulge of the winter of 1891-92, not enough to stop the expansion. There was another drop of about the same extent at the onset of summer. For a time during the fall the downturn appears to have been stalled off by inventory accumulation—a shortage of railroad cars caused a blockade because freight cars were used for storage.[15] Near the end of the year there was yet another drop in exports of about $10 million per month. Then the expansion phase of the business cycle ended, and all the elements of weakness—weak firms, weak banking structure, weak gold standard, and weak investment opportunities—began to interact.

Contraction

The contraction of business proceeded in three well-marked stages. Although the first fits some of the dictionary meanings of the word "crisis," it does not fit the primary meaning of a "turning point." The turn was already past when the pyrotechnical stage began with the Reading failure on February 26. During this stage the contraction gathered momentum, accentuated by panics. It ended with the gold imports of August. During the ensuing fall, winter and early spring—the second or quiet stage—business activity was marked by cross currents with little decline in aggregate output. The third stage, which began in April, was characterized by labor troubles.

13. Ordinarily the crop situation of 1893 would have been satisfactory. The fact that a return to normal could constitute a deflationary shock was beyond the ken of people of the time.

14. If the multiplier were as low as 2 and if there were no repercussion on investment, the shock would temporarily reduce the rate of growth to zero. Since the multiplier operates only with a lag and there was a slight rise in exports in the next fiscal year, expansion need not cease entirely. But the assumption that investment would be entirely unaffected is drastic.

15. *Bankers' Magazine,* XLVII (Nov. 1892), 328-29. Statistics on visible stocks of wheat, oats and corn (but not cotton) seem to bear this out.

The pyrotechnical stage was above all characterized by failures, notably failures of railroads, iron and steel companies, and banks. The first spectacular failure, that of the Philadelphia and Reading on February 26, was in some respects typical. Its difficulties stemmed from two serious errors. On the one hand, it had attempted some fancy empire building in New England railroads, during which it incurred too much debt. On the other hand, as the leading figure in the anthracite coal cartel, it held up the price, enabling outsiders to cut into its business while the Reading piled up stocks of coal. Apparently it failed to cut production because it wanted its annual statement to make a good showing in terms of tonnage. To cap its troubles, early in 1893 the Reading borrowed $3 million in order to pay interest on its income bonds. When the end came, it had a floating debt of $18.5 million compared to cash and bills receivable of little more than $100,000.[16] That the failure involved railroads makes the Reading case typical of 1893. But the coal-cartel aspect differentiates it; and even the general recklessness with which the Reading was operated, although far from unique, does not seem to have been altogether characteristic.

Although the Reading failure precipitated trouble on the stock market, presumably led to liquidation of its anthracite inventories, and helped bring on pessimism, it was not a major factor by itself. It was merely an example which was repeated in ensuing weeks with variations and with smaller firms.

As time went on, failures became more and more associated with the financial situation. In the first quarter of 1893, net exports of gold from New York amounted to $29 million. In April the gold reserve of the Treasury fell below $100 million. In accordance with law the Secretary of the Treasury had to suspend issuing gold certificates for gold deposited with the Treasury. This caused "doubt, fear, and semi-panic"[17] which were temporarily exaggerated by belief that the Secretary would not draw upon the gold reserve to redeem the Treasury notes of 1890 (silver notes issued under the Sherman Act). While it lasted, the semi-panic caused gold exports and frightened

---

16. For the Reading story, see the London *Economist*, CXCVIII (Feb. 13, 1892), 209-10; *ibid.*, CXCIX (March 18, 1893), 319; *Chronicle*, LVI (March 18, 1893), 437-39; *Bankers' Magazine*, XLVII (Jan. 1893), 492; *ibid.*, XLVII (Feb. 1893), 569; *ibid.*, XLVII (March 1893), 546-47; *ibid.*, XLVII (April 1893), 734; *ibid.*, XLVII (June 1893), 892-93; and Oliver M. W. Sprague, *History of Crises Under the National Banking System*, 61st Congress, 2d Session, Senate Doc. No. 538 (Washington, D. C., 1910), pp. 162 ff.

17. *Bankers' Magazine*, XLVII (May 1893), 805.

banks so that they did not make new loans but called in old ones. Failures became more frequent. Some of the failures undoubtedly would have occurred anyway sooner or later, but the stringency tended to precipitate them.

Despite Cleveland's reassurance that the gold standard would be defended, gold exports and money stringency continued. Early in May the National Cordage Co. failed because it lacked working capital. Ordinarily this did not matter, but in the conditions then prevailing in the money market the company could not raise sufficient funds to meet its obligations.[18] Thus credit contraction forced an apparently sound company of great prominence into failure. This precipitated panic on the stock market. There was a rash of failures, largely confined to unsound firms.

Gold exports ceased early in June when Cleveland announced a special session of Congress for September to repeal the Sherman Silver Purchase Act. This allayed fears that the United States would go off the gold standard, but the New York banks were forced to continue contracting credit. Their reserves declined because of a drain to the interior caused by numerous bank failures in the rest of the country, which in turn were the consequence of business failures. The bank failures were due mainly to violations of law and imprudent policies, so that their closing was merely hastened and bunched by the general situation. Although the New York banks still had excess reserves, they set up machinery for issuing clearing house loan certificates as early as June 17. Loan contraction continued all over the country, with reserve ratios outside New York rising as individual banks attempted to improve their own positions at the expense of accelerating the contraction of business. All the usual phenomena were present—hoarding, runs, credit rationing as well as high interest rates, and forced liquidation of inventories.

When at the end of June Cleveland issued his call for a special session, the deteriorating situation which nearly everyone blamed on the silver law impelled him to schedule the session for August rather than September. But the prospect of repeal did not avert a final wave of distrust of banks, which spread over the South and West during the third week of July, intensifying the drain on New York banks. The drain fell unevenly and forced some banks partially to suspend

18. See Report of Reorganization Committee to creditors and stockholders of the National Cordage Company, June 15, 1893, as it appeared in *Chronicle*, LVI (June 24, 1893), 1058.

cash payments. Suspension quickly spread throughout the country, intensifying depression by making it hard to meet payrolls.

The stock market inevitably had been doing badly. By the end of July it had fallen far enough to lead foreigners to buy our securities at bargain prices. This, together with declining imports of merchandise, rising exports in consequence of falling prices here, reassurance about the gold standard, and high money rates, brought more gold into New York in August (net) than had left in either the first or second quarters of 1893. The reserves of the New York banks rose rapidly in the last two weeks of August, restoring the reserve ratio to the legal minimum of 25 percent. Cash payments were resumed. On August 28 the House voted to repeal the silver purchase law, and it was generally (and correctly) assumed that the Senate would ultimately do likewise. The pyrotechnical stage of the contraction was over.

The magnitude of the debacle is indicated by the fact that outside clearings fell 30 percent between February and August. (See Chart 11.) During 1893 one sixth of the railroads, whether measured in terms of capital or mileage, went into bankruptcy. More than 600 banks and other financial institutions with liabilities of more than $200 million failed. Some thirty-two iron and steel companies suffered a similar fate.

To what extent must the debacle be attributed to the underlying business situation, to the weak banking structure, and to the silver law respectively? What Schumpeter called the competing-down process was clearly due to bring about numerous business failures, and these in the best of circumstances would have dragged down other firms fully capable of surviving indefinitely under ordinary conditions. There would have been a contraction of more than minor proportions in any event.

The numerous small, weak, and mismanaged banks so characteristic of the United States during the nineteenth century were bound to aggravate the situation by failing, locking up deposits, adding to general distrust, and forcing liquidation as they themselves were liquidated. Yet one element of weakness in the American banking system—seasonal inelasticity in the money supply—played no part. Contrary to the usual rule that American banking panics occurred in the autumn, stringency and contraction culminating in suspension of cash payments came in the spring and summer.

Severe stringency at a time when seasonal patterns and declining activity would ordinarily produce ease must be laid at the door of the silver policy. In part, the gold exports should be attributed to the decline in merchandise exports and the decline in attractiveness of American securities to foreigners for other reasons than fear for the gold standard. Nevertheless, lower interest rates than actually prevailed ordinarily would have been enough to attract capital to this country.[19] That gold exports stopped when Cleveland announced he would call a special session to repeal the silver law was more than coincidence.

How much difference did silver make? An element of speculation must enter into any judgment, but the following three statements seem justified. (1) The threat to the gold standard made the contraction more rapid and violent during the months of March through August. (2) If the silver problem had never entered the picture at all, the contraction after August would have been more rapid. This follows from the fact that money stringency bunched failures that would have occurred sooner or later anyway. (3) The silver situation probably resulted in deeper contraction by causing failures among firms and banks that could have survived if the kind of money market characteristic of cyclical contractions had prevailed. The evidence for this lies in the high ratio of assets to liabilities among the failures.

The preceding paragraph regards the silver problem as the variable, holding everything else constant. If one reverses the procedure, holding silver constant and inquiring how much difference the underlying business situation made, one might easily come to a different conclusion. The monetary and fiscal policies actually pursued, together with the banking structure, might have produced panic and severe depression in any event. The argument must be a bit arbitrary, since the result would have depended on how the President and Congress reacted to the emergency; but in the political situation of 1893 nothing short of disaster would probably have sufficed to make effective action possible. In this sense, one can assign the leading role to monetary factors, which would have caused strong firms to fail had there not been plenty of weak ones.

When there are two deflationary forces acting simultaneously, the resulting deflation is not the sum of the deflations that each would have caused alone. Two forces, each by itself minor, may in combination be enough to precipitate a panic. Or two forces, as in this case, either of which by itself could bring down the banking system, may in combination be little worse than each alone.

19. Cf. *Bankers' Magazine*, XLVIII (Aug. 1893), 90.

The N.B.E.R has selected June 1894 as the date of the cyclical trough. This accords well with the findings of most other investigators. At about this time the number of series with good conformity to business cycles which were rising reached the 50 percent mark, as should be the case. Clear evidence of improvement in business as a whole, as distinct from sectors, cannot be found before then in contemporary journals. Freight ton-miles reached bottom in July. In view of the rules and purposes of the N.B.E.R. in dating troughs, there can scarcely be any quarrel with its choice.

Yet for present purposes the date is quite misleading. If the evidence in favor of revival is not clear before June 1894, neither is the evidence for contraction clear after August 1893. After the difficulties experienced in meeting payrolls in August had cleared away, numerous plants resumed operations. By January 1894 outside clearings had risen 14 percent from the trough in August. (See Chart 11.) The troughs in a number of significant series came in October— pig-iron production, building permits, number of incorporations, national banks' loans, investments and discounts, and deposits of individuals. The trough in Jerome's index of factory employment (Massachusetts) came in September. Frickey's index of employment in the third quarter was virtually as low as at the trough in the first quarter of 1894. If there were no other evidence than the facts just stated, the upturn might be dated before the end of 1893.

In truth, the period from September 1893 until April 1894 was transitional. Failures were still occurring in reduced but abnormal amount, plants were shutting down or reducing output; but at the same time other plants were starting up or expanding. It was not a dead center but a time of rearrangement and adjustment. It calls to mind the years 1877 and 1878, another period of transition when the evidence is not clearly in favor of either expansion or contraction. But the similarity stops right there. The transition of 1877-78 was marked by contraction in money series (e.g. clearings and prices) and expansion in output series. No such neat classification can be made for September 1893–April 1894. Hence, the analysis must be different.

Unlike 1877-78 the transition of 1893-94 cannot be identified with the depression phase of Hicks's theory, the period when output is creeping along the floor or lower equilibrium line which itself slopes gently upward.[20] When excess capacity gets worked off, Hicks's recovery begins, characterized by interaction between the multiplier and the accelerator under the stimulus of autonomous investment. Ordinarily the date selected by the N.B.E.R. as trough comes near the beginning of Hicksian depression. That is, Hicksian depression is a period when revival has begun but is proceeding very slowly. Moreover, the transition cannot be analyzed in Hicksian terms. Excess capacity in railroads was being worked off neither by a slow growth in output (freight ton-miles did not rise) nor by wearing out (railroad capacity is too long-lived). It appears that excess capacity was eliminated because it was obsolete.

The stormy period from February through August, on the one hand, had not done fully the job of cleaning out firms which needed to be reorganized or liquidated (e.g., the Atchison, which failed in December) but had paralyzed businesses capable of surviving. While liquidation of the first type continued, reorganization and expansion of the second type began. The two for a time very nearly cancelled each other out.

The third and final stage of business cycle contraction was due to labor troubles. By far the most important was the bituminous coal strike of some 150,000 to 200,000 miners. It lasted from April until June 18, virtually shut down the industry, halved the output of pig iron, and made it difficult for the railroads to run their trains. On June 27 the American Railway Union called a strike to aid workers of the Pullman car shops, who on May 11 had struck against a wage cut. This accounts for the trough in freight ton-miles in July. A strike on the Great Northern from April to May 2 also deserves mention. This was the time of Coxey's famous "army," although the event has no significance for business cycles other than as a symptom of deep depression.

Strikes, even on this scale, usually mean little for business cycles. Whatever movement was in progress before the strike, whether up or down, usually is resumed once the strike is over. In this instance the disturbances came at a time when there was no pronounced move-

---

20. *Contribution*, p. 111: "The fourth [phase] is the Depression, in which output has ceased to fall absolutely, and will soon be rising absolutely, but in which it has, as yet, no tendency to rise relatively to the equilibrium level. Once that rise does begin the depression is over, and we are back at the starting point of the next cycle." The words "will soon be" make the passage a little ambiguous; presumably Hicks means that the depression phase encompasses the entire time output is at the floor or lower equilibrium line (and is therefore rising slowly) plus the short interval before the floor is reached but after output has stopped falling absolutely.

ment in either direction. Hence, the depression of output by the bituminous strike and resumption of output when it ended account for the date of the cyclical trough. If the strikes had not occurred, the N.B.E.R. would undoubtedly have had to date the trough earlier, perhaps as early as February, even under its rule to give preference to later dates.

Whether the labor troubles are regarded as exogenous or endogenous is a matter of choice. They were unquestionably a response to the depression itself. How deep the depression was and how severely it affected workers cannot be measured. The highest guess at unemployment I have seen—3 million, by Gompers—is not implausible for a country with a nonagricultural work force of some 15 million or more. Given an inexperienced labor movement which had not learned to avoid sympathetic strikes, strikes were for the time an understandable reaction—but hardly a typical reaction such as might be incorporated into a theory of the business cycle.

On account, no doubt, of its violence, the contraction had an unusually prompt effect on immigration. Already in fiscal 1893, net arrivals (i.e., total arrivals of aliens minus departures) declined to 381,000 from 480,000 the previous year. In the fiscal year 1894, immigration amounted to only 137,000, in 1895 only 95,000. It continued low for the rest of the decade. Residential construction hence declined irregularly after 1892.

Upturn

In a sense, the upturn has already been accounted for by the resumption of business after the strikes. But this is not enough. It merely explains why July and August (especially the latter) were better months than June. It does not explain why business kept on improving for the rest of the year. At a time of excess capacity such a small shock could hardly launch an upward movement.

Other external factors could hardly be called propitious. The threat to the gold standard had returned. Although Congress had repealed the silver law in 1893, it had done nothing to replenish the gold reserve or to protect the Treasury from the silver notes already outstanding. Net gold exports from New York were resumed in December 1893 and became large in May and June of 1894. Twice during the latter year the Treasury had to sell bonds for gold. Foreigners were still distrustful, still taking capital out of the country.

Crops were not good.[21] Congress considered tariff legislation for almost eight months, finally passed a bill on August 13 which pleased few. It became law on August 28, President Cleveland not deigning either to sign or veto it. The *Chronicle* thought it an unsettling factor while under consideration (so did the *Economist*) and attributed improvement in trade after it was passed to the ending of uncertainty.[22] But this is hard to credit.

Except for the precise location of the cyclical trough, external events cannot account for the lower turning point. One must look for internal developments. This involves a good deal of guesswork. Railroad investment, although at a very low level in comparison with two or three years before, presumably made a small comeback as the process of reorganizing bankrupt roads went on and as conditions in the money market became more favorable for raising capital. Liquidation of inventories was undoubtedly attempted during the contraction, probably with little success during the pyrotechnical stage but with considerable success later. Diminution of inventory disinvestment could have had a favorable influence. Rents probably behaved in a sticky fashion during the deflation of 1893.[23] Their relative rise, together with easy money, accounts for the rise of construction.[24] Such developments would be adequate to generate halting revival during the second half of 1894.[25] In any event, the turn was primarily endogenous.

21. Mitchell presumably was wrong when after describing the other adverse events of the year he said, "Worst of all in its effect upon business was the failure of the corn crop . . ." (*Business Cycles*, p. 59). But the crop situation must be put on the debit side of the ledger.

22. *Chronicle*, LX (Jan. 5, 1895), 11; *Economist*, CXCVIII (Feb. 16, 1895), Supplement, 1.

23. *Bankers' Magazine*, XLVIII (Sept. 1893), 182-83.

24. In 1894 interest rates were low in comparison with those in 1890 and 1892, not to mention in 1893.

25. Once again the recovery is more apparent in the statistics than it was to contemporary observers. Cf. *Chronicle*, LX (Jan. 5, 1895), 9.

11

THE CYCLE OF 1894-97

The 1894-97 cycle was confined to the United States. Although France, Britain, and Germany all had troughs early in 1895 (less than a year after the American trough), their upswings continued without interruption until 1900, whereas the United States suffered a serious contraction in 1896.

Upswing

The cyclical expansion that extended from the middle of 1894 to the end of 1895 is analogous to the unsatisfactory recovery of 1933-37. Both expansions occurred during a longer period that was generally depressed. Both were incomplete, just about regaining the previous cyclical high. Both were seriously disturbed by external events, which were political in their immediate origin, although they could be traced back ultimately to economic causes. They differ chiefly because the expansion of 1933-37 was propelled primarily by government spending, whereas that of 1894-95 was endogenous.

Of course, comparison of the peaks of 1893 and 1895 cannot be documented fully. There are no annual statistics on gross national product in print and no statistics whatever on unemployment.[1] But both employment indexes show the later peak as virtually the same as the earlier. Since population and productivity were growing, it may be inferred that unemployment was still abnormally high at the end of 1895. Outside clearings (undeflated) did not regain the previous high, a corollary of similar behavior of prices. (See Chart 11.) Railroad freight ton-miles also failed to regain the previous

---

[1]. Simon S. Kuznets has prepared annual estimates of GNP, but he has so far not published them.

high. Of the important series available more often than annually, only pig-iron output rose substantially—nearly 20 percent. Clearly the recovery was unsatisfactory.

Since the expansion of 1894-95, like that of 1933-37, followed a severe contraction, the extent of the expansion was considerable even though incomplete. Freight ton-miles rose 25 percent, considerably more than during the cyclical expansion of 1891-92. (See Chart 11.) Outside clearings rose one third, compared to a rise of little more than one fifth in the preceding cycle. Pig-iron production nearly tripled. The index of value of buildings permits rose two and a half times from the worst month to the best. This is an example of the tendency for contractions of large amplitude to be followed by expansions of large amplitude.[2]

The expansion proceeded in spite of severe financial disturbances which seriously hindered expansion of the money supply and discouraged capital imports. Although the Silver Purchase Act had been repealed in 1893, the threat to the gold standard continued. The Treasury notes of 1890, based on silver purchases made prior to 1893, continued to circulate and could be presented to the Treasury at any time for gold. The federal surplus, which had troubled the money market prior to 1890 by periodically locking up funds, had been replaced by a deficit, thanks partly to a change in fiscal policy, thanks mainly to the depression. But under the new conditions, a deficit was worse than a surplus, since it reduced the Treasury balance and made it more difficult to hold an adequate reserve of gold. In November 1894 the Treasury had sold bonds with a market value of not quite $60 million for gold. The gold came from within the country. There was nothing to prevent the purchasers of bonds from later buying the gold back from the Treasury. The scheme was at best a palliative which did nothing to keep gold from leaving the country, and it was a short-lived palliative at that. By the beginning of January the need for action was obvious; by the beginning of February the need had become acute.

The problem was entirely unnecessary. A central bank could have solved the problem by raising short-term interest rates and attracting foreign capital. Nor would the remedy, in the conditions of 1895, have seriously damaged business. Because business was depressed abroad, interest rates were low. Not much tightening of credit would have been needed. Once gold started flowing in, the danger that the

---

2. Arthur F. Burns and Wesley C. Mitchell, *Measuring Business Cycles* (New York, 1946), p. 460.

United States might leave the gold standard would have been removed. Then foreigners would have been willing to buy American securities instead of wanting to sell them, credit conditions would have become easy again, and nothing would have stood in the way of business expansion.

Even without a central bank, there should have been no problem. If the Treasury had had the legal power to issue bonds payable in gold instead of coin, it could have sold them in any amount abroad, probably at 3 percent.[3] A clear determination to do so would have restored confidence. But the silver forces, although not strong enough to compel adoption of their program, had enough votes in Congress to defeat any solution other than their own. To trace the relation of this political deadlock to economic conditions would be interesting but is outside the scope of this study.

At no time during the nineties, not even in 1896, did majority opinion among investors, at home or abroad, hold that the United States would actually leave the gold standard. Estimates of capital movements and volume of American securities abroad are good enough to establish that only a small fraction of such securities returned to the United States. If the threat to the gold standard had really been considered dangerous, the outflow of gold would have assumed proportions great enough to have forced its abandonment. As in the political sphere, there was a near balance in the economic sphere. Capital tended to flow in or out of the country depending on whether short-run conditions turned favorable or unfavorable. But the balance was not exact. Over a period of years a large quantity of capital—several hundred million dollars—left the country. This should not be blamed entirely on the threat to the gold standard. The extraordinary failures of 1893, which in part are attributable to other causes, made American securities unattractive.[4] In fact, it is extraordinary testimony to the vigor of capitalism that foreign investment was so little deterred. In the spring of 1895, when the dollar temporarily looked a bit more secure, it became possible to float American railroad securities in London.[5]

To deal with the decline of the gold reserve to $42 million, President Cleveland in February 1895 negotiated with a group of bankers

---

3. *Bankers' Magazine*, XLIX (Jan. 1895), 157.
4. *Ibid.*, XLIX (Feb. 1895), 315.
5. Without necessarily agreeing with Schumpeter on the "march into socialism," one can understand why one with his knowledge of nineteenth-century capitalism felt that in the twentieth century life was going out of the system. Joseph A. Schumpeter, *Capitalism, Socialism, and Democracy* (3d ed.; New York, 1950), Part II.

known as the Morgan-Belmont Syndicate for the sale of additional bonds. The syndicate undertook to float half the bonds in London, pay the gold into the Treasury over a period of months, and undertake for a time to protect the Treasury from further losses of gold. The syndicate was astonishingly successful. Mere news that the great financial houses of Morgan, Belmont and Rothschild were coming to the rescue sufficed to stop gold exports. The syndicate bought the bonds at 104½, sold them at 112½, and saw their market price immediately jump to 119. For six months the syndicate protected the Treasury, whose gold reserve went above the $100 million mark.

Contemporary observers dated business improvement from this event. In the sense that an obstacle had been cleared away that otherwise would have led to relapse, they were right. Gold hoarding, which had set in by the end of January, disappeared, and it became possible to float American securities abroad. But this is not to concede that confidence is the all-important variable governing business conditions. Some hesitancy may have caused investment projects to be postponed prior to the syndicate, but the expansion of 1895 should be attributed to the familiar cumulative mechanism of the business cycle rather than to the whims of business sentiment.

Gold exports were resumed in July, at first on a small scale. The immediate cause was not lack of confidence but the rise of imports, normal in a cyclical expansion, coupled with the failure of exports to rise. (See Chart 9.) The syndicate continued to supply gold to the Treasury, but on September 13 one of the syndicate members exported gold. This caused a break on the stock market, but confidence soon returned after the syndicate announced it would continue to support the Treasury. Gold exports then abated as merchandise exports began to revive, partly for seasonal reasons.

As a result of these troubles, currency outside the Treasury contracted seriously during 1894 and 1895. It is remarkable that such a strong deflationary force had so little effect on the business cycle. In spite of it, easy money conditions prevailed until almost the end of 1895, a number of factors absorbing the deflationary impact. Expansion by the banking system must have been a factor, since currency in circulation (i.e., outside banks) was stable and the money supply (deposits plus currency in circulation) recovered to the 1892 level. In view of the secular tendency for velocity to decline, a money supply in 1895 the same as in 1892 might not have supported a level of output as great as that in 1892 if prices had not fallen meantime.

At any rate, in spite of all the financial trouble on the surface, a shortage of money and credit did not interfere with the expansion of 1894-95.

It is less easy to see why expansion was so vigorous while it lasted. No strong autonomous force was obvious. There was no stimulation from either merchandise exports or capital imports. Any recovery that took place in railroad investment must have been meager and in part induced. The only areas of obvious expansion were building construction and steel, and the former probably did not regain the level of 1892. Iron and steel expanded because they were replacing other materials in building and because a new tin-plate industry was growing up behind tariff protection. Presumably numerous small investments made up the gap left by the decline in railroad investment between 1892 and 1895. This is entirely plausible—although the United States had come a long way in economic development, it was still a young country with plenty of need for capital.

Downturn

The date for the cyclical peak given by the N.B.E.R. is December 1895. It would be convenient to accept this finding, since the downturn could then be blamed readily on the Venezuelan crisis in that month. Nevertheless, statistical information clearly points to an earlier date. The number of series with acceptable conformity to business cycles that were still expanding in December was far below the expected 50 percent.[6] May marked the peak for building permits and wholesale prices of building materials; June for wholesale prices generally; August for factory employment in Massachusetts and New Jersey; September for common stock prices and the price of steel billets; the third quarter for cash from new security issues and for orders of both rails and railroad equipment; October for outside clearings, value of imports, number of incorporations, and the price of pig iron; and November for pig-iron production and gross earnings of railroads. The only important series with a later peak was freight ton-miles (February 1896), a series that normally lagged at peaks. The peak should be dated in October or possibly November.[7]

6. Geoffrey H. Moore, "Statistical Indicators of Cyclical Revivals and Recessions," N.B.E.R., Occasional Paper 31 (New York, 1950), p. 14. Why the expectation is 50% is explained in detail in my appendix on the month of the 1887 peak.

7. True, contemporary observers did not seem to notice any decline of business until the Venezuelan affair, but this can be discounted. They would not be apt to notice a small decline promptly. Moreover, it was convenient for them to date a change in business by some well-known outside event, even when, as in the case of Garfield's

The lag between the cyclical peak and the event to which contemporary observers attributed the downturn was so short that it may not mean anything. Economic series typically exhibit a saw-tooth outline. The business cycle as a whole does not proceed smoothly and without interruption in the course of expansions and contractions. There is nothing paradoxical in the cause's following the downturn, since without the adverse event expansion might otherwise have been resumed after a scarcely noticeable pause. Nevertheless, the lag suggests that one look first for other causes of the turn.

The early peak in value of building permits is noteworthy. The building cycle was in a downswing which continued for several years more, 1895 representing a recovery that was partial and temporary. Probably the supply of buildings was high enough to put a damper on further construction.

With railroads also a poor field for investment, expansion may have run out of steam. According to one's biases one might say either that investment opportunities were inadequate or that the accelerator coefficient was too low to generate more than a weak cycle. Certainly the expansion was not killed by colliding with a ceiling. Full employment probably was not reached. Money conditions never became tight prior to the Venezuelan crisis. Commercial paper rates, although higher in the fall than during the preceding year, were low in comparison with years other than 1885, 1876, or 1858. (See Chart 3.)

The downturn cannot be blamed on poor crops, because the crops of 1895 were exceedingly good. (See Chart 6.) Output was one sixth greater than in 1894 and surpassed every preceding year except 1891.[8]

In November, gold exports resumed. Collapse of speculation in "Kaffirs" (South African mining shares) plus an unsettled political situation caused stock exchange panics throughout Europe. The financial troubles in Europe soon passed away, but not before they had led to foreign selling of American securities, gold exports, and —because gold was being exported—further sales of securities based

---

assassination, it was less plausible than in 1895. And the tendency to attribute business developments to external factors was strong in the 1890's, a kind of thinking that was served by dating the change in business immediately after the adverse event.

8. But bountiful crops did little good. Their aggregate value was the lowest since 1889. They resulted in little expansion of the value of American exports, crude plus manufactured foodstuffs rising only $30 million in the fiscal year 1896 compared to the $180 million jump in fiscal 1892.

on fear for the dollar.[9] Such events could not be blamed for the downturn, but they did prepare the way for further troubles.

On December 17 President Cleveland sent a message to Congress announcing that the United Kingdom had rejected arbitration of a boundary dispute between Venezuela and British Guiana. He recommended that the United States appoint a commission to determine the correct boundary and enforce it against any attempt by Great Britain to overstep the line. Within three days both houses had passed unanimously a bill appropriating a million dollars to defray the commission's expenses. The message was quite properly interpreted as a threat of war unless the British gave in.[10] Sales of securities both here and abroad produced panic on the New York Stock Exchange, with rates on call loans jumping to 80 percent and in a few cases 100 percent per annum. (See Chart 3.) There was a rash of failures in New York, Philadelphia and Boston. The clearing houses in all three cities voted to issue clearing house certificates, and only in New York was their actual use avoided.[11] But the British were conciliatory. The threat of war gradually subsided, although it hung on for months.

Business does not seem to have any standard reaction to war or threats of war. The outbreak of the Korean War in 1950 brought inflationary expectations, and a boom preceded the military spending that was expected to cause it. The outbreak of the first world war in 1914 had a depressing effect for several months in the United States. An economist familiar with the universal tendency for wars to generate inflation has a hard time understanding how the threat of war could fail to be stimulating (except on the stock market, where foreigners have an obvious reason for selling while they can, giving Americans a reason for trying to sell first). Yet there are reasons why the heads of particular firms should contract rather than expand. They may think gold a safer protection against inflation than other commodities and move first to improve their cash position, particularly if they believe that inflations ultimately result in depression. If bonds are the chief form of investment, hoarding gold is a more natural alternative than investment in equities. War brings both destruction and taxation.[12] It also causes uncertainty, since not all firms will necessarily find their position improved; it may be more obvious which ones will

---

9. *Chronicle*, LXII (Jan. 4, 1896), 15.
10. *The Investor's Monthly Manual*, London, XXV (Dec. 31, 1895), 666.
11. *Chronicle*, LXIII (Jan. 4, 1896), 15-16.
12. For a contemporary statement of the adverse effects of war, see *Bankers' Magazine*, L (March 1896), 289-90.

be worse off than which ones will be better off, and those with unfavorable expectations have more incentive to react quickly than the others.

Hence, if contemporary sources blame contraction of business on the threat of war, one cannot dismiss their interpretation out of hand. The Venezuelan incident could have led to enough liquidation of inventories to throw the business cycle engine into reverse, even though it could hardly have had much effect on fixed forms of investment. But to concede the possibility is not to admit probability. The business cycle contraction of 1949 is known as an inventory recession. It was started primarily by a decline of inventory investment between the last quarter of 1948 and the first quarter of 1949 of only $3.4 billion.[13] Yet in the third quarter of 1951 inventory investment fell $5.6 billion, and in the following quarter contracted an additional $5.7 billion, without precipitating a downswing. In the first quarter of 1953, inventory investment contracted $4.7 billion, again without starting a recession, whereas when recession did begin, in the third quarter of 1953, the decline in inventory investment was only $3.4 billion. Due allowance must be made for attempted reduction of inventory investment greater than what was actually achieved. Even so, in the years 1948-53 gyrations in inventory investment clearly caused contractions in business only when accompanied by other unfavorable developments—in the case of 1953 reduced military spending plus a decline in construction resulting from credit restrictions.[14]

Fluctuations in inventory investment may have had either more or less influence on business conditions in 1895 than in 1948-53. But the Venezuelan crisis probably could not have caused the downturn unless the expansion had already died out or unless the crisis was accompanied by other unfavorable developments. The crisis might have been the marginal factor, making the difference between continued expansion and the beginning of contraction. But if GNP was still growing at a rate of 3 percent a year on December 16, the belligerent message delivered the next day could not by itself have caused a reversal.

The Venezuelan incident did not stand entirely alone. On December 20 Cleveland asked for legislation to improve the gold reserve.

---

13. U.S. Department of Commerce, *National Income: A Supplement to the Survey of Current Business* (Washington, D. C., 1954), pp. 224-25.

14. Credit restriction can also be blamed for part of the decline in inventory investment, but for purposes of the discussion in the text, it does not matter what caused the latter.

THE CYCLE OF 1894-97   201

The Ways and Means Committee of the House responded, not very helpfully, with a bill to increase the tariff. By the end of the month the gold reserve was down to $63 million, and another crisis was approaching. The *Chronicle,* after observing that business conditions were much better than during the gold crisis of the preceding February, commented, "every condition favors progress except the currency embarrassment, which has recently been made so irritating that conservative classes are . . . again thoroughly anxious, most departments of business are dragging, and new enterprises at this critical period of the year are waiting—waiting for what? Waiting until they can have some assurance that their work will not be arrested before its fruits can be secured by that worst of all disturbing influences— worst because so absolute and general—the dislocation of our measure of values. But the better conditions of trade make the call for relief even more earnest. 'He that is down needs fear no fall.' It is the recently sick man trying to walk that must have support or tumble."[15]

This passage can be interpreted to mean that the expansion since February was generated in part by investment activity that would not have taken place if doubts about the gold standard had not been allayed by the Morgan-Belmont Syndicate, and renewal of fears on this score were therefore quite enough to reduce investment significantly. This is quite possible, but it sounds convincing only if investment opportunities, though not dead, were weak. This is reasonable. Besides the factors discussed previously—the railroad situation, the decline in immigration and building, the absence of any obvious, strong autonomous force—the panic and severe downswing of 1893 must have inhibited investment even as late as 1895 both by the blow to confidence and by creating excess capacity. The combined effects of the Venezuelan incident, recurrence of monetary fears, and the weak underlying situation are sufficient to account for the downturn at the end of 1895.

Contraction

Hansen has stated that major expansions are often interrupted by minor contractions but major contractions are rarely interrupted by minor expansions. He has cited the expansion of 1894-95 as one of the rare cases.[16] He considered the entire period 1893-97 as a major

15. LXII (Jan. 4, 1896), 4.
16. Alvin H. Hansen, *Business Cycles and National Income* (New York, 1951), p. 20.

contraction, implying that the trough of 1897 was lower than the trough of 1894. This is indeed the case as far as wholesale prices are concerned. Whether it is also true of output cannot be adequately determined.[17] On the whole, the evidence seems slightly on the side of 1894 as the lower trough in output, but perhaps it would be better to say that the two troughs were comparable.

There followed three well-marked stages, which may be called pre-campaign (first half of 1896), campaign (July-October), and post-campaign (November 1896–June 1897) respectively. In the pre-campaign stage, contraction resulted mainly from the internal workings of the cyclical mechanism with comparatively little external disturbance. To be sure, there was a good deal of excitement on the surface. Something had to be done to restore the gold reserve. Since another syndicate was politically impossible, bonds with a face value of $100 million were offered to the public. Once more the response showed that fears for the gold standard did not run deep. The issue was vastly oversubscribed and yielded $111 million, even though purchasers were required to pay gold for bonds which did not promise that repayment would be in gold. Although most of the gold came from within the country, it did not promptly leave the Treasury, as had been the case with the bond issue of November 1894. The contraction of business made it possible to raise this large sum without tightening credit.[18] The net result was favorable in a negative way—it removed an obstacle, ended the disposition to hoard, and made it possible to sell securities abroad. Foreign affairs also provided excitement. As the Venezuelan difficulty subsided, the Cuban insurrection

17. The fact that railroad freight ton-miles in every month of 1896 and 1897 were markedly higher than in any month of 1894 must be discounted, partly because railroading was still an expanding industry, partly because crops were much better in 1896 than in 1893 or 1894. The higher troughs in pig-iron output in the later cycle must likewise be discounted on grounds of an unusually rapid growth rate. The available employment indexes also seem to contradict Hansen, but their scope and accuracy leave much to be desired. Outside clearings in the spring of 1894 were only a few percent lower than in the fall of 1896. (The trough in clearings in August 1893 can hardly be taken as a clue to output, on account of the panic.) This circumstance can be explained on grounds of a rapid upward trend; on the other hand, prices were lower, so that one is again left in doubt. Annual indexes of nonagricultural production are little help. The twelve months of 1894 were probably as bad as any consecutive twelve months that might be chosen between 1893 and 1895, but the twelve months of the calendar year 1896 probably were considerably better than the twelve ending, say, with June 1897. Consequently, the fact that annual indexes of production show 1896 above 1894 is not conclusive. All this ignores farm production as irrelevant. Crops were far better in 1896 and 1897 than in 1893 and 1894.

18. *Bankers' Magazine*, L (March 1896), 298.

took its place. The Senate passed a resolution favoring recognizing the insurgents as belligerents on February 28, the House concurring on April 6. This display of hostile sentiment toward Spain was accompanied by even more hostile speeches and, as might be expected, was called "very disturbing to business."[19] But the administration made it clear that it would not follow Congressional wishes.

With nothing more serious than this to disturb business, the contraction might have run its course some time in the summer of 1896. Exports had started rising at about the time of the cyclical downturn, as a result of deflation in the United States, revival abroad, good crops here, and growing American economic superiority. (See Chart 9.) The rise was to continue for many years and lift America out of depression and into prosperity. By the summer and fall of 1896, the rise had not yet become spectacular. But it was a favorable factor of more than negligible proportions. Unfortunately, it was overborne by disturbances arising from the presidential campaign.

Up to this point the emphasis that contemporary sources had put on assaults on the gold standard to explain all that went wrong is subject to heavy discount. It was compounded of an element of truth and a variant of wishful thinking which may be called wishful blaming plus man's eternal faith that for every effect there is one simple cause. A certain amount of discount is still appropriate for the accounts of July-October 1896, but the rate of discount must be set much lower. Without doubt, William Jennings Bryan gave impetus to the contraction of business.

Bryan's famous cross-of-gold speech won him the Democratic nomination on July 7 on a platform calling for the free coinage of silver at a ratio of 16 to 1. This ratio so overvalued silver that with a victory for Bryan, silver would have replaced gold as the basis for American money. Prices would have risen in terms of paper and silver money.

If Bryan had generally been expected to win, there would have been such a rush to convert paper money into gold that the United States would have been driven off the gold standard long before election day. Under the fractional reserve banking system, pressure on the banks might well have caused panic and paralysis. Such disaster did not befall because McKinley, the Republican gold standard candidate, was expected to win. But any nominee of a major party has a chance, as Truman's election in 1948 later proved. Hoarding of gold began as early as June in anticipation of how the Democratic

---

19. *Chronicle*, LXIV (Jan. 2, 1897), 10.

convention would behave. Enough hoarding occurred to drive interest rates skyhigh even before crop moving time and to make loans almost impossible to negotiate even at the prevailing rates. (See Chart 3.) Banks built up reserves in an effort to protect themselves. Just before the election, gold was selling at a small premium.[20] Desire to hoard induced, and loan contraction compelled, depletion of inventories. Cash raised from new security issues on the New York Stock Exchange fell to very low levels. Allegations that investment projects were being postponed because there was a threat to the gold standard sound more convincing in this context than in the context of 1894 and 1895.

While the internal drain of gold went on, the external drain was reversed. Imports of gold were substantial in September and October. The merchandise balance moved favorably to the United States, imports falling and exports rising. (See Chart 9.) High interest rates helped keep capital in the country; moreover, the British seem to have felt that any withdrawal of securities would add to the American depression and play into Bryan's hands.[21] After midsummer the Treasury gold reserve was never in danger. But matters were delicately balanced. A poor harvest or better Democratic prospects could have started a disastrous hot money flow.

Upturn

Although monetary contraction resulting from the campaign accelerated business contraction, the triumph of McKinley and the gold standard did not restore prosperity. According to the N.B.E.R., the post-campaign stage was part of the "contraction," but "stagnation" would be a more accurate word. During the next eight months wholesale prices and outside clearings behaved irregularly, without displaying any real tendency to rise. (See Chart 11.) Contemporary accounts are gloomy. Yet a good case can be made in favor of October 1896 as the trough rather than June 1897. By the earlier date, about 50 percent of series that conform well to cycles were rising, as one would expect at the trough; by the later, the percentage was not only substantially higher but comparable to the highest points of 1892 and

---

20. The *Bankers' Magazine* interpreted willingness to pay a premium for gold as like the willingness to participate in a lottery, where a small amount is risked on the remote chance of a large gain, LI (Nov. 1896), 506. A better analogy would be insurance.

21. *Bankers' Magazine*, LI (Sept. 1896), 272. According to Partington, some American businessmen pursued the opposite policy, cutting production and increasing unemployment to warn labor how to vote. John E. Partington, *Railroad Purchasing and the Business Cycle* (Washington, D. C., 1929), p. 270.

1895.[22] It is hard to find any important monthly series that justify the June 1897 date.[23] Pig-iron production, railroad freight ton-miles, building permits, employment, railroad gross earnings, number of incorporations, individual deposits, investments, loans and discounts of national banks—even outside clearings—had their troughs in late summer or early fall. The views of contemporary observers can be written off on grounds that small improvement where great improvement was expected could scarcely be differentiated from no improvement. In outward appearance, at least, the period is like Hicks's concept of a depression.[24] For present purposes the upturn may be dated from the election.

In effect the upturn has already been explained—cf. the report by the *Chronicle* that 700 establishments either resumed operations or increased them after the election.[25] With confidence and monetary ease restored, with inventories probably low, and with exports still rising, some improvement was inevitable. What needs explanation is why the improvement was so meager.

First, there were three external events (not counting exports, which leveled off and therefore had little effect one way or the other). On December 18, a resolution by Senator Cameron recognizing the independence of the "Republic of Cuba" was reported favorably by the Senate Committee on Foreign Relations. By virtue of the peculiar logic of Wall Street, a break in the stock market ensued. But as the measure had no chance with Congress, the administration, or the public, it cannot plausibly be blamed for stagnation in business over the following half year. Neither can any lasting effect be attributed to bad weather and floods. They undoubtedly made business worse in the regions affected for the time being, but that is all. The discussions that led to a new tariff bill's becoming law on July 24 (it had been passed by the House on March 31) were described as unsettling to business. Now, any change in a tariff duty is likely to hurt some business interest. The business interest likely to be helped will take little action before the bill becomes law, whereas those in danger of being hurt will draw in their horns at once. If tariff discussions get opened up, any particular duty is in danger of getting changed in an unpredictable way. In spite of these concessions, tariff

---

22. Moore, "Statistical Indicators," p. 14.
23. Chief exceptions are the prices of pig iron and steel billets. Imports can hardly be called an exception since they were disturbed by tariff legislation.
24. *Contribution*, p. 111. For Hicks, depression is a time when output creeps along the lower limit while excess capacity gets worked off. Output rises but not vigorously.
25. LXIV (Jan. 2, 1897), 16.

discussions that were obviously leading to more protection all around could not be very damaging to business even in the short run. Neither can much net effect be ascribed to the big jump that imports took in anticipation of the new duties. The inventory investment involved benefitted only foreigners, and since money was easy, the use of funds for this purpose could not have been at the expense of other forms of investment.

How much did the election actually accomplish? It did not prevent a rash of failures in December, presumably a delayed reaction to the previous troubles, but the failures were not great enough to be important. According to one source, 1893 had taught people that under American monetary arrangements money could be superabundant one day and not available at all on the next. Removal of the threat to the gold standard did not correct this defect and therefore did not restore confidence or lead businessmen to expand operations.[26] The source in question is one that seems to put undue emphasis on sheer confidence.[27] In discussions at the time, the

26. "Under the present laws the trouble with the currency is not its fluctuation as compared with the gold standard, but its liability to be locked up or expanded without regard to the wants of business. The fault with the irredeemable currency before 1873 was not noticed while business was booming. It required a crisis and the subsequent depression to impress this fault on people's minds. Once impressed they would do no extensive business until the dangerous defect was removed. In the same manner the crisis of 1893 has taught people to be careful how they expand their business with a currency liable to be redundant one day and not to be had at all on the next. They will not be reassured and give free scope to enterprise until this liability to sudden stringency in the money market has been removed.

"If Congress, therefore, does not do something to radically remedy this defect it will be vain to look for much improvement for a long time to come. In 1879 the people had only to wait until legislation already enacted went into operation on a fixed date. Now they will have to wait for the slow operations of their legislators. Business does not commence to boom with those who handle the greatest enterprises. These use the smallest part of the money or resources of the land. The great bulk of all business is done in small amounts by the masses of the people. Each one has his own little enterprise which, as his profits are small and easily swept away, he hesitates to launch until everything looks secure." *Bankers' Magazine*, LI (Feb. 1897), 186.

27. E.g., "in the heat of political contest the daily press magnify the dangers that may arise from the election of the opposing candidate, and . . . by representations, naturally exaggerated to secure victory, the business situation is much aggravated. The probability is that the asseverations as to the danger to business interests of the country in the election of this or the other candidate, are often the cause of the depression they deplore. The business world will learn in time that very few of the evils prophesied by the partisan or independent press in the heat of a political contest ever materialize. . . . The business world must endeavor to get over the habit of being frightened into a dumb ague fit, that is worse than the active chill of a panic, with every election that takes place." *Ibid.*, LI (June 1896), 707.

I do not mean to deny that confidence is important as the agent for transmitting

financial disturbances of 1893 and 1896 were associated with threats which by November 1896 had been removed. Inelasticity of the money supply did not prevent objective conditions from restoring confidence and prosperity from returning in the latter part of 1897 and enduring for a decade. Another source, noting that the large merchandise balance in favor of this country during 1897 did not cause substantial gold imports, asserted that foreign investors still felt the country's financial system needed to be overhauled; hence, they not only refused to invest here but, when the stock market went up, took advantage of the high prices to dispose of American securities.[28] Since under gold standard conditions capital imports tend to be stimulating, the financial weaknesses in a negative way were unfavorable; yet the behavior of foreign investors in this era makes it hard to believe they would have passed up good investments for such a reason.

Since the eight months under discussion look like Hicksian depression, one should inquire what light Hicks's theory may shed. In his analysis, interaction between multiplier and accelerator causes the upswing. Contraction creates excess capacity. Depression is a period between contraction and expansion when output rises slowly but cannot generate a cumulative expansion because excess capacity keeps the accelerator low. In time, the desired disinvestment takes place; then the expansion phase begins.

Acceptance of Hicks's analysis of depression does not require acceptance of his view about the acceleration principle or the expansion phase. Clearly, excess capacity can be a drag on recovery irrespective of the mechanism that generates recovery. Now, the contraction of 1896 was quite large, comparable to that of 1893. Recovery, therefore, was slow to get under way. Similar periods of slow recovery—almost stagnation—occurred in 1894, 1885, and 1877-78.

Lastly, what was the state of investment opportunities? This topic belongs last because there is danger of faulty reasoning of this sort: investment is low during depression, therefore opportunities to invest

---

objective factors into action or that in the process it sometimes produces effects out of proportion to causes. But the point to the passage quoted is that even where an objective appraisal reveals no substantial danger the business world nevertheless gets frightened into depression by an ordinary election campaign (the passage appeared before Bryan's nomination). This I find hard to believe.

28. *Chronicle*, LXVI (Jan. 1, 1898), 5.

are absent.[29] Since good evidence on the state of investment opportunities is hard to come by, one inquires first if lack of investment can be explained otherwise. I have discussed a considerable number of points which do not individually amount to much; but collectively they may add up to an adverse total that is more than negligible. In addition there was excess capacity.[30] One therefore need not fall back on lack of investment opportunities for want of any other explanation.

Nevertheless, neither railroads nor building construction offered opportunities comparable to those a few years earlier. Without them, or something to take their place, the iron and steel industry could hardly look inviting. New industries that were later to become so important—automobiles and electric power—did not yet amount to much. Investment opportunities apparently were few and uninviting in the first half of 1897.

The United States was finally pulled out of stagnation by another crop coincidence, similar to those of 1879 and 1891. It became clear early in the summer that crops would be good in the United States and poor elsewhere, so that the stimulus from rising exports was anticipated. In the fiscal year 1898, exports were $350 million higher than in the fiscal year 1896. Moreover, business was improving abroad. The tariff of 1897 effectually held down imports and provided a stimulus to investment in the protected industries. The purge of 1893, not to mention the year of depression that followed, had eliminated obsolescent firms in the United States, enabling American industry to compete more effectively. Gold discoveries in Alaska and South Africa increased the money supply for gold standard countries everywhere. The succeeding years were exceedingly prosperous for American business.

29. Following Gordon, we must distinguish between investment opportunities and the inducement to invest. Robert A. Gordon, "Investment Behavior and Business Cycles," *Review of Economics and Statistics*, XXXVII (Feb. 1955), 25.

30. As R. A. Gordon has pointed out to me, excess capacity normally exists when revival begins. Its removal cannot be a necessary condition for expansion.

12

THE DEPRESSION OF THE NINETIES

THE PRECEDING DISCUSSION of the middle nineties has taken a narrowly short-run view. It is now necessary to inquire why the four and a half years from the beginning of 1893 to the middle of 1897 were generally depressed despite the expansion of 1894-95.[1] Four explanations have been offered. Hansen's is in terms of underlying cyclical and secular developments. The explanation of Friedman and that of the contemporary business world both run in terms of monetary factors and external events. Schumpeter's also involves both internal and external aspects. As usual, the explanations are not mutually exclusive. The problem is one of emphasis.

To take up the explanation of contemporary businessmen first, "The commercial bodies of the country, the clearing-house associations, boards of trade, chambers of commerce and exchanges have almost unanimously ascribed the slow recovery since 1893 to the uncertainty as to the future standard of value in the United States. This they say unsettles all investments certainty in regard to which is the prime factor in all business transactions."[2] The same cause operated in the contraction of 1893 and in the campaign of 1896. Both times there was monetary contraction by the banks. But the emphasis here is on lack of investors' confidence as the underlying factor, particularly for the unsatisfactory recovery after 1893.

One's judgment on this view turns on how important one thinks confidence is in business cycles. I have already given reasons why the opinion of contemporary observers must be discounted; wishful blaming is perhaps the most important. Lack of confidence from the sole

---
1. The word "depression" is used in this chapter in its loose everyday meaning except when a technical meaning is expressly specified.
2. *Bankers' Magazine*, LI (July 1896), 15.

cause of worry about the gold standard hardly seems an adequate explanation. But there are elements of strength in the argument. A severe depression is hard to get out of. The violence of the preceding contraction dealt a blow to confidence and revised downward the attractiveness of any investment commitment at any given level of national income. Moreover, national income and output were low relative to national capacity.[3] Under such circumstances one more unsettling factor can make the difference between a dynamic process that gathers momentum and one that is weak and easily reversed. That hesitancy with respect to certain types of investment seems irrational to modern economists does not matter. Investors of the eighteen nineties could not have foreseen consequences that economists of the eighteen nineties did not clearly understand. Besides, there were rational reasons for caution. Prospective lenders at long term stood to lose by inflation, and prospective borrowers at short term might easily have gone under in a banking crisis accompanying the transition from gold to bimetallism. No shift from debt financing to equities could have been expected when a change of standards was a possibility rather than a probability. Thus a case can be made for lack of confidence as a marginal yet decisive influence.

According to Milton Friedman,

On the resumption of the gold standard in 1879, the money stock shot up rapidly for two years, then leveled off, rising during the sixteen years from 1881 to 1897 at the average rate of 5 per cent per year. From then until World War I, the money stock rose at a decidedly higher rate, about 7 per cent per year, thanks to the exploitation of the South African gold discoveries and similar developments. This difference in the rate of growth of the money stock in the two periods, 5 per cent versus 7 per cent, was accompanied by a striking difference in the character of the periods: the first was a period of agrarian unrest, Populist movements, and silver agitation that culminated in Bryan's famous 'cross of gold' speech; the second was a period of general political harmony, economic prosperity, and rising prices. In the intellectual climate of today and the recent past, with its derogation of the significance of monetary factors, it may seem preposterous to attribute this striking difference in the character of the periods to the difference in the rate of growth of the money stock; yet there is good reason to suppose that, if it was not the whole explanation, it was an important factor. . . . The stock of money rises during most of the contractions in general business [in the period 1875-1954] . . . as well as during every expansion. But, first, when it rises during a contraction

---

3. I.e., in terms of a schedule relating investment to national income, there is both a downward shift of the schedule and a downward movement along the schedule.

it generally rises at a slower rate than during the preceding or following expansion; second, and perhaps even more important, every contraction during which it rises is a relatively mild contraction. The stock of money declined for more than an erratic month or so and by a significant amount on seven occasions: 1875-1879, 1892-1893, 1895-1896, 1907-1908, 1920-1921, 1929-1933, 1937-1938. Each of these declines occurred during a severe contraction in general business, and there is no contraction that can plausibly be labeled severe that is not in this list—unless it be 1882-1885. But 1882-1885 is on the borderline in monetary behavior: the estimated stock of money declined negligibly (by less than one-half of 1 per cent) from 1883 to 1884.[4]

These comments appeared in an interim report on research in progress. Friedman and his coworkers had just finished preparing estimates of the money supply which will be very helpful to other workers. At the end of the report, Friedman said, "These bits of history raise rather than settle important questions on money's role in business cycles. We are proceeding with our analysis of the facts, and of the theories offered for their explanation."[5] Friedman's final views will be valuable and penetrating. Meanwhile, one should be grateful for having these first impressions, and it would be ungracious to seize on their details for carping criticism.

Rather, one should reinterpret the details in order to put Friedman's general position in the strongest possible light. In this spirit, after the comeback that monetary factors have made in economic thinking during the past decade Friedman's analysis does not seem at all "preposterous" in the "intellectual climate of today." Moreover, in spite of the work of Hansen and Schumpeter, a monetary explanation for the difference between the years before and after 1897 is traditional. Second, the rate of growth of the money supply between 1881 and 1892 did not differ significantly from the rate between 1901 and the outbreak of the first world war. The striking difference between the 5 and 7 percent rates comes from the decline of the money stock between 1892 and 1896 in the 1881-97 period and its extraordinarily rapid growth from 1896 to 1901 during 1897-1914. With the partial exception of the middle eighties, the years 1881-92 were generally prosperous for business (however the farmers might have felt), a fact entirely in keeping with Friedman's position. His remarks amount

[4.] *35th Annual Report of the National Bureau of Economic Research* (New York, 1955), p. 32.
[5.] *Ibid.*, p. 33.

to explaining the depression of the nineties, particularly the contractions of 1893-94 and 1896, via the stock of money.

The difference between Friedman and contemporary observers is not great. Friedman does not blame lack of confidence for the weak recovery after 1893 as did contemporary observers. As far as 1893 and 1896 are concerned, Friedman talks in terms of the money supply, contemporary observers in terms of the silver problem. Since the silver problem operated *inter alia* by reducing the money supply (a point that contemporary observers could not have been expected to appreciate fully), the two explanations cover much the same ground.

To what extent was the decline in the money stock the cause of contraction and to what extent the effect? My own position has been indicated in previous chapters: monetary contraction aggravated the cyclical contractions of 1893 and 1896; because it made those contractions worse, it indirectly contributed to the unsatisfactory recoveries of 1895 and the first half of 1897; it probably played no more than a minor role in the downturns of 1893 and 1895; other factors would in any event have produced a business contraction in 1893, which would have inhibited the growth of the money supply; the contraction of the money stock was the effect of business contraction also in that withdrawal of capital from America by foreigners was aggravated by the other factors making for business contraction. I agree with Friedman that the stock of money was "an important factor," although he would probably feel I have underrated it.

Now consider explanations that subordinate monetary influences. To recapitulate comments already made on Schumpeter,[6] the prosperity phase of the sixth and last Juglar belonging to the Kondratieff of railroads, steam and steel extended from about the beginning of 1889 to the middle of 1891, although it was distorted by the crisis or panic of 1890 and its repercussions in 1891.[7] Ulmer's figures strengthen Schumpeter's interpretation by showing that the peak in railroad investment came later than the peak in railroad miles added of 1887.[8] To be sure, the figures put the peak inconveniently late, so that it comes in the Juglar recession (from mid 1891 to mid 1893), but this can readily be explained away: in the first place, investment is not

---

6. See Chaps. 9 and 10.
7. Schumpeter, *Business Cycles*, I, 396-97.
8. Melville J. Ulmer, "Trends and Cycles in Capital Formation by United States Railroads, 1870-1950," N.B.E.R., Occasional Paper 43 (New York, 1954), pp. 16 and 19.

identical with innovation even in the industry that sparks prosperities; in the second place, the stimulus from the favorable crop situation of 1891 (an external factor) was felt by the railroads as much as by any other industry. The notable absence of high profits during the expansion of 1892 is what one would expect during Juglar recession. The extraordinary number of failures among railroads and iron and steel companies during 1893 represented readjustments, need for which had been accumulating throughout the Kondratieff, but which were aggravated by the vicious spiral of the Juglar.[9] Juglar depression extended from mid 1893 to mid 1895, with revival until the latter part of 1897 (interrupted in 1896). Although Schumpeter seemed to emphasize the cyclical mechanism, "The currency factor was a major source of weakness during the vicissitudes of 1893 and was primarily responsible for what proved a specifically American catastrophe, not otherwise fully motivated, in 1896."[10] He said nothing specific about Kitchins, but his schema implies that the recession and depression phases of a Kitchin would come during Juglar revival. The contraction of 1896 is an irregularity only in the sense that it was more severe than would ordinarily be expected; and this irregularity according to Schumpeter was due to the currency problem. He had nothing specific to say about the unsatisfactory recovery of 1895.

To sum up: while accepting monetary factors as the main explanation for 1896 and an important influence in 1893, Schumpeter explained 1893 primarily in terms of his schema, i.e., exhaustion of innovating opportunities plus an unusually severe competing-down process. It seems to me that the Schumpeterian process was clearly in evidence and would have generated a depression, albeit a milder one, even in the absence of the silver problem.

Hansen has attributed the chronic hard times of the nineties to the decline of railroad building. The trend of new railroad mileage rose rapidly from the forties to the seventies, then flattened out except for the big spurt in the eighties. This explains why the last quarter of the nineteenth century was generally depressed, particularly the nineties, and why Hansen compared the period to the 1930's. Making use of the acceleration principle, Hansen wrote, "mere slowing down in the *rate* of growth caused an absolute decline in the volume of new investment required in the plant and equipment of subsidiary in-

---

9. Schumpeter, *Business Cycles*, I, 341, 388-89, and 397.
10. *Ibid.*, I, 317.

dustries, such as iron and steel, which manufactured the materials that went into railroad construction."[11]

Although Schumpeter and Hansen both used secular aspects of railroad building, there is a gulf between them. In Schumpeter's thought, there is never a shortage of aggregate investment opportunities, if for no other reason, because much saving is for investment and would not take place if investment opportunities were not available.[12] Opportunities for innovation do get used up during prosperity, so that the propelling force of prosperity gives out, making it possible for autodeflation and the competing-down process to bring on recession and ultimately depression. For Hansen, the explanations of the 1890's and the 1930's are both stagnationist, meaning that investment opportunities in the aggregate were inadequate after the railroads went into a decline.

A comparatively young and underdeveloped country like the United States in the 1890's could hardly have lacked outlets for all domestic savings. On the other hand, investment opportunities at times are more numerous, at other times less. They were comparatively scarce after 1892, and when they are scarce it is easier to get into a depression, so that the economy becomes more vulnerable to deflationary forces such as were numerous in the 1890's.

Is the use of the acceleration principle in the sentence quoted from Hansen two paragraphs back justified? How does Hansen's view differ from Schumpeter's? Schumpeter had no use for the acceleration principle, since the usual model is too rigid.[13] But the acceleration principle formulates a basic economic relationship that no one disputes. Moreover, the peculiar feature of the acceleration principle, namely, that a slowing down in the rate of increase of demand causes an absolute decline in investment, is not necessary to Hansen's explanation of the nineties, since by then railroad construction in terms of miles added had sharply declined; and in any event Hansen's use of the acceleration principle in a context of trends is not open to the same objections as its use for short-run relationships in many modern theories of the business cycle. Hence, there is no necessary antipathy

11. Alvin H. Hansen, *Fiscal Policy and Business Cycles* (New York, 1941), p. 40 (Hansen's italics). The building cycle explains why the depression of the eighties was milder than the depressions of the seventies and the nineties.

12. Joseph A. Schumpeter, *Capitalism, Socialism and Democracy* (3d ed.; New York, 1950), pp. 394-95. Schumpeter recognizes that in a depression this is not so, but the pursuit of saving without investment is then a consequence of depression, not an explanation of how depression arises.

13. *Business Cycles*, I, 191-92.

THE DEPRESSION OF THE NINETIES

here between this part of Hansen's interpretation and Schumpeter's general position. Nevertheless, there is a difference. For Hansen, the decline of railroad building reduced investment opportunities in subsidiary industries such as iron and steel. If for Schumpeter the decline in railroad building had any impact on iron and steel, it was not via investment opportunities in the aggregate but via railroads' contribution to the numerous failures in the latter industry.[14] Those failures were also the consequence of innovations in the iron and steel industry itself.

What factual basis is there for Hansen's use of the acceleration principle? He wrote before estimates of railroad investment were available and had to rely on figures of railroad mileage built. Nevertheless, in one sense there is no disputing his diagnosis. Following the peak in railroad miles built of 1887, there was a sharp reduction in output of steel rails, a fact implying that the need for investment in that subsidiary industry became exceedingly low. Moreover, the decline of railroad building undoubtedly decreased the need for investment in other subsidiary industries.

The estimates of railroad investment now available in one way strengthen Hansen's analysis. If the peak in railroad building came in 1887, and if the decline in railroad building caused chronic hard times, why did not the hard times commence in 1888 instead of in 1893? The lag could have been explained in part by the crop coincidence of 1891, without which chronic hard times might have begun in 1890; but even so the unexplained part of the lag is awkward, particularly since pig-iron production grew no less than 43 percent between 1887 and 1890. But if the peak in railroad investment did not come till the early nineties, there is no lag to be explained away.

Removal of one difficulty only gives rise to others. No one knows how closely gross railroad investment was correlated with the amount of iron and steel products required for that investment. Moreover, even if the decline of railroad building reduced the need for investment in iron and steel, how much of the iron and steel output went to the railroads? To what extent did the rise of other demands for iron and steel (including foreign demand) fill the gap as railroad demand fell off? To what extent did iron and steel investment depend on output?

14. The crisis of 1893 "was the 'abnormal liquidation' of positions which had become inadaptable in the course of an evolution that primarily centered in iron and steel." Schumpeter, *Business Cycles,* I, 389. In the context, iron and steel includes the railroads.

216   AMERICAN BUSINESS CYCLES

CHART 12. Iron and Steel (*above*) and Railroad Gross Capital Expenditures (5-year moving averages) (*below*), 1884-1900

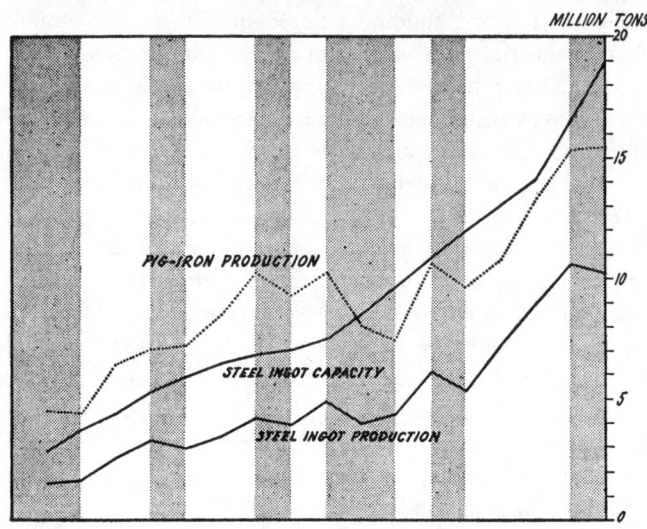

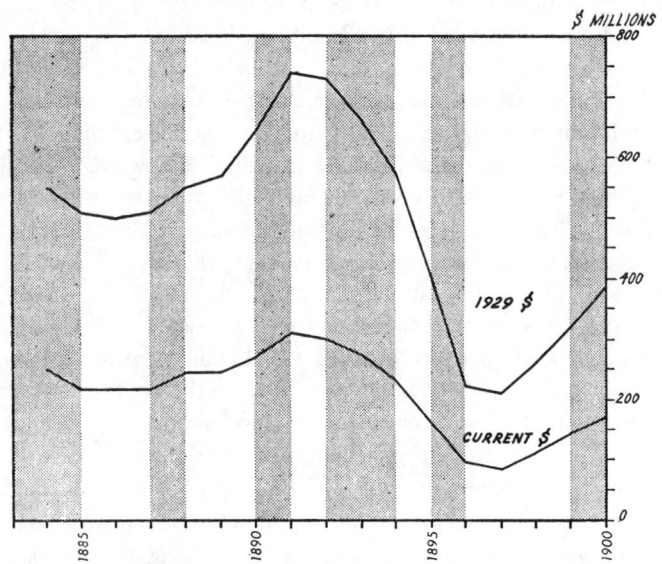

Shaded areas are business cycle contractions (N.B.E.R. dates).
SOURCES: Steel ingot capacity, U.S. Steel Corp., *T.N.E.C.* Papers, II, 140; steel ingot production, *ibid.*, p. 144; pig-iron production, *Historical Statistics of the U.S.*,

Whatever the answers, the correlation is not very good between pig-iron output and railroad investment, under any reasonable allowance for the inaccuracy of the estimates. Pig-iron output was roughly the same in each of the peak years 1890, 1892, and 1895. (See Chart 12.) Railroad investment in each of those years appears to have been quite different; even the five-year moving average shows 1895 little more than half of 1892, and 1892 was considerably higher than 1890. Contemporary sources tell us that other uses such as structural steel were developing. Steel ingot capacity grew more rapidly after 1892 than before (although the upward trend in output did not accelerate until 1899). More precisely, the increase in capacity averaged 342,000 gross tons in the three years 1890-92. During the next six years the increase ran about 1,100,000 per year.[15] To conclude, the decline in railroad building clearly hurt the iron and steel industry; but the matter is too complex to be described in terms of the acceleration principle.

Let us now take up three international influences. The behavior of merchandise exports, except for the downturn of 1893, was unfavorable only in a negative way. In the fiscal years 1893-96 inclusive they were about the same as in 1890-91. Since the secular trend of exports was strongly upward, a failure to rise is an unfavorable though passive factor. One qualification must be made. Exports cannot be taken simply as exogenous even from the point of view of this study. A depression in the United States, *ceteris paribus,* ordinarily stimulates exports, although part of the gain in volume will be dissipated in lower prices. Failure of exports to rise during the depression is evidence that they were in fact a deflationary factor. Although the theoretical argument is somewhat uncertain, the fact that there was a depression abroad too indicates that foreign demand was unfavorable.

More important are capital movements. In so far as they affected the gold supply, they played a prominent role in the interpretation of contemporary observers, but their direct effects tended to be slighted. Under gold standard conditions, capital imports are stimulating directly as well as through the money supply (except in the unlikely case when investment by foreigners is entirely at the expense of domestic

---

15. Allowance for the fact that investment in a new furnace may be spread over several years does not destroy the conclusion that it went up when railroad investment went down.

p. 149; railroad investment, Melville J. Ulmer, *Trends and Cycles in Capital Formation by United States Railroads, 1870-1950,* N.B.E.R., Occasional Paper 43 (New York, 1954), p. 60.

investment by Americans). Capital exports similarly are depressing unless none of the money would otherwise have been spent within the country.[16] American economic development during the last third of the nineteenth century was financed with a sizable amount of help from foreign capital. The shift from capital imports to capital exports amounting to several hundred million dollars per year in the early nineties was a significantly depressing influence. It was partly endogenous, the result of fewer investment opportunities in railroads and of that part of the depression that would have occurred in the absence of external events. But in the main it was exogenous, the result of the silver problem.

The last of the international influences is immigration. I assume that its short-run changes were endogenous, the result of changes in American business conditions, although this may be an exaggeration. To the extent that it was endogenous it was part of the mechanism whereby business contraction leads to further business contraction, depressing demand for residential construction. But unlike most of the mechanisms of cumulative contraction, it operated only with a considerable lag. It does not explain the contraction of 1893; instead it helps explain how that contraction contributed to making the expansion of 1894-95 unsatisfactory and to aggravating the contraction of 1896. It justifies characterizing 1893-96 as one major contraction interrupted by a minor recovery.

To conclude, cyclical and secular forces—the competing-down process plus relative exhaustion of investment opportunities—had set the stage for a contraction of more than minor severity when the fall of exports brought about the downturn of 1893. The competing-down process in this case was more severe than usual, a factor aggravated by the perennially weak banking structure. But the real villain of the piece was the silver problem, without which the contraction of 1896 would have been mild and the contraction of 1893-94 little worse than 1882-85.

The interpretation just given is no more than a personal judgment. The range of possible explanations for the 1890's is very nearly identical with those for the 1930's. It is almost a waste of time for an economist who has studied the thirties to study the nineties as well, for whatever explanation he has reached for the former he can—and probably

16. To the extent that the capital exports result in additional investment abroad, they ultimately increase demand for goods and services of the home country. But it seems appropriate to abstract from this effect in the context of the hot money flows of the nineties.

will—apply to the latter. Those who stress stagnationist tendencies in the one case will do likewise for the other. Those who blame the unsatisfactory recovery of 1933-37 on governmental policies that destroy business confidence can use the same argument for 1894-95. Those who think monetary and banking disturbances are the key factor in business cycles can find verification in both depressions. In both cases one can see at work mechanisms that make severe depressions difficult to get out of—creation of excess capacity, repercussion of depression on population and of population on residential construction.[17] Schumpeter is less an exception than he at first appears. To be sure, he compares the thirties with the seventies rather than the nineties. But his analysis of 1893 runs in terms of the same kind of scrapping and rearranging plus banking troubles to which he attributed 1929-33. His vague comment on 1895-96 is consistent with an explanation similar to his views on 1935-38. I have not considered that the hypothesis that monopolies cause depression by restricting investment is worth discussing, but some sort of case along that line could be made for the nineties as well as the thirties.[18] In a perverse way, the two depressions are evidence that business cycles over a considerable range of time are fundamentally the same kind of phenomenon.

17. In the case of the nineties population was affected via immigration, in the thirties via the birth rate; and the lags were different. But basically the cause and effect relationship was the same.

18. Some of the severity of the downswing of 1929-33 I attribute to unfortunate behavior of prices and wages, which at first resisted decline and then gave way in a destabilizing manner. The same cannot be said of the 1890's, and this is an exception to the point made in the text. It is not an important exception, because it has little bearing on the basic question of why the middle 1890's and the entire 1930's were generally depressed.

13

CONCLUSIONS

THIS CHAPTER has three sections. The first inquires how far the business cycles of 1865-97 were the result of external events. The second deals with internal forces—what theory best fits the facts? The final section takes up the implications of the study for business cycles generally.

External Events

On three occasions, crop conditions exerted a powerful stimulus. All three occurred in the vicinity of a lower turning point. In 1879 and 1897, contraction of business had already ended before favorable conditions in the United States combined with poor crops abroad to give a strong push to an expansion that otherwise might have been weak and slow. In 1891 crop conditions may have caused the upturn itself; and the return to normal conditions the following year helped precipitate the debacle of 1893. Otherwise, variations in crops were an ever present but minor force, affecting the surface of events but not the underlying currents.

Autonomous variations in export markets, except for the three cases where poor crops abroad coincided with good crops here, were never decisive. Nevertheless, the steady decline in merchandise exports between 1880 and 1885 and their relatively depressed state between 1893 and 1895 contributed to two major depressions. Since these declines were associated with cyclical downswings in European countries, they were external events only in a narrow sense. Broadly speaking, they were part of the mechanism that keeps cycles throughout the world roughly together.

CONCLUSIONS

In so far as changes in international capital flows originated in conditions abroad, they had little effect. The chief exception came in 1890, when foreign developments contributed to money stringency and the downturn. The only instance when labor troubles had perceptible effect came in 1894 when important strikes delayed the upturn.

Despite the laissez faire policy of the nineteenth century, the federal government constituted the most important source of external disturbances. In 1865, inflationary fiscal policy suddenly gave way to a balanced budget and currency contraction. A recession ensued. During most of the rest of the century, fiscal policy was mildly deflationary as the government paid off the debt acquired during the Civil War. In 1879, it resumed gold payments (although without immediate effect on business other than to enable the crop situation to have an inflationary impact). In 1890 it began a silver policy that greatly aggravated the debacle of 1893 and the contraction of 1896. Political developments helped bring on the downturn of 1895.

The brief résumé just given suffices to show the importance of external events. Nevertheless, they mattered less than internal forces. Even during the nineties, when for seven years a succession of outside shocks distorted the course of business, they merely altered the timing and severity of what would have been a major cyclical decline in any event. During the preceding quarter century, the internal mechanism dominated the major swings. Of the minor contractions (1865-67, 1869-70, 1887-88, and 1890-91), three were strongly influenced by external events, as was the more severe contraction of 1896.

This is the place to raise the question, is there such a thing as a business cycle? Or better, in what sense are there cycles? If fluctuations resulted from nothing but external events, one would scarcely use the term. But there is a mechanism that tends to perpetuate general movements in whatever direction they have started. There are also internal mechanisms that sooner or later tend to bring cumulative movements to an end and perhaps reverse them. Often (for example, the downturns of 1882, 1887, 1890, 1893, and 1895) the turning point comes because external events reinforce internal developments. Whether such considerations justify using the term "cycle" is a matter of taste. They do not tell what would happen if the economy ceased to be battered by external events. Would fluctuations disappear? If not, how regular would they be? This is the fundamental riddle of the business cycle.[1]

What can be said of the riddle? Given the invention (exogenous) of the railroad, the economic mechanism converted its development into a number of major cycles (which can be grouped in a two-phase Kondratieff). In that sense there were business cycles in the latter part of the nineteenth century. Whether there would have been minor cycles without external events seems much more doubtful.[2]

Internal Forces

All research on business cycles has as its ultimate goal a satisfactory theory. Chapter 2 developed an eclectic theoretical framework compounded from the work of Schumpeter, Hicks, and Gordon. The next step is to assess the usefulness of the various elements in the framework.

Schumpeter. The preceding chapters have shown that on the one hand drastic modifications need be made in Schumpeter's theory, and on the other hand the model is exceedingly illuminating. Innovation in railroads led to the boom of the early 1870's; and when as much had been accomplished as could be, competition of the new with the old brought on panic and prolonged depression. Much the same story was repeated after 1879. By the late 1880's, innovation no longer centered so predominantly in railroads, although the latter still represented a large outlet for investment. However much external events distorted the 1890's, the Schumpeterian process was clearly at work, the panics of 1893 resulting not only from the preceding Juglar prosperity but from the entire Kondratieff.

1. An ambiguity about external events complicates the riddle. To Schumpeter, his theory was endogenous. Others call it exogenous because innovations presuppose creation of investment opportunities, especially invention. Whether a given theory is endogenous is a matter of definition that should not be allowed to obscure analysis. To me, invention is a background feature of modern economic life just as much as banks are. An economy with no invention is a different kind of economy; whether it would have cycles is of no interest. If inventions come in jerks for reasons other than the economic process, the jerks are exogenous. Although invention, particularly minor improvement, is shaped by economic processes, purely technological considerations are important for the advent of great new fields like railroads, electric power, and the automobile. If a Kondratieff containing six Juglars and based on electricity, chemistry, and automobiles began just when a railroad Kondratieff of six Juglars ended, that must be called exogenous.

2. Recent "inventory cycles" seem to have been precipitated by external events, e.g., the tight money policy of 1953 and the cut in federal spending. The same may be true generally (cf. 1887). This does not preclude using the word "cycle" for the minor swings. Such regularity as they have comes from the internal mechanism creating from time to time conditions for external events to do their work.

CONCLUSIONS

Except for exogenous interferences, the four Juglar phases—prosperity, recession, depression, and revival—are clearly evident. For the Kondratieff, a two-phase cycle fits the facts better, with recession lasting from about 1869 to 1897. Schumpeter's Kitchin is not a useful concept.[3]

Gordon. Three major cycles, as defined by Gordon, are as clearly evident as the three Juglars of Schumpeter. During the years preceding the downturns of 1873, 1882, and 1893, investment opportunities were used up more rapidly than they were created;[4] during the following years they were accumulated more rapidly than they were used up. This study has less to say about short cycles, but the minor cycles of Gordon are clearly more useful than Schumpeter's Kitchins. Gordon's hybrids, useful for 1907 and 1920, are not relevant to 1865-97 (with the possible exception of 1879-85).

How, then, do the theories of Schumpeter and Gordon fit together? How should emphasis be distributed? Gordon has provided a catalogue of influences on the stock of investment opportunities that mixes external and internal forces and includes innovation. Schumpeter has provided an endogenous theory centered on innovation.[5] For the ten-year cycles of the last third of the nineteenth century, Schumpeter put the emphasis in the right place—the cycles were primarily endogenous, and innovation was the key variable. The greatest source of the investment opportunities stressed by Gordon was innovation, particularly in railroads, which opened up a host of opportunities in apparently unrelated lines. Schumpeter's theory requires bolstering with respect to minor cycles; and it attached far too little importance to investment opportunities. But the theory applicable to this study is basically Schumpeterian, not only because

---

3. Much to my surprise, I have found three Kitchins to each Juglar, just as Schumpeter claimed. There were not three cycles in the N.B.E.R. sense, but in addition to the Juglar (which masks the middle Kitchin) there were in each case two perceptible deviations from what one would expect from the Juglar alone. For the Juglar that Schumpeter dated from the end of 1869, my finding requires putting the beginning date a little earlier to bring within it the downswing from June 1869 to December 1870, and I count the small revival and relapse of railroad investment in the latter 1870's as a Kitchin. In the next Juglar (1879-88), the two additional Kitchins are the pause of 1880 and the recession of 1887-88. For the final Juglar (1889-97) there were clearly defined contractions in 1891 and 1896 in addition to that in 1893. Finding three Kitchins to each Juglar does not confirm Schumpeter's theory. They were strongly influenced, if not caused, by external events. The finding is merely a curiosity, reminding us that the usual concept of business cycles is somewhat arbitrary, excluding lesser movements.

4. A qualification must be made for 1882 with respect to building construction.

5. Cf. n. 1 above.

innovation deserves a central role but also because the disturbances caused by the fruits of innovation—the competing-down process—were a prominent part of Juglar recession. And the concept of a Kondratieff is helpful.

Hicks. Hicks's theory has contributed less to this study than the theories of Schumpeter and Gordon. Its distinctive feature is stress on the acceleration principle. It is exceedingly difficult to get convincing evidence on the acceleration principle, so that the negative results in this instance are not decisive. Nevertheless, the fact remains that the acceleration principle has scarcely come in for mention in the chronological account of American cycles.

Yet I cannot agree with Burns that Hicks's theory is "a dubious aid to students seriously concerned with the actual alternations of good and bad trade to which the Western world has been subject in modern times."[6] It is not a single hypothesis about business cycles and therefore does not stand or fall with one hypothesis. It is a framework embodying the work of Keynes, Harrod, Domar, and others that accommodates many hypotheses, including that of investment opportunities. It needs further development because it does not incorporate any explanation for cycles of autonomous investment. Moreover, it suffers from the weakness of all aggregative theory, ignoring too much that goes on within the aggregates, such as the partial disequilibria caused by innovation. But even as it stands, Hicks's theory has been suggestive for two different parts of the discussion of Chapter 5 and again in Chapter 7.

Hicks's theory suggested to him that "Really catastrophic depression . . . is likely to occur [only] when there is profound monetary instability—when the rot in the monetary system goes very deep."[7] If 1893 and 1896 are considered part of the same depression, then the most severe depression of the last third of the nineteenth century was the one in which monetary instability was greatest; the 1870's rank second in severity of both depression and monetary disturbance; and 1882-85 comes third in both respects. Unquestionably, monetary disturbances contributed to the long-wave depression. Nevertheless, this study has subordinated monetary to real factors. Monetary disturbances themselves have causes, some exogenous, others endogenous. The banking panics of 1873 and 1884 were primarily endogenous.

---

6. Arthur F. Burns, "Hicks and the Real Cycle," *Journal of Political Economy*, XL (Feb. 1952), 24.

7. *Contribution*, p. 163. It is not clear from the context that Hicks would refer to any historical depression as "really catastrophic" except 1930-34.

CONCLUSIONS

That of 1893 was endogenous in part. Other monetary disturbances were, strictly speaking, exogenous; yet in a broader sense the most important of them—the silver policy of the 1890's—was itself the result of the long period of falling prices, and falling prices in turn were primarily endogenous. Cyclical swings would be reduced in amplitude if monetary problems could be avoided; but depressions of moderate severity could occur anyway.[8]

The lower turning point (or upturn) is the least developed part of business cycle theory. Hicks's theory in this respect is comparatively well developed, suggesting that contraction comes to an end because there is a floor. The floor results from autonomous investment, the limit of zero on induced disinvestment, and the marginal propensity to consume being greater than zero. So far, so good. The analysis of what happens next is less convincing. Output for a time creeps along the lower limit. Vigorous expansion is delayed until excess capacity wears out and disappears. Historically, this is not what happens. Typically the period of time is too short to eliminate much excess capacity in this way, particularly where the capital is as long-lived as railroads. Typically, expansion gets up steam in spite of excess capacity.[9] Perhaps some of the excess capacity is obsolete or obsolescent and does not deter new investment. Here is another instance where Hicks's aggregative approach is inadequate.

Hicks's and other theories imply that the upturn is endogenous. This study provides confirmation. Although in many cases, such as 1879, 1891, and 1897, external stimuli were important, in 1888 the upturn came after a brief contraction without the aid of exogenous forces. The upturn of 1885 also appears to have been primarily endogenous. Other cases are less clear. But even in 1894, when the monetary rot went very deep indeed, contraction to all intents and purposes ended as soon as the monetary troubles were over. The upturn of 1879 might have come sooner except for external events, although on the other hand the upturn of 1897 seemed to wait for something favorable to come along.

To sum up, this study points to a theory basically Schumpeterian (stress on innovations, the competing-down process, four-phase Juglar and two-phase Kondratieff, with monetary forces not unimportant), strengthened by important additions from Gordon (investment oppor-

---

8. Monetary factors sometimes figure prominently in downturns—e.g., 1887, 1890, and to a lesser extent 1873.

9. For this point I am indebted to R. A. Gordon.

tunities, minor cycles) and, less important, by the Hicksian framework (growth, the lower turning point).

International Aspects. This study has not focused on the international equilibrating mechanism nor on the question why cycles throughout the industrial world display a loose correlation, but a few comments can be offered. The classical theory of the gold standard mechanism, as usually expounded, ignored the business cycle and even implied that disturbances such as capital movements would have opposite effects in the countries concerned, the borrowing country receiving gold and expanding, the lending country losing gold and contracting. The modern income effects theory represented an improvement, implying that cyclical expansion in one country (whether or not it was fed by capital imports) would stimulate others. As originally developed, the income effects theory suffered from two weaknesses. By itself, it gave no reason for believing that equilibrating forces would not be either too little or too much. In fact, if a world in international equilibrium were disturbed by a cyclical movement in one country, the ensuing course of events might cause continually increasing disequilibria. Such a theory is inadequate to deal with a world where the gold standard worked satisfactorily for several decades. This weakness is remedied by combining income effects with gold flows. The other weakness was failure to deal with economic growth. International flows of capital, men, and goods are often essential to one country growing more rapidly than others. The income effects theory, supplemented by gold flows, can readily be adapted to deal with growth problems, and some recent work has been done along these lines.[10]

Between 1879 and 1897 many different international forces illustrating effects suggested in the last paragraph were at work. A disturbance in 1891 produced contrasting effects, stimulating business in the United States, presumably depressing it in Europe. This is one reason why the correlation among cycles in different countries is so rough. Much more frequently international flows helped keep cyclical movements in different countries in line with each other. At times poor export markets, as in the early 1880's and 1893-95, helped ensure that the United States would have depression at the same time as

---

10. Alexander K. Cairncross, *Home and Foreign Investment* (Cambridge, Eng., 1953), chap. III, has provided a purely empirical account of Canada from 1900 to 1913 that clearly implies the author was using a theory of the sort suggested above. James C. Ingram, "Growth in Capacity and Canada's Balance of Payments," *American Economic Review*, XLVII (March 1957), 93-104, has contributed to making the theory explicit. See also Chap. 4 above.

other countries. At other times, as in the latter 1880's, expansion in America spilled over to other countries via imports. In other cases, like 1880 and 1890, international forces restrained expansion, keeping the United States in line with others. In 1890 the restraint took the form of money stringency. In a way, 1890 bears out the classical theory—gold flows and the money supply were an essential part of the equilibrating mechanism. Yet the incident was almost anticlassical in flavor. It was not a case of gold flowing from one country, which had to contract, to another, which was enabled to expand. Rather, owing to business cycle developments, money conditions became stringent generally. Throughout the entire thirty-three years of this study, international markets and international flows of capital and men played an important part in the rapid economic growth of the United States.

Despite the power of international influences, they do not adequately account for the degree of correlation of cycles throughout the industrial world. I have argued that major American cycles were primarily endogenous, even under a narrow definition. Even if that is wrong, depression affected the United States in the 1870's at the same time as elsewhere despite the insulation of freely fluctuating exchanges. The explanation must be sought in forces that are worldwide.

The Nature of Business Cycles

The kind of theory sketched above applies to thirty-three years in the history of one country. To what extent does it apply to other times and places? To deal with the question comprehensively is beyond the scope of this study, but something needs to be said.

The suggested theory is basically Schumpeterian. Schumpeter's theory—particularly his Kondratieff—undoubtedly fits the railroad era better than the twentieth century. Schumpeter himself thought that life was going out of the capitalist system. Growth of anticapitalist attitudes was destroying entrepreneurial incentives. The development of trustified capitalism—giant corporations that are shells for a stream of innovators and innovations—would modify prosperity and recession phases. And, it may be added, depression (and revival) can be avoided by government action. To him, it was an open question how long his model would continue to be relevant. Nevertheless, he felt that the theory was standing up surprisingly well. Although the investment opportunities concept and the Hicksian model have origins going back before the first world war, they have been most fully developed only recently and with recent history primarily in view. They might be expected to apply at least as well to the twentieth century as to the nineteenth, perhaps better.

Without going into details, the theory applicable to 1865-97 seems to have some validity for 1945-58 in the United States. Any two cyclical episodes always have great superficial differences; yet, the contraction going on as this is written (March 1958) strongly resembles those that began in 1882 and 1903: a relative exhaustion of investment opportunities in business but not housing, combined with increasing competition from the innovation and investment of the preceding decade.[11] Moreover, the Schumpeterian concepts of prosperity and recession are more widely applicable than is generally realized.[12]

For other countries—the United Kingdom, France, Russia, and the underdeveloped regions—the theory can hardly have much validity in the future. True, there is no escape from the consequences of innovation, and fluctuations in the abundance of investment opportunities can hardly be avoided. Any model, however, embracing nineteenth-century America and the entire world a century later would have to be so exceedingly general that it would have very little interest or use. For a somewhat more limited range of history and geography, the search of the pure theorists for a simplified model seems amply justified.[13]

11. The present contraction (1958) presumably will be milder than that in 1882-85, because structural changes in the economy (e.g., built-in flexibility) and external events (fiscal policy and international trade) on balance are relatively favorable. Nevertheless, if the theory suggested here is applicable, the contraction should be more severe than the downswings of 1948-49 and 1953-54. This will be a test of my conclusion.

12. E.g., the outlook for rubber during the next few years is for Schumpeterian recession. Past innovations have opened up new economic space. Innovators and their imitators will make profits and output will increase at the same time that obsolete producers will be driven out amid considerable distress.

13. The econometricians can be expected to find ever better structures but never to solve their dilemma of changing parameters. Structures embracing a wide range will have to be enormously complicated by rules governing changes in parameters, and at best any structure will predict the future successfully for only a short time before it will have to be modified in the light of new developments. Cycles persist because of a few fundamental forces, making a simple general theory possible; but continuous institutional change and developments that are fundamentally new frustrate a simple general theory that also predicts details.

Appendix I

TWENTY-YEAR CYCLES

FOR THIS STUDY, the twenty-year cycle is an awkward topic. It cannot be ignored, but the literature is not yet at the point where results can be appropriated. To contribute to the discussion would mean reviewing all the literature and dealing with the subject in its entirety, but this would go far beyond the scope of this study. I shall only show how my study impinges on the topic and defend my decision not to go further.

Twenty-year cycles are different from other kinds of cycles. Contemporary observers were well aware of the major cycles of the day. They were also acutely conscious of longer-range phenomena such as the falling prices of 1865-97. Even the minor cycles were noticed. But twenty-year cycles were completely unknown. They are a discovery of the statistical investigations of the last thirty-odd years. In the case of the other cycles, there is surely a problem—the problem of explaining what contemporary observers experienced. In the case of the twenty-year cycles, one must first establish that there is a problem at all.

Twenty-year swings can unquestionably be found in many statistical series. But they may be a red herring. In the period of this study, there were three major depressions. The first was prolonged and in monetary series deep. The second was mild as depressions go. The third was deep. These circumstances alone would be enough to impose twenty-year cycles during the period on certain statistical series. To this extent, the problem of explaining twenty-year cycles is coincident with explaining the characteristics of the three depressions; and there is nothing further to be added to what has been said in previous chapters. This plus the obvious impact of external events accounts for the twenty-year cycle Kuznets reported for net capital imports with troughs at the end of the 1870's and 1890's and a peak at the end of the 1880's.[1]

For another possible red herring, Ulmer and Kuznets found a twenty-year cycle in capital formation by steam railroads, with troughs in the mid 1870's and end 1890's and a peak at the end of the 1880's.[2] But they point out that the cycle is questionable, since the peak in the early eighties was followed by a decline that is quite marked although not as deep as the other two troughs mentioned.[3] Even if one calls this behavior a "twenty-year cycle" (or "swing," to use the more cautious word of Kuznets), there still is no problem beyond explaining the different characteristics of the three depressions.

Kuznets also listed a swing in GNP (1929 prices) with a trough in the early 1870's, a peak in the early 1880's and a trough in the early 1890's.[4] Until he publishes the justification for this, there is not much that one can do with it other than to note some problems. Kuznets has published only decade averages beginning with 1869-78.[5] Underlying the decade averages are annual estimates which he has not published. His dates for twenty-year swings are "based largely on nine-year moving averages"[6] presumably of the annual estimates (or revisions thereof). In his datings, "early 1870's" means 1872-73. If the series begins with 1869, then the first nine-year moving average is centered on 1873. Unless Kuznets has prepared estimates going back a number of years prior to 1869 (as he may have done), he could not establish a trough in the early 1870's in this way, for he has no way of knowing that the true trough did not come earlier. Aside from this, a trough in real GNP on the eve of the longest cyclical contraction in American history is hard to credit. (Kuznets might have dated the troughs in the early 1870's and early 1890's and the peak in the early 1880's in order to eliminate cyclical distortion by putting all three at the cyclical peaks preceding major depressions; but this is not plausible in view of his dating troughs for net capital imports, net immigration, and residential construction all in the late 1870's, i.e., 1877-78—the cyclical trough.) To be sure, I have argued that the contraction of the seventies was more severe in monetary than

1. Simon S. Kuznets, Introduction to Melville J. Ulmer, "Trends and Cycles in Capital Formation by United States Railroads, 1870-1950," N.B.E.R., Occasional Paper 43 (New York, 1954), p. 3.
2. *Ibid.*
3. *Ibid.*, p. 2. See also the charts on pp. 16, 19, and 25 of Ulmer.
4. *Ibid.*, p. 3.
5. Simon S. Kuznets, *National Product Since 1869* (New York, 1946), p. 119.
6. Introd. to Ulmer, "Trends and Cycles," p. 3.

in real series, and I said that Schumpeter and others greatly overrated its severity. Even so, to put a peak in real GNP in 1872-73 is such a remarkable finding that it will have to be thoroughly documented before any attempt is made to explain it.

As far as the swings in net immigration as dated by Kuznets are concerned,[7] I see little more than a combination of major depressions and external events. To stray out of my period and work backwards, the trough of the early 1930's was due to the depression, the peak of the mid 1920's to restrictive legislation, the trough of the late 1910's to the first world war. The peak at the end of the 1900's came too early to be ascribed wholly to the forthcoming war, but clearly the war had something to do with the downswing. The troughs in the late 1890's and late 1870's were partly the result of the depressions. The peak in the mid eighties at first seems difficult to explain, but after a little thought everything falls into place. The depression started the downturn but with a lag; the lag was partly what one would expect in any event, partly a delayed reaction to the small amount of immigration in the seventies. Because the depression was comparatively mild and did not last long, the decline in immigration did not become steep nor culminate in a trough until the nineties.

The only other series that Kuznets in the source cited reported as having long swings was residential construction, which had troughs in the late 1870's and end 1890's and a peak in the end 1880's. This is the familiar building cycle. I suspect that this industry has special characteristics that tend to produce long cycles (although not necessarily of twenty years): the large volume of housing in existence relative to annual output, a lag of rents and construction behind vacancies, the length of time it takes to induce workers to move into or out of the industry, the large number of small, ill-informed producers. That this is so (or at any rate that it is quantitatively important) is difficult to establish, because the swings in construction can be attributed to the swings of immigration, with which they roughly coincide, although with the expected tendency for immigration to lead. If this is not enough, the differences among the major depressions help explain the residential swings for my period as well as for other series already discussed. In spite of my bias in favor of a building cycle, I am bound to conclude that it is a very doubtful hypothesis.

There is quite a bit of literature on twenty-year cycles, but this discussion should be enough to establish that a full-dress review is

7. *Ibid.*

not in order. By way of summary and conclusion, the problem of explaining long swings in the period from 1865 to 1897 to a considerable extent is identical with the problem of explaining the business cycles of that era and it does not constitute a separate problem. If it is desired, the swings in immigration can be considered exogenous (this is not necessary, but is safer than attributing them to cyclical contours); and there may be a housing cycle in addition to the response of house building to immigration and business cycles. It was indicated in Chapter 2 how twenty-year cycles can be incorporated into the Schumpeterian schema in a formal way.

APPENDIX II

THE MONTH OF THE 1887 PEAK

ACCORDING TO THE N.B.E.R., a cyclical expansion reached its peak in March 1887. The Bureau's date is earlier than that assigned by other investigators. Ayres and Persons both put the peak in November, Hubbard in June.[1] Thorp labeled the year 1887 as "prosperity," 1888 as "slight recession."[2] There seems to be no question that the date given by Ayres and Persons is too late in the year and that Hubbard and the Bureau are closer to being correct.

Since many experts collaborated in choosing the dates listed by the Bureau, no one individual is in a position to challenge its decisions on close questions. Nevertheless, March seems one or two months too early under the Bureau's rules for dating, and the matter is worth re-examining. Although the issue is not important for the causal analysis of my study, the precise dating of turning points is important for the field of business cycles generally.

As far as some of the leading series are concerned, outside clearings (series 12,14 in the N.B.E.R.'s files) is ambiguous. It reached its peak in June, but since the use of checks during this period was growing at the expense of other ways of making payments, one might expect this series to reach its peak a little later than the business cycle. Similarly, although liabilities of business failures (series 9,32) reached its peak in the third quarter of 1887, its tendency to lag behind the business peak by two full cyclical stages is consistent with the March date. Orders for rails (series 6,25) with a peak in the third quarter of 1886, wholesale prices of pig iron (series 4,11) with a peak

---

[1] Leonard P. Ayres, *Turning Points in Business Cycles* (New York, 1939), p. 35; Warren M. Persons, *Forecasting Business Cycles* (New York, 1931), p. 198; Joseph P. Hubbard, "Business Volumes During Periods of Decline and Recovery," *Review of Economic Statistics*, XII (Nov. 1930), 183.

[2] Willard L. Thorp, *Business Annals* (New York, 1926), p. 135.

in February 1887, wholesale price of steel rails (series 4,181) with a peak in March 1887, and cash obtained from new security issues on the New York Stock Exchange (series 10,27) with a peak in the first quarter of 1887 all indicate a date at least as early as the one the Bureau chose.

On the other hand, pig-iron production (series 1,130) reached its peak in October. Even allowing for the tendency of a series with a strong upward trend to lag behind the business cycle at peaks, this seems to support a later date. Long's index of building permits (series 2,04), which might be expected to lead, has its peak in March. The Cowles index of common stock prices (series 11,25), which has a tendency to lead, has its peak in May. Federal budget receipts (series 15,04) reached their peak in September, number of incorporations (series 10,35) in April. (It may be noted in passing that the peak of wholesale prices, series 4,48, in January 1888 does not necessarily indicate a later date, since it presumably was strongly influenced by crop production, which fell off a little in 1887.)

For those who like their statistics wholesale, a chart published by Geoffrey H. Moore seems to indicate a later date for the peak than March.[3] In his study Moore selected 404 series with "acceptable" conformity to business cycles. Only 83 of these series extended back as far as 1890. He then calculated the percentage of series expanding in each month and exhibited the results in the form of a line chart. Since the peaks of time series—even when one's sample is limited to series with "acceptable" conformity—are not generally concentrated in the peak month of the business cycle but are dispersed about it, Moore's chart shows a downturn in the percentage of series undergoing expansion prior to each cyclical peak. By the time of the reference cycle peak, as Moore pointed out, it is often the case that only about 50 percent of the series are still expanding.[4]

That this is what should be expected can be shown in the following manner. Suppose there were 100 independent series of equal importance for the business cycle and equally balanced as between series that tend to lead at cyclical peaks and series that tend to lag; suppose further that in a given case 10 series reach their peaks in each of 10 successive months, with the reference cycle peak coming in the middle of the ten-month period. As far as these hypothetical statistics are concerned, the fifth and sixth months are equally good

---

3. "Statistical Indicators of Cyclical Revivals and Recessions," N.B.E.R., Occasional Paper 31 (New York, 1950), p. 14.
4. *Ibid.*, p. 47.

APPENDIX 235

candidates for the title of reference cycle peak; and since the rules of the Bureau call for selecting the later date in such cases, the sixth would be regarded as the peak month. Under Moore's method of computation, in the sixth month exactly 50 percent of the series would be listed as expanding.

But this is an extreme case. To alter the assumptions a little, if there were 110 series, 10 of which reached peaks in each of 11 successive months, then 55 percent would be expanding in the month of the reference cycle peak. Any tendency for the peaks of individual series to be bunched in the month of the reference cycle peak, instead of being spread evenly as I have so far assumed, would increase still further the percentage of series expanding. To conclude, one would normally expect that the reference peak would fall in the latest month in which 50 percent or more of the series were expanding, or in other words that the percentage would fall below 50 for the first time in the month immediately after the reference cycle peak.

Before applying this expectation to Moore's results for 1887, one must inquire whether his sample is evenly weighted as between series that tend to lead and series that tend to lag. Moore stated that for the whole period, 1885-1940, there were somewhat more leaders at peaks than laggards.[5] This statement applies only to the 225 series with consistent timing at peaks and troughs, not to the entire sample of 404 series. The rejected series may contain a disproportionate number of series that lag at peaks (but are rejected because of irregular timing at troughs). For an even more restricted part of the sample (those series that not only exhibit consistent timing at peaks and troughs but have the same kind of timing at peaks as at troughs) Moore stated that there were 23 leaders and only 12 laggards out of the total of 83 series with acceptable conformity available for 1890.[6] A disproportionate number of leaders in the sample would tend to depress the percentage of series expanding in the month of the (true) reference cycle peak. But is the sample sufficiently biased so that we need alter our normal expectation and look for the reference cycle peak in the first month (or later) in which the percentage of series expanding fell below 50? An examination of the behavior of Moore's chart around the other peaks occurring before 1914 does not suggest

5. *Ibid.*, p. 37.
6. *Ibid.*, p. 49.

that the bias is great enough to make any noticeable difference.[7] To the extent that Moore's analysis is useful at all for dating peaks, it would point to the final month in which the percentage of series expanding was 50 or more.

If I read Moore's chart correctly, more than 50 percent of the series in his sample were still expanding in May of 1887, a little less than 50 percent in June. If this evidence could be taken at face value, it would point to May as the reference peak. Of course, it cannot be taken at face value. Aside from duplication and interrelations among the series and aside from the question of bias already discussed, some series are plainly more significant for this purpose than others; moreover, the exact month in which any one reaches its peak may result from chance factors or deficiencies in the series itself or its seasonal adjustment; and in any event our statistical resources for this period are all too meager. Nevertheless, the percentage of series expanding in March 1887 is so very high—nearly 75 percent—as almost to rule that month out of consideration in dating the peak.

Further evidence on the dating of the peak may be obtained from contemporary comments. Some support for the March date can be found in the *Bankers' Magazine:*

The month of May has been a surprise in some branches of business and a disappointment in others. Spring trade started off well in the wholesale and jobbing branches, and was ahead of last year, as country and retail city trade generally bought more freely than for several years, in March, in expectation of a larger business in consequence of the improvement in the times, and also to get the cut freight rates in anticipation of the operations of the Inter-State Commerce law in April. As a result, . . . the April volume of business was lighter than usual; but it was expected to show an increase for May. Reports from traveling men in the Eastern

---

7. I examine only the peaks prior to 1914 because I want a period when the sample was as nearly like 1887 as possible. It should be noted, however, that even in this period the sample grew rapidly—83 in 1890, 140 in 1900, and 175 in 1910. Of the eight peaks between 1890 and 1914, in two cases (1907 and 1913) the peak (as determined by the N.B.E.R.) came in the last month in which 50% or more of the series were expanding. In two cases (1890 and 1895) the percentage is less than 50 at the reference peak. In four cases the reference peak preceded the final month in which 50% or more were expanding. In two of the four cases (1893 and 1910), the lead was only one month; but in one case (1902) there was a lead of three months and in another (1899) a lead of six months. All these statements are based on a reading of the chart and may be inaccurate; but there can be no question about the general conclusion that the chart lends no support to the hypothesis that the sample is biased in favor of series that lead at peaks. If anything, it indicates a bias in the opposite direction. More likely still, as Moore pointed out, it suggests that some of the peaks have been misdated (*ibid.*, p. 47).

APPENDIX 237

and Middle States, show that it has been a disappointment in nearly all lines of manufactured goods, for which the retail demand is said to have been less than for April and May of last year.[8]

But the article goes on to say that this is less true of the West, the far West, and the South; and the above quotation is partly vitiated by its misconception of a fact—if true, the statistics of freight ton-miles (seasonally adjusted) should show a decline in April whereas the figures indicate that April set a new all-time high, not to be exceeded until the following November.[9]

The *Chronicle* was less specific: "One would call the year [1887]—take the average of the whole twelve months—a pretty good one from an industrial point of view. During the first half of it prices of all commodities were well sustained, the quantity of goods marketed being immense, while during the last half production did not decrease, though in many departments prices gradually grew less satisfactory."[10] Thus the *Chronicle* recognized a difference between the first and second half of the year. This could hardly be taken as evidence in favor of June as the peak month, but it does suggest that March may be a little early.

In conclusion, March seems to me the earliest month which could plausibly be defended as the peak, June the latest, with April and May strong candidates for the title. For my purposes, this statement is more helpful than any decision, however trustworthy, as to the precise month to be selected. I would expect that the Bureau's procedure would lead it to prefer May for its purposes.

8. XLI (June 1887), 959.
9. Since the quotation does not imply that April should show a reduction without ambiguity, reference may be made to an earlier article in the April 1887 issue (XLI, 797-800). The Interstate Commerce Law was due to go into effect on April 5. Railroads and shippers alike anticipated that it would raise rates on through business, since the railroads could not cut rates for local business without losing money. Both therefore hurried shipments while they could, the railroads fearing they would lose business to the waterways, the shippers wanting to take advantage of low rates while they lasted. The result was, according to the article, that two months of business were done in one. As pointed out in the text above, the statistics do not bear this out.
10. XLVI (Jan 7, 1888), 4.

INDEX

Abramovitz, Moses, on inventory cycles, 9
Acceleration principle, and long-wave depression, 74; in contraction of 1882-85, 135-36; in 1890's, 213-17. *See also* Hansen; Hicks, cycle theory; Samuelson
Agricultural output, in 1869-1913, 66 (Table 1); between 1866 and 1878, 90; in 1869-97, 91 (Chart 6); in 1879, 111-12, 114-15; in 1882, 126-27; in 1887, 151-52; in 1890, 169; in 1891, 173-76; in 1897, 208
Agriculture, and unemployment, 78-79. *See also* External events, crop conditions
Andrew, A. P., 86n
Astor, J. J., 123n
Auble, Arthur G., 83n, 113n, 119n, 126n
Axe, Emerson W., on severity of 1883-85 contraction, 128n
Ayres, Leonard P., on month of 1882 downturn, 125n; on month of 1890 peak, 166n; on month of 1887 peak, 233; mentioned, 116n

Banks, panics, 73, 98-102, 130-31, 185-88. *See also* Clearings, Money
Bean, Louis H., 91n, 141n, 151n
Bennion, E. G., on Schumpeter and Keynes, 24
Blank, David M., on building construction, 165n
Bond issues, 1865-97, 116-17 (Chart 8)
Boom, in 1879-81, 121-22. *See also* Schumpeter, secondary wave
Boulding, Kenneth E., on price and wage flexibility, 44n, 45

Boutwell, George S., 120n
Brown, E. H. Phelps, on 1873-96, 67n; on long cycles, 81n; mentioned, 68
Bryan, William Jennings, effect on business, 1896, 203-4
Building construction, in 1874-88, 66; in 1865-97, 86 (Chart 4); in 1865-67, 94; in 1871-73, 98; in 1879-83, 123; in 1885, 132; in 1884-86, 140-41; in 1887-88, 148-49; in 1893, 191; in 1895, 198; in 1890's, 218
Building cycle. *See* Twenty-year cycles; Investment, building
Bullock, C. J., 162n, 167n
Burns, Arthur F., *Measuring Business Cycles,* 4, 8n, 9, 24n, 83n, 94n; on Hicks, 12, 224; on deductive approach, 12-13; on building cycles, 85; on 1887-88, 142; mentioned, 67n
Business cycles, definition, 3-4; inductive approach, 4, 5, 8-9, 13-14, 17; econometric approach, 4, 5-9, 15, 228n; deductive approach, 4, 9-15, 17-18; historical approach, 4, 15-21; relation of N.B.E.R. cycle dates to Schumpeter, 24-25; contraction of 1865-67, 92-96; contraction of 1869-70, 96-97; month of 1873 peak, 98-99; downturn of 1873, 98-107; monetary theory of, 103; contraction of 1873-79, 107-12; 1865-79 a major cycle, 112; lower turning point of 1877-79, 113-15; date of 1877-79 trough, 113-14; upswing of 1879-81, 115-24; check of 1880, 124; upper turning point, 1881-83, 124-28; date of 1881-83 peak, 25-26; downswing of 1883-85, 128-31; upturn of

1885, 131-33; expansion of 1885-87, 137-42; contraction of 1887-88, 142-58; month of 1888 trough, 153; and coincidence, 156; upswing of 1888-90, 159-66; month of 1890 peak, 166; downturn of 1890, 166-71, 177; crisis of 1890, 168; downswing of 1891, 171-73; month of 1891 trough, 173; upturn of 1891, 173-76; shortage-of-capital theories of, 178; upswing of 1891-93, 179-83; month of 1893 peak, 183; downturn of 1893, 183-84; contraction of 1893-94, 184-91; month of 1894 trough, 189; upturn of 1894, 191-92; upswing of 1894-95, 193-97; month of 1895 peak, 197; downturn of 1895, 197-201; contraction of 1895-97, 201-4; troughs of 1894 and 1897 compared, 202; date of 1897 trough, 204-5; upturn of 1897, 204-8; depression of 1893-97, 209-19; similarity of 1890's and 1930's, 219; nature of, 221-22, 227-28; month of 1887 peak, 233-37. *See also* Burns, Cassel, Gordon, Hansen, Hicks, Mitchell, Schumpeter, Twenty-year cycles

Cairncross, Alexander K., on gold standard, 226n
Capital movements, in 1865-78, 79-80; effects of, 89, 221; in 1873, 100; in 1880-81, 120n; in 1893-97, 195, 217-18
Cassel, Gustav, cycle theory, 103-5, 112; on 1890, 159n
Clark, Colin, on consumer's goods, 54n; on instability, 157
Clearings, outside New York, 20, 159, 160 (Chart 11)
Clemence, Richard V., 23n
Cleveland, Grover, and Venezuelan crisis, 199; and gold reserve, 200
Commercial and Financial Chronicle, as a source, 113n
Communication. *See* Transportation and communication
Confidence, and railroad investment, 118-19; in 1879-81, 120-21; in 1881, 125; in 1890-91, 171-72; in 1891, 174-76; in 1895, 196, 199-200; in 1896, 203-4; in 1896-97, 206-7; in 1890's, 209-10
Cooke, Jay, and panic of 1873, 99-100, 101, 103
Coulter, E. Merton, 92n

Cuba, in 1896, 205
Currency. *See* Money

Debt. *See* Federal debt
Depression. *See* Business cycles, Long-wave depression
Dewey, Davis R., 97n
Domar, Evsey, 74, 224
Doody, Francis S., 23n
Duesenberry, James J., on econometrics, 7n; on Hicks's theory, 9-11
Dun, Barlow and Company, 123

Eckler, A. Ross, on severity of 1873-79 contraction, 107n; on severity of 1883-85 contraction, 128n; on 1887-88 contraction, 143n
Economist (London), as source, 113n
Entrepreneurs. *See* Innovation, Schumpeter
Equilibrators, in Schumpeter, 35-36; and long-wave depression, 74-80
Equilibrium, in Schumpeter, Samuelson, Keynes, 29-30; in Hicks, Schumpeter, 34, 35, 36
Exogenous factors. *See* External events
Exports. *See* International trade
External events, and prediction, 6n; and business cycles, 14; in Gordon, 37, 40; defined, 55; international trade, 56-60; crop conditions, 60-61, 220; and railroad investment, 111; and upturn of 1879, 111-12, 114; in 1890-91, 176-77; in 1865-97, 220-22

Failures, in 1873, 101; in 1887, 152; Philadelphia and Reading R.R., 185; in 1893, 185-86, 187, 215
Federal budget, 1865-66, 92, 94; receipts and expenditures, 1865-97, 121 (Chart 10); surplus in 1885-87, 150; expenditures in 1887-88, 151. *See also* Federal debt
Federal debt, reduction, 1866-93, 72; increase in value from falling prices in 1870's, 110; in 1880-81, 120
Federal government, as source of external events, 221
Fellner, William, on Schumpeter, 27n; on risk, 72n; mentioned, 24n, 71n
Field, Cyrus W., 123n
Fisk, Jim, and panic of 1869, 96
Four-cycle schema, 28-29

INDEX

France, 1865-79, 83; 1865-67, 94n; 1879-85, 113; 1882-90, 137; 1894-1900, 193; and Schumpeter's theory, 228
Frank, Isaiah, on 1865-69, 94n
Freight ton-miles, 1875-97, 160 (Chart 11)
Frickey, Edwin, 66 (Table 1), 83n, 93n, 94n, 153n, 166n, 173, 189
Friedman, Milton, on econometrics, 7n; on econometric and inductive approaches, 8; on testing theory, 13n; on money supply in the 1890's, 209, 210-12

Garfield, J. A., President, and downturn of 1881-82, 125n, 126, 197n
George, Henry, on unemployment in 1883, 125n
Georgescu-Roegen, Nicholas, 7n, 53n
Germany, 1865-79, 83; 1879-85, 113; 1882-90, 137; 1894-1900, 193
Gilbert, Donald W., on 1866, 94n
Gold exports, in 1895, 198-99. *See also* Capital movements, Money
Gold panic of 1869, 96-97
Gold premium. *See* Paper standard
Gold standard, theory of, 56-58; resumption of, 72-73, 110, 111; equilibrating mercanism, 123-24, 150, 177, 226-27. *See also* Silver
Gompers, Samuel, on unemployment in 1893-94, 191
Goodwin, Richard M., on deductive approach, 13
Gordon, Robert A., on econometrics, 7n; on historical approach, 16; on major and minor cycles, 22, 37-42, 84, 106-7, 223; on contraction of 1882-85, 134; mentioned, 34, 43, 208, 222, 225
Gould, Jay, and panic of 1869, 96
Graham, Frank T., 90n
Great Britain. *See* United Kingdom
Gross national product, rate of change, 63-67, 66 (Table 1); 1874-83, 80; twenty-year cycles in, 230-31

Haberler, Gottfried, on cycle theory, 43; on price and wage flexibility, 44n, 47-49; mentioned, 103n
Hansen, Alvin H., on depressions of 1870's and 1890's, 73-74; on major cycles, 84n; on acceleration principle, 85; on 1893-97, 201-2; on depression of 1890's 209, 213-15; mentioned, 44n, 75, 81, 211

Harris, Seymour E., on federal debt, 72; mentioned, 49n
Harrod, Roy, 74, 224
Hayek, Friedrich, 103n
Hickernell, Warren F., 97n
Hicks, John R., on econometrics, 7n; cycle theory, 9-13, 22, 30-37, 105, 189-90, 207, 224-26, 227; theory compared with Gordon's, 40-42; on monetary factors, 68-70; on contraction of 1882-85, 135-36; mentioned, 15, 39, 43, 222
Higgins, Benjamin H., 49n
Hoarding, in 1873, 102; in 1896, 203-4
Housing, rents, 86 (Chart 4). *See also* Building construction
Hubbard, Joseph B., on severity of 1873-79 contraction, 107n; on severity of 1883-85 contraction, 128n; on 1887-88 contraction, 143n; on month of 1890 peak, 166n; on month of 1887 peak, 233
Hultgren, Thor, 147n
Hume, David, 14

Immigration, and Hicks's theory, 10; and long-wave depression, 76-77; in 1870-97, 86 (Chart 4); in 1865-67, 92; in 1880-82, 124; in 1893-95, 191; in 1890's, 218; twenty-year cycles in, 231, 232
Imports. *See* International trade
Ingram, James C., on gold standard, 226n
Innovation, in Schumpeter's theory, 23n, 24, 25, 34, 40n, 223-24; endogenous, 40n; in 1873, 106; in railroads, 118, 134-35; in 1889-91, 169-70; in 1865-97, 222
Interest rates, on municipal bonds, 62; on prime commercial paper, 62, 64-65 (Chart 3); on call money, 64-65 (Chart 3); an equilibrator, 77; on railroad bonds, 66 (Table 1), 116-17 (Chart 8); in 1880-81, 120
International trade, exports and imports, 119 (Chart 9), 142, 151, 162, 165, 169, 183-84, 203, 217, 220. *See also* Capital movements, External events, Gold standard, Paper standard, Silver, Tariff
Investment, autonomous, 33-34, 35, 75. *See also* Building construction, Iron and steel, Railroads
Investment in inventories, farm products, 61; in 1869-78, 97; in 1880, 124; in

1885, 133n; in 1886, 141; in 1887, 151-52; in 1888-89, 163-64; in 1890, 170; in 1892, 184; in 1895, 200
Investment opportunities, in long-wave depression, 73-80, 82; 1865-73, 105-7, 112; in 1890, 170; in 1894-95, 197; in 1895, 201; in 1897, 207-8; in 1890's, 214; in 1865-97, 223. *See also* Gordon, major and minor cycles; Railroads, investment
Iron and steel, in 1865-79, 90; in 1864-65, 92; in 1872, 98; in 1872-73, 105; in 1880, 122; in 1883, 129; in 1887, 140, 148, 153; pig-iron output 1865-97, 159-61 (Chart 11); in 1889, 163; in 1891-92, 181-82; in 1890's, 215-17; output 1884-1900, 216 (Chart 12)
Isard, Walter, on transport-building cycle, 84; cited, 85n

Jerome, Harry, on migration and cycles, 76n, 124n; on employment, 166n, 173, 189; mentioned, 92n
Juglar cycles. *See* Schumpeter, theory; Schumpeter, three-cycles schema

Kepler's laws, 4, 5, 14
Keynes, John M., on equilibrium unemployment, 30; on suddenness of downturns, 124n; mentioned, 37, 74, 177, 224
Kitchin, Joseph, on month of 1882 downturn, 125n; on contraction of 1887-88, 142n
Kitchin cycles. *See* Schumpeter, theory; Schumpeter, three-cycle schema
Klein, Lawrence R., 7, 9n
Kondratieff cycles. *See* Schumpeter, theory; Schumpeter, three-cycle schema
Koopmans, Tjalling C., Koopmans-Vining controversy, 5, 8n
Kuh, Edwin, 9n
Kuznets, Simon S., on Schumpeter, 24, 29; GNP estimates, 63-66, 80, 97n, 115n, 193n; on twenty-year cycles, 67n, 229-31

Lange, Oscar, on Schumpeter, 24n, 29
Lauck, William J., 131n, 167n
Lewis, W. Arthur, on Schumpeter, 23n
Lloyd, Henry D., 122n, 124n
Long, Clarence D., 140n, 141, 148, 169n, 173, 234
Long-wave depression, 1873-97, characteristics of, 62-68; money supply in, 68-73; investment opportunities in, 73-80; Schumpeter's explanation of, 80-81; conclusions on, 81-82

McCartney, Ernest R., 83n
McKinley, William, 203
McKinley Tariff Act, 165-66, 168, 170-71
Major cycles. *See* Business cycles, Gordon
Manufacturing, output, 66 (Table 1), 93 (Chart 7), 107
Marshak, Jacob, 24n
Martin, Robert F., on national income, 92n, 108n
Mason, Edward S., 4n
Means, Gardiner C., on price and wage flexibility, 44n, 46
Methodology, 3-21
Metzler, Lloyd A., 42-43, 58n, 170
Meyer, John, 9n
Mining, output, 93 (Chart 7)
Minor cycles. *See* Business cycles, Gordon
Mitchell, Wesley C., *Business Cycles*, 16; on costs-prices-profits, 35, 181; on 1865-78, 83n; on crops in 1891, 173, 174, 176; on 1891-93, 182n; on crops in 1894, 192n; mentioned, 109n, 142. *See also* Burns, *Measuring Business Cycles*
Money, in cycle theory, 43, 103; in 1865-73, 70; and long-wave depression, 81, 82; in 1865-69, 90, 92, 95-96; in 1873, 99, 100, 103; in 1880-81, 119-20; in 1885, 132; in 1887, 149-51, 153; in 1888, 164-65; in 1890, 167-69, 177-78; in 1893, 185-88; in 1894-95, 196-97; in 1890's, 210-12; subordinate to real factors, 224-25
Moody, William Godwin, 129n
Moore, Geoffrey H., on statistical indicators, 142n, 153n, 197, 205, 234-36
Morgan, J. Pierpont, 123n, 196, 201
Morgan-Belmont Syndicate, 196, 201

National Bureau of Economic Research. *See* Burns; Business cycles, inductive approach; Business cycles, month of 1887 peak
National Cordage Co., failure in 1893, 186
Neal, Alfred C., on price and wage flexibility, 44n, 46
Net national product, 66 (Table 1)
Newton's theory of gravitation, 4, 5, 14

INDEX 243

Northern Pacific Railroad, and panic of 1873, 99, 101, 106; in 1880's, 115

Ohlin, Bertil, on gold standard theory, 177
Ozga, S. A. *See* Brown, E. H. Phelps

Panics. *See* Banks, Gold
Paper standard, theory of, 58-60; and capital imports, 79-80, 89; in 1865-78, 87-90; gold premium, 88 (Chart 5); in 1873-78, 109; and international correlation of cycles, 227
Partington, John E., on railroads, 98, 145, 146n, 147; on month of 1882 downturn, 125n; on 1887-88 contraction, 142n; on month of 1890 peak, 166n; on 1896 election, 204n
Patterson, Robert T., on money supply, 95n
Pearson, Frank A., 98n
Persons, Leonard P., on month of 1882 downturn, 125n; on severity of 1883-85 contraction, 128n; on month of 1890 peak, 166n; on month of 1887 peak, 233; mentioned, 83n, 93n, 94n
Poor's, 147n
Population. *See* Immigration
Powderly, T. V., 129n
Price and wage flexibility, two problems distinguished, 44; monetary and physical aspects, 45-46; definition, 46-47; wages, 47-52; overhead-plus-profit margin, 52; selective cuts, 52-54; and long-wave depression, 71-72; and equilibrium, 77-78; in 1870's, 109-10
Prices, wholesale, 1865-97, 63 (Chart 2); wholesale, 66 (Table 1); wholesale, 1865-79, 89-90

Railroad investment, rate of change, 66 (Table 1); bond yields, 66 (Table 1); in 1890's, 73-74, 213-17; in 1865-73, 99-100; in 1869-73, 105-6; in 1873-79, 110-11; in 1879-82, 115-19, 122; in 1881-83, 126-28; in 1883, 129; in 1883-84, 130; in 1885, 132-33; in 1885-87, 138-40, 155-56; in 1887-88, 143-48; miles of track laid on main lines, 1886-87, 144, 145 (Table 2); in 1888, 161; in 1890-92, 180; in 1884-1900, 216 (Chart 12); twenty-year cycles in, 230

Railroads, freight ton-miles, 160 (Chart 11)
Rents, 1860-80, 86 (Chart 4)
Rezneck, Samuel, 83n
Rostow, W. W., on Schumpeter, 23n; on money in long-wave depression, 68-70, 81; mentioned, 108, 136n
Rothbarth, E., 24n
Rubin, Ernest, 87n

Samuelson, Paul A., multiplier-accelerator theory, 29
Schumpeter, Joseph A., on econometrics, 7-8; his three-cycle schema, 8-9, 24, 25-28, 42, 182-83; his cycle theory, 23-30, 40, 87n, 154, 222-24, 225, 227, 228; on cycle dates, 24-25, 84n; on secondary wave, 25, 26, 27, 29, 34, 37, 106, 166; his theory compared with Hicks's, 34-37; on investment opportunities, 42, 214; on long-wave depression, 80-81; on 1869-73, 105-6, 112; on 1873-79, 108; on 1879-85, 134-35, 136; on railroad construction, 139n; on 1885-88, 155-56; on 1889-91, 169-70; on socialism, 195n; on acceleration principle, 214-15; on depression of 1890's, 212-13, 219; mentioned, 14, 15, 16n, 18, 22, 43, 77n, 83n, 113n, 176, 187, 209, 211, 231. *See also* Innovation
Secondary secular fluctuations, 67n
Sherman Act. *See* Silver
Shortage-of-capital theory. *See* Cassel
Silver, in the 1890's, 72, 82, 210-12, 213, 218; in 1884, 130-31; Sherman Silver Purchase Act, 165-66, 167, 171-72, 186-87, 188; in 1893-94, 191; in 1894-95, 194-96; in 1896, 202, 203-4
Slichter, Sumner H., on selective price cuts, 52; mentioned, 16n
Smithies, Arthur, 30n
Sprague, Oliver M. W., on 1891, 174n; mentioned, 99n, 131n, 168n, 185n
Stability, in the American economy, 157-58
Steel. *See* Iron and steel
Stocking, George W., 44n
Strauss, Frederick, 91n, 141n, 151n
Strikes, in 1893, 190-91

Tariff, of 1890, 165-66, 168, 170-71; of 1897, 205-6
Terborgh, George, on investment, 85

INDEX

Theory, defined, 4. *See also* Business cycles, Gold standard, Paper standard
Thomas, Brinley, on Schumpeter, 23n; on twenty-year cycles, 76n
Thorp, Willard L., annals, 16; on 1887 peak, 233
Tinbergen, Jan, on econometrics, 6n, 7n; on historical approach, 17; mentioned, 16n
Tobin, James, 49n
Transportation and communication, output, 66 (Table 1), 93 (Chart 7)
Transport-building cycle, 84, 98
Truman, Harry S., 203
Tucker, Rufus S., 162n, 167n
Tuttle, Pierson M., 83n, 94n
Twenty-year cycles, in building, 28, 74, 85, 231, 232; in immigration, 76, 85, 231, 232; transport-building cycle, 84, 98; relation to major depressions, 229; in railroad investment, 230; in GNP, 230-31

Ulmer, Melville J., on railroad investment, 115, 144, 161n, 180n, 212, 217n; on twenty-year cycles, 230
Unemployment, in 1878, 108; in 1879-82, 123; in 1885, 129n; in 1893-94, 191
United Kingdom, wholesale prices in, 63 (Chart 2); long-wave depression in, 67-70; 1865-79, 83; 1866-68, 94n; depression of 1870's in, 108; 1879-85, 113; 1882-90, 137; 1894-1900, 193; and Schumpeter's theory, 228
Upgren, Arthur R., and Schumpeter, 23n

Venezuelan crisis, 197n, 199-200, 201
Vining, Rutledge, Koopmans-Vining controversy, 5

Wage flexibility, 47-52. *See also* Price and wage flexibility
Wages, 1865-97, 63 (Chart 2)
Warburton, Clark, on role of money in downturn, 178n
Warren, George F., 98n
Watkins, Myron W., 44n
Wells, David A., 92n
Weston, George M., 120n, 123n
Williams, John H., 162n, 167n
Wolf, A., 12n
Wright, Carroll D., on unemployment in 1878, 108; in 1882-85, 113n, 127n, 128-29